CHASING CLOUDS

CHASING CLOUDS

An Invitation to Travel
With Heart

KRISTIN MURRAY

PARTRIDGE

To order additional copies of this book, contact
Toll Free 800 101 2657 (Singapore)
Toll Free 1 800 81 7340 (Malaysia)
orders.singapore@partridgepublishing.com

www.partridgepublishing.com/singapore

Contents

This book is dedicated to all the children less fortunate than I.
They are all little heroes.

I've been through valleys where the children had no clothes,

Slept on boats heard the prayer call rising,

Seeking people who are not afraid to show love,

Who can undress their soul.

Are you one?

Naked Soul

Preface

I was teased a lot when I was a child.

"Hey Peacemaker, we saw your mum the other day. She's a hippie, isn't she?"

Perhaps, I thought. I guess by some people's standards she was.

Sitting in our living room after school, I picked up Cosmic Creepers, our cat. He gave a small meow of protest as I sat him in my lap. I was snuggling deeper into the couch, ready to watch some mind numbing TV, when my mum walked into the room and sat down beside me.

"Hey, darlin', how was your day at school?" she asked. There was rarely a day that she didn't ask me this question, usually over cookies and our one glass of milk for the day—all we could afford at the time.

I looked up into her deep blue eyes. "It was OK, I guess." I kept my voice as neutral as possible and looked slightly past her so as to not give away how upset I was.

"Really?" she quizzed me, trying to find my eyes.

The sun was setting. The light from its rays hit one of the crystals hanging in the window, casting small colourful reflections of light over the living room walls.

My mum stood up from the couch and walked to the window to spin the crystal, causing the reflections to dance about the walls. Then she walked over to the bookshelf. After a minute of scanning the books, she found what she was looking for.

She came back over to me. "Read this, Krista," she smiled, calling me by my pet name—one that I actually liked.

Bridge Across My Sorrows, I read aloud. "What's it about? If it's sad I don't want to read it."

"Yeah, it is sad, but it's a story that will help you to see just how fortunate you are in life," she replied. "And," she added, "it has a happy ending. I know you love a happy ending."

How she could have been so intuitive about what I needed to read that day and at that time in my life, I still don't understand.

The book was about a woman by the name of Christina Noble, who had come from an extremely impoverished childhood. Without education, money or support, she had started a foundation to help street children in Vietnam.

After reading that book, something inside me not so much changed as ignited. I thought, if one woman who had nothing could save thousands of children from a life of torment, then I had to try my hardest to do something, anything, no matter how small, to change at least one person's life for the better.

Five years experience of travelling overseas taught me valuable lessons. My mind and heart opened to the world and the people in it, and I gained a deep understanding of the oneness present in the human experience. For the last two years, I have been studying for a Bachelor of International Relations, and am excited about the doors these credentials will open for me on my journey.

With this story, I hope to inspire young people to chase their dreams, to have faith and trust in their paths, to be aware of the magic that happens along the way to our destinations. I hope that my travels can inspire others, so that their hearts and minds can open to the differences that seemingly separate us, to dissolve the illusion of us and them and unite us with our global brothers and sisters. I also hope my story will encourage the traveller to travel consciously, to realize that countries are not something to "do", that they are to be lived and felt and held close to our hearts.

1

Outta here

My heart pounded in my chest, my palms were clammy. I was nervous, excited, scared and ecstatic all at once. I had never been overseas before; I hadn't even been on a plane. I was eighteen, a little lost and very unaware of what to expect when I landed in Indonesia.

After leaving school, I had begun to work for my dad at his bakery while I figured out what I wanted to do with my life. While everyone else seemed to have already chosen the path they were going to take, I had no idea what I wanted to do. I knew that I wanted to see the world, and that I wanted to help people—but how? I had barely put a foot out of my home town since my family had moved there. What did I know about places unknown, other tongues and traditions? About how to help people in need? And in the teenaged, confused-about-life rut I had found myself in, I seemed to be the one in need of a little help.

When two of my good friends, mother and daughter, told me they were going for a trip to Indonesia and invited me to go with them, I didn't think twice. I began saving money the day I made the decision. Each day I marked off on the calendar at work seemed to bring more purpose than ever before. I had spent so many hours working away with no idea of what I was working for, what I was living for. Looking back, that invitation to Indonesia was the first of many doors to open for me, inviting me to step through and chase my destiny.

My trip to Indonesia was not such an adventurous trip. The two girls I went with had been to Indonesia before; they just wanted to relax. As I had absolutely no idea of how to travel, I went along with them. This was a lucky thing, as it would prove to be one of the only relaxed overseas travels I would ever have.

Although we stayed in a more westernized area of Indonesia, I was able get my first taste of how people less well-off than I were living.

Christina Noble's story of travelling to South East Asia was in my mind as I walked through the dusty streets of Seminyak, dotted with people who sported brilliant smiles when our eyes made contact. Stray, underfed dogs scurried away from the heels of passersby. There didn't seem to be any road rules or rules as to how many people were allowed on a motorbike at any one time. I was invited into houses and shops with dirt floors, confronted by men, women and children all looking for a spare rupiah. I had been in the country less than two hours when I first saw children dressed in rags, covered in dust from head to toe. Blood rushed to my face. I felt embarrassed and extremely self-conscious. I had nothing on me to give to them, I felt dreadful and utterly helpless. Even though these children had nothing, the smiles they flashed me were bright enough to light up a football field. I didn't like this first taste of many people's reality, but I got addicted to it just the same.

The overwhelming smell of incense from the day's offerings found its way through streets. The town's sewage and the aromas from the women's pots and pans was in itself addictive. I knew that after this experience I wouldn't return to Australia the same. I had just turned eighteen and was only just beginning to find my feet in this world, although I was very far from understanding it.

I spent the nights in bed replaying the scenes of the day, the faces and the sounds of this new land. My mind started to wander to other parts of the globe. What was out there? I wanted to see it all. I wasn't interested in anything that was remotely similar to what I knew or had seen on TV. I wanted to see more diversity, to hear people speaking other languages, to try different food. What more was there on offer to experience? I thought of my heritage: Canadian-Indian, German, Irish and then some. What was Germany like—what was their food like? The people? I could barely sleep during those nights from excitement at the prospect of travelling!

My friends and I returned home two weeks later. Although I had been gone such a short time, I felt that I had changed entirely. Suddenly I found my home town profoundly boring, meaningless. Even after I met my boyfriend Taylor I felt lost in my own home town.

I returned to work but did not feel the same as I had before. I started to work in a Spanish restaurant to spice up my life a little, something I discovered the Spanish certainly know how to do! My bosses and I became very close. They even tried to get me to go on holiday to Spain with them. I think they could see that I had so much to learn. My home town didn't offer a very wide variety of cultures and traditions. After experiencing in Indonesia something very different from what I was used to, I knew I needed more than what home had to offer, but I couldn't see myself saving as much as I thought I would need to go to Spain with my bosses.

Even though it was great living with the Spanish chefs, I still felt as though I was missing a very big part of the picture. I wasn't at all thinking of university, I was determined to find whatever it was that my soul seemed to be chasing.

It turned out that I couldn't save enough money in time to go to Spain with my bosses. My flatmates had bought a van and started travelling around Australia. I decided to do the same with Taylor.

I searched for the most affordable van I could find, trembling as I drove it the thirty kilometres home. I felt as if I was driving a bus and that every gust of wind was going to blow me off the road. It was white with a brown interior and was in great condition. I was filled with excitement of the unknown, and of all the possible adventures that lay before me. I had driven the same streets, shopped at the same supermarket and clothes stores, and eaten at the same restaurants almost all my life. I was feeling like I was living in the movie *Groundhog Day*. The prospect of getting out was soul-shifting to my core.

I fell in love with being in new places all the time while on the road with Taylor. My previous boyfriend of just over a year had been an emotional nightmare; I was left heartbroken. Now I found myself enjoying being with someone who was as devoted, honest and sweet as Taylor.

Our two major worries were where we could park my van without the rangers moving us on, and where we could find a public toilet so we didn't have to poo in the open. I was nineteen, it felt amazing to be alive. We were showering at a new beach every day, cooking fish we'd caught ourselves on the public barbecues or meals on a small gas stove, and having petrol- station pee stops.

When we got to North Queensland, we ran out of money so we decided to stay in Cairns, as I had a friend living there. Taylor got work in different labouring jobs around the city, and I got a job in a Thai restaurant getting paid about half of what I'd been earning back home. But I was content. I was fortunate enough to meet a young girl by the name of Ali at my new underpaid job. She would contribute to the next big change in my life.

Ali was a sweet brunette from Canada. She looked my age although she was twenty-five, five years older than I was, and had travelled much of the world alone. To me, my short trip to our neighbouring country had been life changing, but this little Canadian had lived and worked in other countries! Korea had been one of them, a country whose language she couldn't even speak.

To many people of my age and younger, who have already been there and done that, this is nothing new, but for me it was like someone had just turned on a light. What secrets about the world and about life did this world traveller know? If one two-week holiday had turned my life upsidedown, what events had occurred during this girl's adventures?

I realized then that I knew less than nothing. How was I ever going to be able to make a positive change in the world if I knew nothing about it? I was determined to follow in Ali's footsteps. She told me about a course she had taken called TESOL, which gave her a certificate to teach English to students of other languages. It sounded perfect, I could travel and earn money at the same time. And wouldn't you know it, a week or so after meeting my new globe-trotting friend, I found an advert in the paper advertising a TESOL course for the following month. I took a loan from Taylor and applied for the course.

The teacher was Australian, although she didn't have an Australian accent. She was in her late thirties, early forties—it was hard to tell. She was very pretty, fine boned and with long blonde hair. Her name was Jenny. She seemed to take a liking to me from the start, which made it much easier when I had to present my mock lesson to the rest of the class. Normally I'd die of embarrassment if I had to do public speaking, but with Jenny's reassuring gaze I felt completely comfortable. This stayed with me throughout my teaching career. When telling us of the opportunities afforded by the TESOL certificate, Jenny gave us some examples from her own experience. She had travelled to all corners of the world, could speak ten different languages and had lived in Italy for eight years. I decided there and then that I wanted to do what Jenny had done. What better way to learn about the world?

Life got in the way of this happening straightaway. During the two years after completing the TESOL course and working and saving, Taylor and I began to realise we had different ideas about what we wanted from life. It was a sad break-up (as they always are), but I knew it was for the best, and soon after I booked my flight to Europe—not necessarily to teach English just yet, but as a new adventure I knew I had to do for myself.

2

The bug

Standing at Immigration at the Sydney International airport, I was holding my brother so tight I thought I would crush him. I was twenty-two years old with next to no travel experience and I was going alone to the other side of the world. My mum had insisted that for the first month of my two-month trip I go on a tour to learn the ropes and meet some people, which turned out to be yet another life changing event: I wasn't expecting to meet my next love on that tour, or so soon!

I had no idea what the procedures were for Immigration, or anything to do with airports for that matter, and somehow or other I accidentally brought my brother inside Immigration. Security came up to us and told my brother that he wasn't supposed to be there if he didn't have a ticket, which hurried our goodbyes. I decided to call him two seconds after he had left so we could have a proper goodbye. Security guards rushed towards me, looking as though they were about to tackle me to the ground. I soon found out that it is against the law to use a phone in that area of the airport. Looking around, I saw enough signage to realise I should've known. Needless to say, I have been a bit wary about where I use my phone in an airport ever since, even if everyone else is using theirs.

The following eleven-hour-plus-thirteen hour flight from Australia to Europe was something of a nightmare. Every time I woke up, I thought at least ten hours must have passed since I got on the plane, but it would only have been half an hour since the last time I checked my watch. Another thing that was worrying me was that at times the plane looked to be on a sharp angle with the front descending. The fact that I had the song "Ironic" by Alanis Morissette in my head for the entire flight made me feel even more on edge.

My stopover was in Beijing as I was flying with Air China. As I collected my things from the overhead compartment, I could feel a migraine coming on, something I had begun to experience over the past year. It was just what I needed, facing the second thirteen-hour leg of flight, along with an eight-hour stopover in the Beijing airport.

It was only six a.m. when we landed; most of the stores were still closed. Thankfully the pharmacy was open and I bought some painkillers, receiving my change back in yen. My first lesson in travelling: check currencies and exchange rates before leaving. I'm almost sure the lady in the pharmacy didn't intend to rip me off, I just don't think many people paid in Australian dollars and, with the confusion of the exchange that always comes along with paying in the wrong currency, it saw me getting substantially short changed.

My head was pounding too much to care as I searched for somewhere with Internet to let my mum and brother know that I had landed in Beijing safely. I logged on to Facebook and wrote them a quick message, before heading off to find somewhere to rest. I was freezing, so I found a place by the windows where the sun came through. I was too scared to lie down: my brother had gotten a fine in Australia for having his feet on a train seat.

Soon I became bored and decided to take a look in the cosmetics stores. I was surprised to find that almost every product in the store was to whiten your face. This was something entirely strange for me. Why would anyone want to whiten their face? In Australia, practically everyone wanted to be brown! I looked behind me at the two Chinese girls who had also been in the store since I entered. Sure enough, their faces were glowing white.

Check-in time finally dragged around. I found my desk and checked in awkwardly, trying my hardest to look like an experienced traveller. Then I made my way to the gate and found people relaxing with their feet all over the chairs.

The meals on the flight were something of a lucky dip. Each time my fork went into the foil container some strange part of a sea creature came out. I hadn't eaten much seafood in Australia, so even this was a new experience for me. The most adventurous I had previously been with seafood was to eat oysters, which I hadn't really liked. Come to think of it now, it was pretty elaborate to have a seafood dish for an in-flight meal.

My migraine had subsided. I slept for almost the entire flight. On arrival in London I woke with a numb leg and one billion butterflies in my stomach. As I made my way through the gates and to Immigration I started to have a liberating feeling that just would not go away. It was a feeling that I had never had before.

I collected my backpack from the baggage belt and made my way to the information desk. The boy working there was extremely friendly. He even went to the trouble of getting me a sim card for my phone, which I had been sure to unlock. I only realized after he gave it to me that he did so to get my phone number. He told me when I was leaving the airport that he would call me in a few hours to see if I "got along orright".

Despite the fact that I liked the British accent (as I had just found out) and that he was handsome, I became incredibly paranoid. I had just seen the film *Taken* and was completely freaked out, thinking I was going to be abducted by the young Brit. I messaged my brother the name and description of this guy just in case.

Better safe than sorry—right?

When I eventually checked into my hostel and found my room I caught a glimpse of myself in the bathroom mirror. My long blonde hair was a mess; I was leaning forward as I lugged my big backpack on my back and carried the small one across my chest. Still I felt that same overwhelming feeling of freedom I had felt on arriving in the city. I was so excited about the people I would meet and the experiences I was about to have. Oh and the Eiffel tower! The idea of moving from place to place around this continent filled with history, tradition, countless cultures and languages just seemed utterly surreal.

I began the guided tour, arranged for the first three weeks of my trip around Europe, with a busload of fifty other tourists. Most were from Australia, New Zealand and America; I didn't quite get the cultural experience that I was looking for, so at every stop along the way I tried to interact with the locals as much as I could. The architecture and sheer age of the buildings lining the cobblestoned streets were impressive enough in themselves, let alone the different foods, cultures and lives that existed among them. I began to fall even more in love with the idea of travelling across this glorious earth.

We had started our tour in London and were to do a loop of Western Europe as far as Germany and back, visiting eleven countries along the way in just over three weeks. This fast pace meant many early mornings and long hours of travel by bus. I was excited at the prospect of visiting one of the countries in my heritage. But I was just as excited to see all the countries along the way and what each crossing of the border would bring.

We had snails and French onion soup in France, and a French picnic with delicious cheeses and meats, and wine that was cheaper than water. I visited the Eiffel tower on dusk when the sky was an array of pastels, and returned at nine o'clock that night to watch it light up with hundreds of white fairy lights. Watching the tower in awe of its beauty, I felt as though I was in a dream.

We had pizza and pasta in Italy and watched old men with strange hats play the accordion. We partied 'til all hours of the morning in Spain and drank sangria to our hearts' content. We had pork knuckles and sausages as big as our heads in Germany, went paragliding in Austria, ate fondu and drank delicious hot chocolate in Switzerland. On the way, we passed three of the smallest countries in the world: the Vatican city, Liechtenstein and Monaco. We were lucky enough to arrive in Amsterdam for Queen's Day, where we partied with the rest of the country, wearing the customary orange in honour of the queen's birthday.

Not long into the trip I started to feel something of a crush towards our tour manager Luca. I could feel some kind of chemistry between us. By the end of the tour, we were officially an item. We hid this for almost the entire trip. Only at the final dinner together did we let everyone know. Luca was a smiling, sweet Italian, twenty-six years old, with big brown eyes. He was of small build and had a lovely face, a fit body and a matching personality.

Luca invited me to his home town for the week he had free between the tour we were on and a training week in Spain, and I said yes. Once we were in Switzerland, in a small, smokey bar over a glass of orange juice, I booked a flight to Luca's home town. I was so excited. I had loved Italy so much. Now I was about to stay with Luca's parents in the south of Italy, close to Naples—a place we had missed on our tour. Wow.

I had always thought that Neapolitan ice cream came from Napoli. When I asked Luca he told me that no, in fact it did not. I couldn't help but be a little disappointed as well as embarrassed for asking. The tour had been a great experience but not what I had been hoping for. Still, it seemed like fate to have met this new loving soul I had started to fall for along the way.

After the tour we spent a few days in London before our flight to Napoli. Our relationship was already intense, and I was beginning to wonder what would happen when I went home in a month's time. Luca had accommodation provided by the tour company while in London and snuck me into his room for those nights. We made beautiful love and stayed up until all hours of the morning, talking about anything and everything, even though he was supposed to be studying for the training trip in Spain. I was worried, however, that our relationship might be a summer romance—perfect in the moment, but maybe in reality not so perfect. But I put what was unsettling me down to the language barrier (or paranoia, or skepticism), threw caution to the wind and jumped right in.

Our flights to Naples were at different times; he had booked his flight before we met. He was due to arrive about two hours after me. The morning of my flight, I woke up around three o'clock in the morning, walked to the bus stop and waited. A big red bus came charging down the freezing cold London street, splashing the night's rain out of its way as it went. It was postcard perfect. I pulled my suitcase onto the bus, but I wasn't sure that it was the right bus. I asked the bus driver, who had no interest in answering me. The few people already on the bus kindly advised me that yes this was the bus to the train station for Gatwick airport.

I got to the train station, found my platform and waited. It was freezing. I had a little picnic on the train platform to keep my mind off the cold and fill my grumbling tummy, and revised the few Italian phrases I was trying to learn to say to Luca's mum. "Nice to meet you," was one. "Thank you for picking me up from the airport," was another. "Thank you so much for lunch. It was delicious." That last was something I could not get off my mind: a home-cooked lunch. Better still, a home-cooked lunch in *Italy*.

When the plane landed two hours later, everyone erupted in applause. One very cute, short, balding old man was screaming, "Nap-ol-i! Nap-ol-i!" Going through Immigration was as easy as the walk through Hyde Park I had taken earlier that week. The officer didn't even want to look at my passport. I hadn't travelled very much but I did know that was a little bit too relaxed, even by Italian standards. I had only seen Luca's mum on Facebook, so I was a bit worried I wouldn't recognise her at the airport. There was no need to worry. She recognised me the minute I walked out to the arrivals gate.

"Kri!" came a voice from somewhere in front of me. I knew already from Luca this Italian nickname for girls with a name like mine and knew that the call was directed at me. I smiled at Violetta as our eyes made contact. She was really beautiful with long dark hair, full lips, a stunning smile and warm brown eyes that told you she had a deep, big personality. After a kiss on each cheek she grabbed me by the arm and led me out of the airport to her car. I tried to produce the words I had been repeating earlier, but I felt so uncertain that I just sat in silence, looking as if I was about to say something, but didn't.

Violetta tried to have a conversation with me. This quickly fizzled once she realized I couldn't understand a word she was saying, let alone reply. I could tell that she desperately wanted to converse with me. I felt exactly the same; still I felt completely comfortable in her presence. So the radio was turned on and Violetta sang for most of the way home.

My heart was in my throat as she sang, steered, smoked, talked on the phone and dodged cars coming and going from every direction. It was incredible, I had never seen anything like it before. Once we got to Castellammare di Stabia, Luca's home town about an hour's drive from Napoli, Violetta pushed a button on the dash that said *city* and began the process of parking her small car in a space that seemed even smaller. I later learned that a click of this button allows the steering wheel to turn around as much as the driver likes to fit into such spaces, but at the time I was certain there was no way the car would fit. But it did—with a bump to the car in front and a bump to the car behind.

I got out of the car, knees shaking. Violetta grabbed my arm and pulled me into a fruit shop. I walked around the store awkwardly, feeling completely out of my comfort zone. The store vendor motioned to me, saying something along with the word *bellissima*. I was soon to find that Italians gave great importance to appearances and beauty. Violetta nodded in approval with the storekeeper, and bought a small bag of tomatoes, along with a bunch of basil. She took me by the arm again and led me out of the store, leaving my suitcase with the store owner. We walked to a nearby seafood market. I found myself looking over my shoulder, hoping I would see my suitcase again.

The seafood market was half-indoors, half-out. Displayed out the front in large buckets of seawater were all kinds of seafood I had never seen before. Violetta chose a bag of something that resembled pipis, which I later learned go by the name of *vongole,* then we were off again to pick up my suitcase, which was still with the trusty store owner Violetta obviously knew. We rounded the corner to the block of apartments where Violetta lived. The street we had bought the seafood and fruit from seemed a fairly busy area and I assumed we were somewhere near the centre of the city. What little I had seen so far of Luca's home town I really, really liked.

We took the elevator to the eighth floor. Violetta handed me the ingredients for our lunch while she found her key. After much jiggling of the keys, we burst into the flat to find Luca's nan, who would turn out to be one of my very good friends. Her name was Rosaria. She was a character all on her own. She wasn't like anyone in particular, but she certainly fitted the criteria of a typical Italian mama—loud, exaggerating, intense, an amazing cook, and oh, so open, especially about the problems she had with her husband. Rosaria was eighty years old. She came up to my chest and had dyed platinum-blonde hair. The first day I met her with Violetta she was cleaning the house in her nightgown with her hair a mess. She was obviously unimpressed when she saw that her daughter had brought company with her looking like that! Of course I didn't understand a word that came out of her mouth, but I got the picture.

We were shooed out of the house and walked upstairs to Violetta's flat, which had previously been the roof terrace of her parents' apartment. Violetta's flat was illegally built. To keep the neighbours quiet about it, she and another lady who had done the same thing had paid for a new lift to be installed in the building. Violetta was hoping, I later found out, that the government of Campania would, when in need of money, pass illegally built houses such as hers for a small but substantial price.

Welcome to the south of Italy. The first-world, third-world country.

Violetta told me to have a shower while she prepared lunch. As I walked through her flat I realized just how beautiful this illegal building was. The walls were painted in oranges and reds, the kitchen was red and the floors were timber. There were indigenous masks and paintings on the walls. The small living room had a cream leather couch that I was tempted to fall in a heap onto. The house had the most amazing smell, so fresh and clean.

Her balcony looked over the whole Bay of Naples. Vesuvius, still active, was standing its ground at the end of the bay. A few illegally-built houses climbed its slopes. It was spectacular. I was told later that the people living in this area strongly believed in the Latin phrase *carpe diem,* meaning "seize the day". The volcano could have erupted at any time without warning, covering its neighbouring inhabitants in ash and rock as it had done in the past, leaving behind the famous ruins of Pompei.

After a shower I walked into the kitchen. Sitting at the table was Nonna Rosaria, completely transformed. Her hair was up in a French knot, and she was wearing make-up, along with a beautiful black dress. This eighty-year-old woman made me feel incredibly daggy in my Amsterdam radio T-shirt and tights. I looked around the kitchen and saw Violetta was serving up three bowls of pasta. On the table were large platters of food that made my mouth salivate. There was cheese as white as snow, cut into thick slices, along with a plate with some strange, gigantic green and red bumpy tomatoes cut into slices as thick as the cheese and covered in oil, oregano and basil, and a bottle of white wine.

As soon as I sat down, she handed me a large bowl filled to the rim with pasta and the pipis she had bought earlier, some squashed tomatoes and oil. That was it. I was absolutely ravenous, but looking at the plate in front of me, I worried about eating this pasta with practically no sauce, filled with pipis, and having to pretend that I liked it. There was no need to fret. As soon as that pasta touched my tastebuds, all my worries disappeared.

What had I been missing out on all of my life? I'd spent the last twenty-two years thinking I knew what pasta was. I had literally no idea. And the bread and cheese and tomato situation was just the icing on my first real Italian-feast cake. There was no looking back from there.

After the most amazing meal I'd ever eaten in my life, I was told to go have a rest in Violetta's bed while I waited for Luca to get home. I crawled into her big, comfortable crisp-smelling bed and felt like I was in heaven.

The next week in Castellammare di Stabia was as romantic as you can imagine. By the end of the week I was madly in love with Luca, Italians, Castellamare di Stabia and with life itself. We spent most of our time zipping around the city on a Vespa, eating pasta and pizza to my heart's content, picking up a few words in Italian, making love day after day, learning the meanings of the romantic statements graffitied all over the city's walls.

Ti amo, Rita. I love you, Rita. *Sei bellissima, Maria.* You're beautiful, Maria. The declarations of love scrawled over the city's walls were a nice change from the usual form of graffiti back home.

After a week of bliss Luca and I flew back to London. We spent the next two days together before he left for his training in Spain, and I left for a week in Crete.

Flying over Crete, I began to feel extremely excited about my new adventure. The sea surrounding the island was emerald green, the land looked as if it were dry and perhaps a little barren. Although there were trees and bushes to be seen, these, too, seemed to look dry and somewhat dusty.

I had booked a small apartment for my week in Crete along with my flight, a package deal. It was small and a little rundown, although it had a view of the sea and was clean enough. There was a pool and a bar at the complex, and no one to be seen. It was May and still off season. It seemed as though the only occupants of the premise were myself, the owners and a frail old woman staying next door to me.

I spent the days chatting with locals, swimming in the sea, walking unknown paths to unknown places, all the while ignoring the men wolf whistling and trying to chat me up as I walked around the town. For every lunch I went back to my apartment to cook my new favourite dish, pasta with olive oil and tomato. I was yet to learn the seafood part of the recipe, but it was still a delicious combination.

This was my first real experience travelling alone and I hadn't the faintest idea what to do with myself. I knew I wanted to explore but I had no idea how. I went to the travel agency and asked a curvy Greek goddess what I should do and see. She booked me into a traditional dinner and show for the following night, and a tour of the ancient ruins in Heraklion the next day.

The day of my dinner and show I crossed paths with the elderly lady I had seen staying next door; she was still the only other soul in the complex. She was over eighty years old, had been one of the first female pilots in Australia, and had once worked for the Flying Doctor Service. We went to lunch together and shared some succulent souvlaki. She saw me off on my tour and told me to be sure not to get too drunk. I tried to follow her advice but the wine was included and it looked as though they were going to ask people from the audience up onto the stage. Knowing my luck, plus the fact that I was one of the only people on the tour without silver hair, I didn't like my chances of not being selected. Sure enough, after my fourth wine and a shot of ouzo, I was the first to be called onstage. I was dizzy from the wine and even dizzier after I had been thrown around the stage by one of the performers, who was apparently "dancing" with me.

After the show, as we were preparing to go back to the bus and drive back to our respective hotels I could feel the boy who had thrown me around staring at me. One of the girl performers suddenly appeared at my side.

"Hi," she smiled.

"Oh, hello." I smiled back at her. I had admired her beauty on stage and was suddenly made shy by her closeness and attentiveness towards me.

"My name is Alena. My friend thinks that you are very beautiful. He cannot speak English but would love to get to know you better. We are all going out for a drink in about an hour or so, would you like to join us? Do you have a phone number?"

"Uh, yeah, sure." I fished out my phone and read it out to her as she pinned the numbers into her phone. I was still using the sim card I had been given in the UK although I was almost sure it no longer had credit and that I could no longer receive calls outside England. I didn't mind: I was far too skeptical to go partying with these guys. Much as I wanted to hang out with some locals my own age and make new friends, my paranoia after watching *Taken,* the fact that I was alone, that one of the guys was interested in me, that it was night and I was a little drunk left me knowing I would not be going for drinks with these (more than likely) innocent people.

Arriving in my room, I showered, ate some chocolate and flicked on the television. Just as I was about to snuggle into the sheets, I received a text message.

Where are u staying? We will pick u up at 11.
Alena.

I replied telling Alena that I was just going to bed as I had a tour in the morning. After pressing Send on my phone, I received a message informing me that I did not have enough credit to send the text. So that was that. I drank two glasses of water and fell into a deep sleep.

I woke next morning feeling better than I had expected and got ready for the tour of Heraklion and the ancient ruins of Knossos that lay within the city. Knossos is considered one of the oldest cities in Europe. I felt overwhelmed at the thought of the history the worn walls of the city held. We spent half the warm spring day in the city, learning about Knossos and I returned to my apartment happy to welcome the siesta I could feel coming on.

Next day I was to fly out of Crete and back to London. To my surprise, waiting for the transfer bus was my Australian pilot friend. After an impossibly quick flight across countries, we said our goodbyes at the airport. At the ATM, for some reason I could not withdraw the little money I had left in my account. Then I realized that I only had around forty dollars left. Even if I could withdraw it, it wasn't going to do me much good, considering I still had two days left in London. I couldn't understand how I had spent all my money, how I had lost track so easily.

I found the nearest payphone and called Luca's friend Antonio. I was supposed to be staying with him for the night, and I hoped he would pick me up from the airport. The number didn't connect so I dialled Luca's Spanish phone number and told him what was going on. He told me to call him back in ten minutes; he should be able to organise something by then. I waited the ten minutes and dialled Luca's number again, all the while looking around the airport, wondering if I would have to stay there for the following two days. Luca answered the phone sounding upset. He told me that Antonio was still in Italy with a terrible flu and was not returning to London until he felt better.

Then it was time to panic. Where was I going to stay for the next two days with only forty dollars? Even if I could find somewhere that cheap, I wouldn't be able to eat, let alone take any public transport. How had I done this? Would I have to make the dreaded call to my parents and admit I had been unsuccessful in my travel planning?

Although I hated doing it I told Luca of the predicament I was in.

"Uh oh, Kri," Luca breathed into the phone.

"Yep, I don't know how I did this," I replied, trying not to stumble over my words.

"Wait five minutes and call me back, OK?" he asked.

"OK," I answered, my ego falling somewhere around my feet.

I waited ten minutes to be sure Luca had time to figure something out and dialled his number again, all too aware of the cost of the phone calls.

"Allora," Luca's voice came through the receiver, "Antonio is taking a flight back to London tonight. You can take the tube to his house now and his flatmates will let you in. He should be home by nine o'clock."

"No way!" I responded.

"Yes, way," Luca said.

"Thank you so much, Luca! Please call Antonio and thank him for me! I don't know what to say, I am so grateful for this!" I could feel the anxiety in my stomach start to ease.

"It's not a problem, Kri. Antonio is a good guy, he's happy to help."

"So I'll see you in two days?"

"Sure will, *amo*. See you in two days," Luca used the nickname he had given me, meaning love.

I hung up the phone with a deep exhalation. I was relieved, but I felt incredibly stupid for making such a rookie mistake, and guilty for making Antonio fly home when he was unwell. Big lesson number two: keep a very close eye on savings when travelling; they do indeed run out.

I made my way to Antonio's apartment and was let in by a sweet girl from South Africa by the name of Anna. She showed me to Antonio's room and the bathroom and I stayed there, waiting for Luca's sick friend's return. Just after ten o'clock that evening I heard a gentle tapping on the door. I sat up quickly.

"Hello?" I called, wishing the earth would open up and swallow me whole.

"Kristina, it's Antonio. May I come in?"

"Of course, please, come in." I got up from the bed and made my way to the door, but Antonio had beaten me to opening it.

"Ciao, Kristina, how are you?" Antonio asked. He leaned in for a hug and the traditional two kisses I had still not gotten used to.

"Never mind about me, Antonio, how are you? I can't explain how—" I began.

"Don't worry about it, Kristina, I told you that you could come here. I was just feeling unwell and thought that you would be OK, and Mamma's cooking is a little hard to leave when I'm feeling sick. Not to worry though, I am here now and all is well."

Antonio's English was impressive and his accent was adorable. He was of medium height and medium weight and had piercing blue eyes.

"I'm sure you are hungry. Let's go downstairs and have dinner. I think I have some salmon in the fridge," he said.

"OK, sure," I said. Hungry was an understatement, but there was no way I was going to let that show.

The day of my flight back to Australia Luca got to London from his training trip in Spain just two hours before I was to leave for the airport. I had my new favourite pasta waiting upon his arrival, but with one look at each other we ran to the bedroom before he got a chance to see my attempt at a replica of his mum's pasta.

He ate it cold, telling me that it was *deliziosa*. I found that hard to believe, considering it was cold, but took the compliment anyway.

Luca came with me to the airport to bid me farewell, which proved much more difficult than I'd imagined. He gave me a small stuffed tiger before I boarded the plane, and told me that we would see each other again if I wanted to. I told him that of course I wanted to.

I boarded the plane, trying to hold back tears, found my seat by the window and snuggled in for the dreaded flight ahead of me, holding the tiger close. Some twenty-four torturous hours later I was back home.

Standing in Immigration surrounded by Australians was an unforgettable experience. Wow, I thought, do we really sound like that?

"I know, I know, my passport photo doesn't look like me. That's when I used to be fat," a young blonde woman explained in a thick Australian accent to the Immigration officer.

The entire queue burst into laughter as the girl who was explaining her picture turned and faced everyone.

"I was!" she assured us.

Ah Australians, I thought, you just have to love us.

After seeing arrival signs all over the place I couldn't help but have the song "At the Arrivals Gate" by Ani De Franco stuck in my head. It's a beautiful song about people meeting their loved ones at the airport.

I took out some of the remaining cash I had left in my bank account to buy my train ticket home. The money the ATM machine spat into my hand felt completely fake! The colours seemed too bright to be real. It was weird. After a mere eight weeks away from Australia, the money I had used for my entire life felt completely foreign to me. It was bizarre.

I made my way to the platform among the all-too-much familiarity and, before I knew it, I was back home. Where we drive on the left side of the road—and sensibly. Where I could see the same cars parked out the front of the same houses in the same streets. Where when I spoke to a waitress I knew she would understand what I was saying because we spoke the same language.

Although it was nice to be back home for a little while, and I could have stayed and started projects and studying here, I couldn't swallow the feeling of needing to get back out.

3

Together again

The next four months were difficult. Luca and I stayed in contact over the phone. Although it was hard, we were determined to see each other again. He booked a flight to Australia for September. We planned to do a road trip around Australia as well as a trip to South East Asia. I worked day and night for those four months to save up as much money as I could before Luca arrived.

The week before we would finally see each other again I started to feel extremely nervous that things weren't going to work out, that it had all been a fairy tale that we had invented. This boy, after only five weeks together, was flying to the other side of the world for me. The pressure of this realisation was heavy; I almost wanted Luca to stay in Europe. What if I wasn't what he had expected, or vice versa? There were countless *what ifs* rolling around in my mind as I drove to the airport to pick him up. But once I saw him standing there, I knew everything was going to be OK. Even if we didn't work, Luca was a beautiful person that I was excited to see and have in my life.

I rented a small apartment for us to stay in for the two weeks I had left at work. Luca spent some serious one-on-one time with my dog

Lucy, and getting to know my Groundhog Day town. When the two weeks were up, we said goodbye to my family and friends and took one of the two roads out of town, heading north in the Ford Falcon my dad had given to me as a parting present. We were on the same route as the one I had begun with Taylor and never finished four years earlier.

Our first stop was in a small town fifteen minutes north of Forster. It was just Luca, Lucy, me, the Ford and our two-man tent. The feeling of freedom couldn't have been stronger. It was such a liberating feeling to say goodbye to that town and hello to the road ahead. We stopped at the supermarket and bought some semi-dried tomatoes, camembert, crackers and a bottle of red wine.

Lucy snuggled up in the tent with Luca and me, although Luca wasn't so fussed on having a dog in the tent with us. We played the game Guess Who, without the board game. It goes something like this:

"Are you attractive?"

"Yes."

"Are you an actress?"

"Yes."

"I give up. Who are you?"

"Demi Moore."

"Ahh, OK."

We spent many nights and rainy days like this in the tent and, over the next few weeks, we made our way up to where my mum was living. We stopped at some beautiful small beach towns along the way, setting our tent up in gorgeous places with priceless views, but also hidden so the rangers wouldn't see us. This was always a bit stressful.

"*Amo*, it's getting dark. Where are we going to park?" is what I frequently heard from Luca.

This was our biggest problem usually, but after a while we realized that No Through Road signs were our new best friends. As soon as we saw a No Through Road sign we knew we had more than likely found our place to set up camp.

Once we left my mum's place and left my dog Lucy with Taylor, we had around two weeks to drive some three thousand, five hundred kilometres to Darwin for our flight to Singapore. During those three thousand, five hundred kilometres Luca and I had time to get to know each other, and to begin to understand just how crazy we could make each other.

Driving along yet another barren road in the middle of the outback, Luca and I started to fight. I can no longer recall what it was about but I'm sure it was ridiculous. Suddenly, without even realising it myself, I grabbed the cap off Luca's head and threw it out the car window.

"*Amo*! But are you fucking crazy?" Luca screamed, screeching the car around to go back to pick up his cap.

"Yeah, I'm crazy! Keep calling me names, Luca, I love it!" I screamed back.

It wasn't that we weren't an amazing couple; at the time I thought we were the most beautiful couple in the world. We loved being around each other, we were interested in many of the same things. Luca had said that he also wanted to do volunteer work, and I had not met many people with that interest. More than anything, though, we just clicked. But as often as we clicked, we hit heads just as much, if not more so. And for a long time. I'm not sure if it was the language barrier or a cultural barrier. There was just something about each other that seemed to drive us crazy, and not in a good way.

A few days later we were driving through dry, grassed plains with Sarah Blasko's voice belting out of the tape player for the umpteenth time. There was no radio signal where we were, and I had made only two mixed tapes for our trip. Big mistake. Suddenly a huge bang came from one of the tyres.

"*Amo*, what's going on?" Luca half-whispered, squeezing my thigh.

"I think we might have a flat tyre," I replied, noting that we seemed very far from civilization.

I swung my door open as we came to a bumpy stop. Stepping onto the melting hot asphalt, I realized that the temperature must have been in the forties. Sweat began beading on my top lip and making its way down my cleavage. There was no dry breeze to stop it in its tracks. I looked at the breathtakingly bare landscape around us. The plains stretched as far as the eye could see, split in two by the empty road we had been driving down only minutes before. The sun beat down on us, the sky seemed to be a darker blue than I had ever seen.

My stomach fell to the floor when I realized that we hadn't checked the spare tyre before leaving, and we had passed maybe two people during the entire morning's drive.

We circled the car. The front right tyre was blown to shreds. We popped the boot and, fingers crossed, I helped Luca to fish out the spare. It looked to be OK, and we went about the job of changing the tyre on a road that was too hot to touch.

Once the job was done, we went back to our route, aware that if there was another blow out, we would be in a lot of trouble. It was two hundred kilometres to the nearest town and one hundred kilometres since the last one. We made it to the next town without mishap, bought a spare tyre and felt more at ease as we hit the road. Our relief was short-lived. No more than one hundred kilometres later, BAM!

"No fucking way!" I screamed.

"Another tyre, *amo*. What should we do? How long until the next town?" Luca asked as we piled out of the car.

"I can't remember. I think pretty far. Should we turn back?"

"I have no idea." He looked panicked.

We set about our next tyre change, the second for the day, and came to the decision to keep moving on. We made it to the next petrol station, which thankfully sold tyres. It seemed that all of these remote towns had at least one tyre store, if nothing else. There were no tyres the right size, so we settled for a brand new tyre the closest size we could find. The man we bought the tyre from told us the tyres were most probably busting because of the heat of the road. We decided to stay put until dark and drive only at night, even though we still had a very long way to go.

We sat outside the petrol station and watched as the sun sank into the horizon. That sunset was one of the most beautiful I have ever seen. The grassed fields around us were barren and burnt yellow. The sky slowly turned pink as did the sun. It was like a bright pink balloon sinking to the other side of the world.

We waited for as long as we could, testing the asphalt every twenty minutes. When we judged the road was cool enough, I hopped into the driver's seat as Luca had been driving most of the way.

"Luca, I'm scared I'm going to hit a kangaroo, they're attracted to the headlights."

"*Vaboo,*" Luca said, an expression in Napolitano that has an array of meanings, this time meaning, "We will drive without the lights on."

That was that. For rest of the journey, we drove only at night, with no headlights, beeping the horn every ten seconds, in hopes of scaring off roos. During the scorching hot days, we sat inside air-conditioned malls trying to escape the heat.

We stopped at the city of Katherine for the day and rented a canoe at the famous gorge. We were told not to go close to the banks marked CROCODILE NESTING AREAS as it would disturb nesting crocs.

The size of the red rocky gorge is impressive, and the beauty of it breathtaking. There wasn't a noise to be heard apart from our paddles slapping the surface of the still water. As we sat in our canoe, red rock cliffs on either side, I had the grounding sensation of insignificance. That feeling that I am so small, that on a larger scale of things I am totally and utterly unimportant, that my worries and problems and stories and dramas are just stories. That the rocks around me were more real, alive and important than the little story that I call me.

We were splashing around, close to the small caves along the rock face when suddenly Luca stopped.

"*Amo*, I think I just saw a crocodile."

"No way." I suddenly felt anxious.

"I swear, *amo,* right over there." He pointed to the inside of a cave we were close to. We looked at each other and paddled a little closer.

As we approached I heard a loud noise from the area like the pressure of expelled air. Seconds later I saw her. Only her eyes at first, then the nostrils and the top of her head as she slowly started to surface. We began paddling frantically in the direction from which we had come.

"Oh my god, Luca! It was a crocodile! Did you hear the noise she made?" I asked.

"That wasn't the crocodile making the noise, *amo*," Luca answered.

"It was the crocodile, Luca! Are you kidding me? Did you not hear that?" I said.

"No it wasn't, *amo*, no way. Crocodiles don't make sounds. It was probably just the water against the wall."

I persisted. "I promise you, Luca, it was the crocodile."

"OK, let's go back."

Eager to prove Luca wrong, I agreed. We turned the canoe around towards the cave and slowly made our way back to the crocodile, stopping closer than we had before. We were maybe two metres away from her when suddenly … "RRRRAAAAAAWWWWWWWWWWW!"

The crocodile lashed out at us as fast as the blink of an eye, jaws wide open and then retreated, sliding back beneath the surface.

Not that we hung around for any goodbyes. I have never seen anyone move as fast as that cute little Italian did that day. His mouth was in the shape of an O, his frantic arms were pulling at those paddles like his life depended on it. I couldn't stop laughing.

That would teach him for not listening to me.

We made it to Darwin with no more flat tyres, so we didn't have to abandon the car, something I had been fearful of having to do. Two days before our flight to Singapore, we woke up in our tent early and began the process of packing it up, along with all our things, before heading into town to have some breakfast. Luca went off to do a wee and ran back quickly with a look of disbelief on his face.

"They took everything, *amo!*" he exclaimed.

"What do you mean?" I asked, my stomach falling somewhere between my feet.

"They took everything. They smashed the windows and everything is gone."

"WHAT?" I ran out of the tent and looked at the car. The back door didn't open by the handle, so the thieves had smashed the front window as well to get in, not realising they could have simply put their hand through the back smashed window and opened it from the inside. All of our things were gone. I began searching desperately through the car, as though if I just kept looking I would find our belongings.

We still had our big backpacks, but everything else was gone. Phones, cameras (along with many, many photos), iPods, toiletries— all gone. Luckily we had taken our passports and credit cards into the tent with us.

I was standing by the car, my hands to my mouth, trying not to cry, when the police happened to drive past. They pulled over, our situation apparent, asked us some questions and began to make some phone calls.

We waited for quite some time until the forensic team came. Once they had fingerprinted the car, we finished packing up our tent and drove into town for breakfast, feeling depressed and a little against the world.

As it so happened, I was supposed to sell the car that very afternoon. I gave the guy a call and told him the situation. To our surprise he still bought it, although for less than we had expected, of course.

We stayed the night at a hostel and tried to forget the negative situation we'd experienced. Things could have been much worse. What we had lost we could make up again, apart from the photos; that was what stung the most. However, we did have an adventure ahead of us with plenty of opportunities for new photos and memories.

We focused on this instead.

4

Second time around

My second impression of Asia wasn't exactly what I had been expecting. Singapore is far from being like its sister countries. For one thing most people speak English. Still, I knew what was in store for me over the next two months and my love affair with South East Asia had already begun all the same. For dinner, we ate for less than five dollars in a soup restaurant by the name of Fishheads. The restaurant consisted of five plastic tables covered in blue-and-white floral plastic tablecloths and strewn across the front of the store; it was too hot to eat inside. Each table had a hole in the middle with a gas bottle underneath. We chose from a menu, ticking the boxes on the small form on our table with our options for the soup, and yes, the fish head option was there. Once we had chosen, they brought out a large stainless steel bowl divided into two portions for two different types of soup. The waitress lit the gas bottle and there you had it, a mini gas-stove top as your table. Then our choice from the menu arrived raw on a plate, and we cooked it ourselves in the soup. Amazing! And it was delicious.

After dinner we went to the hostel we had already checked into. Our room was at the top, and only half-enclosed, with another fourteen or so backpackers who had also decided to take the cheapest option. Early the next morning we took our flight to Bangkok, and then a bus to the place we had found on the couch surfing website—a website where it is possible to stay at other member's home, or where travellers can come and stay at your home for free. It is a fantastic way to meet people and to learn more about different cultures.

This, however, was a hostel, although it did have a free-of-charge dorm room with around fifteen beds, as well as having private bedrooms for less than five dollars. As the free dormitory was full, we got ourselves a private room for three dollars a night.

On seeing the rooms I could understand why they were so cheap. First of all we climbed the five flights to our room, which had no bed as it was drying out from beer spilt on it by the previous tenants. We put our bags in our glorious room that smelled of damp towels, cigarettes and old beer. Then I made my way to the bathroom, something I already knew was going to be a nightmare.

I have never seen or even imagined a bathroom as disgusting as those in this hostel. There was poo all over the toilet bowl and seat. It looked mouldy, it smelt horrendous. I was gagging the entire time I was peeing. There was liquid all over the floor; I could only imagine its origins. I just had to put myself in a distant place in my mind not to scream.

At that point in time, the worst toilets I had seen were the public toilets in the main street of my home town, which now seemed five-star in comparison. I had a lot to learn about third-world countries' toilet management. Since then there has only been one other toilet that ranked as high on the horror-story scale as that one in Bangkok. Sure, the squat toilets were different and may have smelled strongly, but most were kept extremely clean—especially if ignorant travellers hadn't tried to flush toilet paper down them.

I made my way back to our room feeling weak in the stomach. The room wasn't much of a comfort. It was dark even with the light switched on and its maroon walls and musty tiled floors looked as though they had not seen a cleaning implement in their entire existence. We decided not to wait in the shit hole for our mattress and went out for a walk. If we hadn't already had such a trek to get from the airport to the hostel we would have left straight away, although we only had five days in Bangkok until we had a flight to India, and would be returning to see the rest of Thailand in a month's time. With such a short amount of time in the city we didn't want to bother looking for another place to stay and moving all our things. Instead, we spent as little as time possible at our hostel, and spent most of our time visiting the sights.

Bangkok is a magical city; you just have to know how to work it. Luca, being the tour manager and traveller that he was, knew how. We visited the giant buddhas nestled away in pockets of the city, whose viewing took my breath away. We visited a floating market, passing through its "streets" by canoe, buying fruit from the fellow canoeists, many of whom were old and grey, sporting pointy round hats and toothless grins. We went to the night market, where we found the rest of the tourists we had barely seen anything of during our stay.

As I was walking through the market I misjudged a step and rolled my ankle. Two Israeli boys who'd just finished their service in the army strapped my ankle up for me. I had never heard about the Israeli army and the problems that Israel and Palestine had. I was surprised to hear that all young men and women had to go into the army after school, two years for women and three for men. I thanked my saviours and limped back to the hostel with Luca's help. This was going to make getting around the city incredibly difficult.

We were lucky enough to be in Bangkok for the king's birthday, an enormous celebration. Everyone celebrating the day wore pink because the king was sick; normally they would have worn yellow. We ate at small food stalls with the locals, watched with them as the Thai people paraded through the town and joined in with our fellow celebrators in waving the Thai flag high in the air. We made our way through the sea of pink shirts to the king's palace, and were accosted by teenage girls and boys wanting to take photos with us. Later I would learn that this was quite normal in South East Asia, and felt a little more at ease with the process.

The day after the king's birthday we took our flight to India, checking Luca's emails beforehand to see if the guy we would be couch surfing with in Delhi that night had written us anything, and he had. He couldn't host us after all. So we were arriving in India in the middle of the night, with no accommodation booked.

Not the best idea, we soon found out.

We pored over the *Lonely Planet* we'd borrowed from our hostel, reading up on places to stay in Delhi. We also read up a little on India:

Don't believe what anyone tells you at the airport.

Don't believe what the taxidrivers tell you.

Check where you are taken, as it may not be where you want to go. And so on.

OK, I thought. I felt pretty sure I knew how to handle my new Indian friends. On arrival we took the first public bus we could into the centre, feeling the sooner we found a place to stay the better. The horn honking in this city was unbelievable. Every millisecond someone blew their horn.

A big truck with an open trailer filled with men pulled up beside us at the traffic lights. The men's faces were covered with scarves, their eyes stared out into the cold night. I started to feel that most of those eyes were on me. I tried to shake off the feeling and kept my gaze anywhere but on the truck. But everywhere I looked, I could feel eyes on me and I realized that it wasn't just a feeling: all eyes *were* on me. Although in Thailand and Indonesia people had looked at me more than I was used to, it was nowhere near as intense as I found it that night and for the rest of my stay in India. I was later told that it wasn't seen as rude in India for people to stare, but that night I was not aware of this and I felt extremely uncomfortable. Hindi music had been blaring from the bus's speakers and I felt for the first time culture shock. Sure I had experienced cultural differences a little already, but all of the places I had visited so far were fairly westernised.

Hindi music? It didn't feel real. I guess in my bubble of existence Hindi music and Indian culture was like some fantasy. People didn't actually listen to that, did they? As I looked around me I had a dawning realisation. Yes, people did listen to that music. And some Indian women did wear saris, and they spoke a language that I would probably never understand. Not everyone lived like me.

Wow, wake up call. Now I understood the meaning of culture shock.

Once we arrived at the centre, we took a rickshaw to the hostel we had chosen. Our Sikh driver informed us that we had come at a really bad time of year. Now it was the Muslim festival and all the hostels were likely to be booked out.

"No, really?" Luca asked.

"Yes, rilly," our driver told us, shaking his head. In our culture this means *no,* but in Indian culture it affirms the answer.

"Wamana *amo,* we came exactly at the wrong time," Luca said.

Our driver took us to two different hostels. Both told us that they and everyone around them were full.

"I can take you to the twenty-four-hour tourist information office if you like," the driver offered.

"OK, let's do that. Thank you so much."

It was quite a ride to this twenty-four-hour tourist office, where we were hoping that we could solve our problem. As we arrived I realized that it was almost midnight.

"What do we do, Luca, if we can't find somewhere?" I asked as we made our way to the tiny, lighted room I guessed was the twenty-four-hour tourist office.

"It's OK, *amo*. Don't worry, I will find us somewhere."

When we entered the small room we were greeted by a boy who looked to be no older than eighteen.

"Yes, my friend, it is correct. Everywhere is very, very full," he said, before we could even ask.

"OK, wait a second," Luca said as we pulled out the guide book and flicked to the pages for accommodation in Delhi. "Can you please call here for us?" he asked, pointing to a number on one of the pages.

"Not a problem. I can call them and you can ask them yourselves."

It went on like this for the next hour or so, our new friend calling the hostels and passing us the receiver with a sad look. Suddenly two men appeared at the entrance to the small office. Both possessed a strong air of arrogance and looked as though they were a part of Delhi's mafia.

"Ah, here are my friends. They can take you to a hotel, somewhere not too expensive. You can't stay here any longer and you can't go out on the street." He paused for effect. "You," he said, pointing to Luca, "will get beaten and robbed. And she," he said, nodding to me, "she will get beaten, robbed and raped. So you really have no choice." He emphasised the last three words and the severity of the situation with a head wobble.

So that was that. Our bags were loaded into the back of a car belonging to the travel agent's friends, the ones who had the appearance of the local mafia.

"Are you OK?" Luca asked.

"Not really," I answered.

But we got into the car anyway, and to this day it remains the scariest ride of my life. For the entire drive I looked left and right, frantically searching for landmarks and street names so that I would have an idea of where we were if something went wrong.

The streets we sped through were spotted with figures living in cardboard boxes and makeshift shacks. Their gaunt faces showed contempt more than curiosity as we drove past them. I searched the driver and his friend for any distinct features or for a sign that they were people that we could trust, but I got no more out of my searching than I already had. Both wore thick gold chains around their necks and wrists and gold rings, each ring sporting different coloured large stones in the centre. Their dark hair was combed and slicked back with oil. I could only see part of the driver's face in the rear view mirror, but it was too dark to make out his features. Bollywood music blared from the car's speakers as we flew down the dark, narrow streets littered with rubbish. We screeched to a stop in front of a luxurious looking hotel. I blinked in disbelief at our good fortune and my stomach went back to normal, rather than being in thirteen thousand knots.

"Hahaha, would you like to stay the night here?" the driver asked with one quick backward glance. The brute beside him roared with laughter.

"It's just five hundred euros, not too bad, hey?" the friend chimed in as the driver punched the car into reverse and sped backwards out of the driveway of our mirage.

"It's OK," I exclaimed. I would have been happy to pay five hundred euros just to get the fuck out of that car.

The driver didn't hear me or he pretended not to. He took off, leaving behind the safe walls of the hotel behind us. Two blocks and two heart attacks later we stopped in front of a sagging hotel. Luca and I burst out of the car before it had come to a complete stop, not letting the opportunity slip this time. The hotel manager was conveniently waiting out the front. After negotiating the incredible price down from three hundred euros per night to one hundred and fifty for a room of not much higher quality than the one we had stayed at in Bangkok, we exhaustedly followed the gentleman who had appeared out of nowhere and kindly offered to carry our bags for us upstairs. Placing our bags beside the lumpy-looking bed, he showed us around our room, which was coloured from floor to wall to curtains to bed in the same shade of pink. The pink room.

He gave a demonstration (he couldn't speak English) of the hot and cold taps in the bathroom, how to pick up the phone and dial reception and how to turn the TV on and off. After multiple demonstrations he just stood staring at us. Eventually he held out his hand and said a word we were not expecting to hear.

"Tip?"

A tip. After we had obviously been taken for the ride of our lives.

"Go and ask your boss for your tip!" Luca told the man as calmly as he could.

We stayed in our pink room for only six hours. We wanted to get out of there as soon as possible and it had been two o'clock in the morning by the time we had checked in. Next morning I asked a fellow backpacker I ran into in the hallway how much his room was. Fourteen euros he said. We had been slaughtered.

We drank our included Thumbs Up (the Indian version of Dr Pepsi) and Coke to get as much as we could for our money, and made our way to the real tourist information office the man at reception told us of.

Surprise, surprise, who was our driver from the hotel to the real tourist office? The little jerk from the "twenty-four-hour tourist office" of the night before. How convenient. Once we got to the government tourist office, we had everything laid out for us.

The Muslim festival that everyone had been carrying on about the night before had finished a month earlier. Bullshit number one.

The people who had told the rickshaw driver they were all full were all in on the scam. Bullshit number two.

The twenty-four-hour tourist office was illegal and fake. Bullshit number three.

That rickshaw driver! He had us so fooled with his sweetness. All the hostels the kid at the twenty-four-hour tourist office was calling were probably his friends or family members telling us they were full. Of course! He dialled the number for us and spoke to the person on the other end before we did. Bullshit number four.

While the real tour agent behind the desk was enlightening us I had a flashback to a moment when the jerk kid had picked up our copy of Lonely Planet's publication of *India,* as we were both sitting across from him, utterly helpless. He'd pointed to the title on the cover and had said:

I ... **N**ever ... **D**o ... **I**t ... **A**gain.

Well, we'd had a first-class experience of what the guide book had warned us about, and what we had thought we were prepared for. Those people were so tricky—and believable! For the entire remainder of my trip in India I found myself second-guessing absolutely everything I was told by anyone.

I turned my attention back to the real tour agent in front of me. He had offered us a tour that included a personal driver and accommodation throughout the Rajasthan area, the part of India in the desert bordering Pakistan. He had also included train tickets from Agra, where the Taj Mahal was, to Varanassi, the place for Hindi people to visit at least once in their life, and especially when dying.

After our previous night's experience, and given that we had only three weeks to see India, we decided we didn't have time to sort the bullshit from the truth for the rest of our trip—or the money to be ripped off again—and booked the tour with our new-found friend. We paid the hefty price for our tour, even though we were both skeptical, and were told that it would be two hours before our driver arrived to pick us up and start the tour, a twelve-hour drive to our first stop in Mandawa.

We decided to go and get some lunch. The walk of two blocks from the travel agency to a small restaurant gave me my first real taste of India. The crowded streets were filled with makeshift stalls selling samosas and snacks. Just like the night before, all eyes were on Luca and me. Mainly me. Looking around, I could barely see a woman in sight.

For the entire five-minute walk we were constantly approached by a variety of men trying to sell us one thing or another, or to take us somewhere or other. Personal space didn't seem to be considered and I found myself feeling a little overwhelmed, if not frightened. We went into the first restaurant we found to escape the madness and ordered some thali—a dish typical of southern India. I didn't know what any of the dishes were except the dahl. It was delicious.

As we were eating, a man in his mid-forties to early fifties made his way over to the table beside us. He started up a conversation with us and began asking us some rather strange questions. We were already paranoid after the night before and decided not to give him too much attention. Looking back now, he was probably just a guy wanting to be friendly.

After lunch we made our way back through the crowded streets to the tourist office, happy that indeed it still existed, and that we hadn't just paid some random man sixteen hundred dollars for a tour, only to have him run off on us. We met our driver in the small office and with great relief got the hell out of Delhi. We drove well into the night, Luca and I both in the back seat of the car, me lying in his lap: the bumpy roads we flew down were making thali milkshake in my stomach. I was sure it would come up the moment I decided to sit up.

Around nine o'clock that night and seven hours into our drive, we started to get hungry. Luca asked our driver if there was somewhere close by where we could get something to eat.

"Yes, sir," he answered. He had been doing that for the entire trip. My comments seemed to go unnoticed, Luca would have to repeat them to get an answer. "In approximately one hour we can find a restaurant for you to eat."

What seemed to be an eternity later, we pulled up in a dusty car park before a building that looked very old and empty and far from being a restaurant.

"We are here, sir."

We got out of the car and were met by a thin, dark man dressed in the typical desert attire—long white robes and an off-white turban. He showed us through the front door and we saw, after he turned the lights on, that there were three men asleep on the restaurant tables. Groggy with the sudden shock of the neon lights in their faces, the men pushed themselves into a seated position, swung their legs to the floor and made their way to the kitchen, still half-asleep.

I didn't want to stare but I couldn't help but be fascinated by the clothes they wore, which were the same as the man's who had met us at the entrance. They looked ... beautiful. In Delhi the dress code had been fairly westernized, especially among the younger generation, the men wearing mainly trousers and a shirt buttoned until the last button. They were very smart looking with a hint of retro, and most of the men were sporting moustaches. The women in Delhi wore mainly jeans and T-shirts.

We ordered our meal. It was expensive, but at that time of night and the fact that it was tasty and safe looking it was worth the price. We set off for the remainder of the drive to our first stop, the fort city of Mandawa. We arrived in the early hours of the morning, checked in to our guesthouse and were shown to our room. It was jaw-droppingly gorgeous. I felt as if we had just flown a magic carpet into a sultan's daughter's lair. The entire room was covered in tiny pieces of cut mirror, spreading the walls with tones of green and silver. Unfortunately we had an early morning the next day and were exhausted. The most our eyes saw that night were the backs of our eyelids.

Early the next morning we woke for the guided tour around the ancient city of Mandawa. The streets were of sand, the mode of transport was by donkey and cart or camel. I noticed as we walked the streets that most of the older women still covered their faces with their colourful saris, and that the men here wore turbans and desert clothing.

Mandawa is famous for its walls painted with well preserved frescos called havelis. The havelis tell stories of how to give birth, when the British invaded, wars and elephants and other animals. They were beautiful and fairy tale-like.

Halfway through the tour I had a desperate desire to pee. Our guide told a young boy who happened to be standing nearby to show me where the toilet was. I followed the boy to a small out building made of rotting planks of wood forming a rather slanted cubicle.

I took a hesitant step inside and was almost knocked over by the stench. Although I was already bracing for it, I still had to give my nostrils a small test to see what I was in for. It seemed the plumbing here in Mandawa was not as advanced as the places I had previously visited in my life. I took a long breath through my mouth and held it for the entire time I was in the cubicle.

It was a squat pit toilet and I found it extremely difficult to juggle myself over that thing without part of my being or my baggy, non-revealing clothes touching the damp ground. There was no toilet paper and, while I was silently thanking the heavens that it wasn't a number two, I mentally noted to always carry toilet paper while travelling. Sitting under a tap was a bucket of water with a plastic scoop. I gathered it was to flush down my stuff and wash my hands. I fumbled with this new-found technology while my face turned pink from lack of oxygen and tumbled out of there as fast as I could.

The young boy was waiting for me, waiting for his tip. I soon learned that tipping here was just a way of life if you were a foreigner. Get used to it, and carry rupees on you always. A rupee can go a long way at the worst of times.

After our tour we left for the next town, and then the next. We went on like this for two or three days at a time in each town around the Rajasthan. Along the way I started to feel the effects of culture shock. I couldn't find any comfort in Luca, who was more at ease with our new surroundings. He had been to India before and had travelled much of the world, which made me feel even more lonely. After a few days, though, I started to get the hang of things and even started to fall in love with this new-found way of life. And a new-found life it was. Anyone going to India must forget what they think they know about life. Try as they might, it just will not work like that there.

5

Incredible India

From elephants in the traffic to women working in construction, their bright saris scattered through the fields we passed, nothing can compare to incredible India. As the days wore on I fell more and more in love with this country—the colour, the music of the daily grind. And the people. They are funny and sweet and giving. As in all places around the world we had to be careful about where we went, but in general the people were just as incredible as the land they resided in.

We took a camel tour into the desert and watched the sun set over the dunes. We went to a monkey temple and then to a rat temple, where hundreds of rats crawled across the floors, through the offerings and windowpanes, balancing on the sides of the dishes of milk left out for them. The most off-putting experience however was not the stickiness I felt under my feet but the sight of a woman kissing the ground in honour of the smelly little guys.

Very young kids working in all types of jobs were common, from fruitsellers to little mini chefs. I haggled with a child who barely came up to my belly button over the price of a bra. In the golden city of Jaisalmer I bought a leather shaving-kit case for my brother. The store clerk, an enormous ten years of age, asked me the famous question that Indians love to ask.

"Which country?"

"Australia."

"Ahh, Australia, yes yes. I have business in Australia." The boy smiled up at me, shaking his head in confirmation in that confusing way Indians have.

Seeing first-hand, children having to work to survive, without the opportunity of an education or better yet a childhood, was heartbreaking. The future for these children was not much more than years and years of hard work, quite possibly for the rest of their lives. My heart was beginning to open to this country, and possibilities were starting to run through my mind. Maybe India was the place where I could make a difference. Could I handle this intensity? The food here certainly wasn't my favourite. Could I live here, could I eat Indian food for long periods of time? These were questions I would have to address later.

We stopped in the holy town of Pushkar for one night. Everyone was supposed to be vegetarian as Pushkar was believed to be a holy city because of the lake the city is built upon. It is surrounded by fifty-two bathing ghats, where just one dip is believed to cleanse sins and cure skin diseases. Over five hundred Hindu temples were situated around the lake.

We went for a walk along the ghats and met a holy man along the way. Who, of course, tried to take advantage of us.

"Fifty two ghatsss," he hissed. "Five hundred temples."

He repeated his mantra to us until finally we stopped to humour him. After all he did look thin and in need of some food. The holy men as they are called usually live at the temples, dedicating their lives to God.

He seemed very happy that we'd finally stopped to listen to him.

"This is your passport all over the world for your spirituality," he said as he wrapped two pieces of yellow and red cotton around our wrists. "Now you pay," he said, when he had finished the knot on my arm.

We were already expecting a price for our new passports and had fished out our wallets.

"How much?" Luca asked the holy man.

"Oh nothing, just something, nothing really, just something like five hundred dollars?"

Aha. We weren't expecting that.

Some time passed before we eventually got his price down to something a little more reasonable for the two pieces of string he had tied around our wrists. We ended up paying around five dollars each, a very good price for a world-wide spiritual passport, we were told.

We walked to the city's famous temple. Once in the temple I immediately felt a strong calmness running through my veins. On our way around the temple we were offered some kind of candy, which I ate. I only realized that it was probably supposed to be an offering when it was too late.

All of a sudden Luca began to feel sick, so we went home to bed. We ordered room service. Two hours and many phone calls to reception later it came. I was almost fainting with hunger. We soon learned when in India to order food at least an hour before we would be hungry.

The middle of the night rolled around. I was woken by the sound of Luca heaving. I pushed open the door a crack and saw that he was vomiting standing up.

"Are you OK, Luca?"

"Yeah, *amo*, I'm OK. Go back to sleep."

As sorry for him as I felt, I couldn't help but be impressed by his ability to vomit standing up. How could he aim?

When we got to Agra we said goodbye to our driver, and gave him his well-earned tip. Dropping our bags at the hostel, we made our way straight to the Taj Mahal. The difference in the price of admission between foreigners and Indians was somewhere along the lines of ten to one. But it was worth it. Upon seeing that shining, perfectly symmetrical building something inside me moved. If I hadn't been so doped up on migraine tablets, I would have cried. It was just ... spectacular.

Unfortunately, being a foreign woman attracted a lot of unwanted attention. Men, teens and parents wanted me in their photos with the Taj Mahal. An Indian couple who lived in England asked Luca if I was famous. A group of boys even hired a professional photographer to take a photo with me, along with the Taj Mahal in the background.

I just didn't have the heart or the energy to say no.

The Taj Mahal, meaning "crown of buildings", was built by Moghul emperor Shah Jahnan for his third wife Mumtaz Mahal, as her resting place after her death.

After the exhausting afternoon we returned to the hostel. On our way we stopped for a pizza. I was happy to have food without spices—and even then I think there were some sprinkled in the mix. Something that really disturbed me was the way a few of the men dining treated the waiters. Only the wealthier Indians ate at places like this, and the hierarchy was only too visible. It took all my might not to tell those stuck-up men where to go.

One other impressing personality we met who didn't reach the height of our shoulders went by the name of Bahia. We were in Khajuraho, the town of the Kama Sutra temples. We had hired a driver and were visiting the temple ruins, stopping to buy snacks from roadside sellers along the way. After one such stop a young boy who looked no older than twelve jumped into the front seat of our rickshaw beside the driver. Neither of them exchanged a single word as the young boy answered a phone call on his mobile phone. Luca and I were both thinking the same thing: commission kid.

We had been riding for around five minutes before the boy turned to us.

"Would you like to see the real Khajuraho? The old city?"

"Sure." Luca and I smiled back at him, intrigued by this little tour guide's offer.

After some communication in Hindi between the driver and the boy, he turned to us and asked that favourite question.

"Which country?"

We found out that our new friend's name was Bahia and that he was thirteen years old. He was incredibly cute, I could tell he was a smart kid.

He jumped out and held my hand as I got off my seat. "Follow me."

We walked through the narrow, dirt streets with our new friend. The old city was so beautiful. We walked past a small door and I peeked inside. It looked like a laundrette. A dark-skinned woman in a pink sari was ironing some material. The iron looked to be from the middle ages. The room she stood in was small and filled from bench to ceiling with piles of what seemed to be linen. We kept walking and with every turn my eyes feasted on the delights that make India: a woman tapping a donkey loaded with bricks on the backside, kids playing cricket in the street, a little boy and an even smaller girl pumping water. I felt a pulling urge to stay here for a long time.

Bahia had been very patient with our stopping and taking photos and asking him questions, which he had all the answers to. Finally we came to a stop outside a school.

"This is my old school, we have volunteers working here sometimes. Would you like a tour?"

"I would love a tour," I exclaimed.

Bahia made an excellent guide. At the end of the tour we found ourselves in the principal's office.

"You don't have to, but if you would like, you can make a donation to the school so that more kids can have the opportunity to learn like I did."

We made a small donation; we were tight for money. I had a feeling that someday I would come back here and make a real contribution to these gorgeous kids.

"That's the end of our tour. I am not asking you for money. If you would like to donate some, you can. I just do this because I know that education is very important and I want other kids to have the opportunity that I have had."

This kid was really special.

We exchanged email addresses and phone numbers as we had an Indian phone. To this day some five years later, I still write to Bahia. Unfortunately I haven't yet had the opportunity to go back.

The next morning we navigated our way to the bus station, then on to the train for our trip to Varanasi. We sat on the two spare seats at the back of the bus. I was positioned between Luca and a friendly fellow who was doing his best to keep the conversation rolling.

"So ... which god do you have?"

"Oh, I don't really have a god in particular."

"What do you mean—are you Christian?"

I shook my head.

"Buddhist?"

I kept on shaking my head.

"Muslim then? Which god?"

It was a nice change from which country.

"None, my friend, no god in particular," I answered.

"No god?" he replied, and with that looked to the front of the bus, total and utter confusion plastered on his face.

There were so many people living around the train station and in the street. I wanted to give them all something to eat. I bought a nann for one guy who looked as though he was particularly in need, and a packet of crackers for a little boy. It wasn't much, but I felt better knowing that at least two tummies were fuller than before.

In my lack of experience I had brought a suitcase with wheels. It was very heavy and impossible to carry. I had to drag it through a considerable amount of I have no idea what for the entire trip, and that walk to and around the train station was no exception.

The train ride to Varanasi was something I will never forget. There were about eight narrow beds in each carriage, and I was the only girl in mine. In India it's not at all rude to stare, a lesson I learned in detail on this train ride. I felt long-lashed brown eyes on me every move that I made. Twice I woke up in the night to find someone different sitting on my bed staring at me. All I could do was roll over and try to focus on the sounds of the train. Sleeping on the train, I found, was an extremely soothing experience.

We arrived at the Varanasi train station at an unimaginable hour in the morning. We mustered all our strength, collected our bags and hailed a rickshaw to our (thankfully) pre-booked guesthouse. We unloaded our bags in our room and, not wanting to miss the included breakfast and the first day in Varanasi, we made our way to the restaurant. Then we sat at a table and waited the usual hour and a half for our breakfast to arrive.

First comes the pepper and the salt. Then the cutlery. Then the drinks, and finally ... the food. Feeling more and more at home in India, I gobbled my meal as fast as I could so we could go explore this city I had heard so much about.

Varanasi is to Hindus what Mecca is to Muslims, Bethlehem to Christians and the Wailing Wall to Jews. Walking through the streets on our way to the Ganges, the sacred river that runs through Varanasi, in our exhausted state we decided to take the lovely mode of transport of a horse and cart. We hopped in, turned a few corners and were set down a short distance from the Ganges. From our elevated position we could see the life pulsing below us as thousands of people went about their business. There were women washing clothes, holy men smoking pipes, men bathing in the river or playing cricket on the ghats, sellers with their small stands of thousands of prayer beads.

We started walking towards the ghat where the ceremony for the dead takes place. Along the way I bought a small glitter set for my sisters from a very enthusiastic guy. Five blocks later I found the same product for a third of the price. At one of the ghats we met a sweet little girl selling bread from a basket. She was eight years old and chatted with us nicely until we got to the next ghat. She told us she couldn't keep walking with us because it wasn't her area to sell.

The Ganges was a mess, but a beautiful mess all the same. There was rubbish everywhere, there were cows *everywhere*. The cows were eating the rubbish along with old flower offerings. The ghats were painted an array of colours, one wall having a giant *om* splashed on the side of it.

Hindus believe the Ganges to be water from the head of Shiva, one of the most important of the thirty-six-thousand-and-four gods they have. It is a place that most Hindus want to visit at least once before they die, and especially when they die. If you die here that's it, you have finished with reincarnation. Another way to reach paradise is to have your ashes thrown into the Ganges by the eldest son. But the ritual for those who die in this magical city is much more ceremonial than a mere sprinkling of ashes.

The body of the deceased is wrapped in gold, cellophane-like material, and then dipped in the Ganges. After this the body is placed beside the Ganges and covered in the best wood the deceased's family can afford. The eldest son then has his head shaved before he lights his father's funeral pyre. We didn't linger in this area out of respect to the grieving families.

Small makeshift barber stalls strewn through the streets were filled with brave men preparing for the duty that lay ahead of them. The barber stalls were coupled with wood stalls for the funeral pyres. Woods of varying quality were sold to accommodate all levels of income. Needless to say, it seemed that running a business here would have to desensitise your relationship with death just a little.

As we were leaving the open-air crematorium I almost tripped over the most adorable thing I have ever seen. It was a calf the size of a German shepherd! It was impossible for me to drag myself away from it. This beautiful little baby was born into the right country, where no one will eat him because he is holy.

Another amazingly cute and beautiful being we found on the banks of the Ganges went by the name of Siddharta. Like the Buddha. He was a small, ten-year-old boy whose job description was commission kid. He was one of the children who worked for businesses that were not on tourist routes. He would roam the streets, find some tourists and ask them to go back to his shop. If there was a sale, he would get a small percentage from the shop owner. These shops mainly sold pashmina scarves, perfume, tea and herbs.

We went to look at this boy's shop. Luca bought scarves for his mum and nonna. We got to chatting to Siddharta for quite some time. He told us other kids were mean to him because he was a commission kid. He said he didn't care, if they were mean to him once; it was OK. But if they were mean twice, they were his enemy. It was hard to imagine this cute little kid with his pierced ears and brilliant smile being anyone's enemy. I wanted to take him home. We said goodbye to Siddharta and hoped we would see him again before we left.

Later that evening we made our way back to the Ganges where a daily sunset ritual dedicated to the river would be performed. There were countless women and children walking about with baskets of candles for people to buy for puja. Puja can be made in a variety of ways. This particular puja was in the form of a lit candle floated out on the Ganges.

We bought a small bundle for our puja. It consisted of a leaf with a candle in the centre, surrounded by colourful flowers, and we floated it out into the Ganges before the ceremony began. Then we took a seat as close as we could to the ceremony.

Lined in a row facing the Ganges were seven wooden platforms. Seven men slowly started to cover the benches in red and yellow flower petals. Then they lined the platforms with candles and lit them one by one. Everyone was silent as the men stood calmly at the front of their platforms. They were wearing beautiful, flowing pastel pink and golden robes. Each then picked up a huge sea shell and started to blow it. The sound that came out was long, low and peaceful. I felt goosebumps spread before I had a chance even to register what I was hearing. What was this? Where was I? I found it hard to control my emotions and wished at that moment that all the people I loved could be with me to share this other-worldly experience.

Something incredibly strange during my travels through India was the fact that when I would come across another foreigner, he or she wouldn't make eye contact. They would act as though I wasn't there having the same experience. This happened during the ritual. A foreign guy sitting tall, blond and fair-skinned right beside me would look everywhere but in our direction. We were witnessing something we would likely never see again, and this guy didn't want to acknowledge this fact with a smile or nod or even eye contact! I would later find this to be true in many other foreign countries, where I along with my fellow travellers would stand out like sore thumbs. They would do their best not to make eye contact while passing each other at a distance of around thirty centimetres.

I came back to my surroundings in the here and now and tried to forget the foreign guy sitting next to us. After the blowing of the shells, the men continued with a succession of rituals. I found it hard to believe that they went to this trouble every night. While the ceremony was under way, a boy of about seven was trying to sell me the same glitter the guy who had ripped me off earlier that day had sold me—for even less than the one I'd found.

The cutie kept telling me "No problem" when I told him I didn't want to buy the glitter materials. "No problem, lady," he would beam at me and then proceed with yet another demonstration of different ways to use the glitter. In the end I bought a stack of postcards from him that were really beautiful. He was so happy with his sale that, after shoving the cash for the postcards into his tiny bag, all the while looking left and right to make sure that no one saw his profits, he gave me a packet of bindis for free and made me put one on my forehead.

It was Christmas Eve. We decided to go home early so we could wake for the sunrise the next morning. We planned to watch it from a boat on the Ganges. Just after we hopped into bed, we realized we didn't have any water to take our malaria tablets with, so we swallowed them dry. Big mistake. We woke up in the middle of the night with an indescribable pain in our chests, the kind when you swallow a hunk of bread without chewing it properly and it gets stuck in your oesophagus, slowly and painfully making its way down. Once it's down is the most relieved feeling in the world. It was like that, except from the relief part.

Luca got up and went to get water. He couldn't find any at that hour and came back with Coke. We gurgled the Coke down with high hopes but to no avail, the pain just would not go away. And it wouldn't for the next ten days or so.

We stayed in Varanasi for Christmas and Boxing Day. On the afternoon of Christmas Day, we happened to run into Siddharta.

"Hey, guys," he said sadly when he saw us.

"What's wrong, Siddharta?" I asked him.

"Nothing. It's just that ... I know that Christmas Day is for Christians, but it's still a special day, you know? Everyone is with their families and ..."

"Where is your family?" we prompted Siddharta, eyeing each other as we did.

"My mum died when she gave birth to me, and my dad is a holy man. He lives in a temple two hours from here and I never see him."

Here sat this sweet ten-year-old kid with a massive responsibility: making it in the world.

"Maybe we can buy you a bus ticket?" we asked him.

"No, it's OK. You guys have helped me enough already by buying from my boss. Besides, even if I left now I wouldn't make it there and back in time for school."

The part of me that was yearning to help kids like Siddharta hurt at hearing this.

6

Nepal

We said our goodbyes to the delight that was Varanasi, caught a bus to the border of Nepal and then a jeep from the border to the nearest town. When we arrived at the town, we booked a ticket to our final destination. We were exhausted and, just as we were about to hop onto the bus, the guy who was checking the tickets pulled us aside and pointed to the roof. We looked at each other and came to the same realisation: it wasn't our luggage he wanted to heave onto the roof; it was us.

We climbed shakily to the roof of the bus and took our places wedged as safely against the suitcases as we could. Once we were settled, we started calling out and waving down to the passengers below. We stayed that way, riding on the roof of the bus for the next two hours until we got to the birth town of the Buddha, Lumbini.

We walked through the mass of rainbow-coloured prayer flags blowing in the breeze to the Buddha's birthplace. A Japanese woman sat on a grassy hill among the flags, performing some kind of ritual that involved lighting incense only to put it out on her forehead. She repeated this action over and over, only stopping to take hold of her breast, stomach or crotch while almost screaming a mantra. I got the feeling that she had an illness and was doing this ritual to try to heal it.

We left the lady in peace and wandered through the rows of colourful prayer flags. The gentle breeze was blowing them against my cheeks. They felt rough on my skin. I inspected them more closely. I had read that prayer flags were considered sacred and were never to be put on the floor or worn as clothing and that old flags should be burned rather than thrown away. Each flag consisted of a picture and a mantra in beautiful Hindi writing. There are some four hundred different mantras to different deities, to be carried to them on the breeze.

We spent the entire day at the supposed birthplace of the Buddha, then wearily made our way back to our guesthouse, stopping for a small plate of food on the way. So far Nepal seemed to be a world away from the chaotic throb of incredible India, it was a welcome change. However, we did take a bus ride that would prove to be the longest night of my life.

First of all, the bus had been overbooked. Although we had almost certainly paid much more for our ticket than many of the other passengers, we were squashed in the front area of the bus beside the driver with no space to lean anywhere, especially for us who were the foreigners. Meanwhile another young Indian couple were given our seats; no doubt it was because we were foreign.

We knew we were being taken advantage of and, after our time in India, we had learned you had to stand up for what was right or you were doomed. As soon as the bus had a pee stop, we took our opportunity and sat in our seats. There was a time and a place for being giving but when a twelve-hour bus ride was at stake it was everyone for themselves. We held our tickets firmly in our hands ready to show any protesters the seat numbers, but when everyone got back on, no one said a thing, and we knew we were right in taking back our seats.

Turned out it wasn't much better in those seats. We were sitting directly behind the driver. For some strange reason, in the biting cold of a Nepali night, he thought it a good idea to have his window wide open. For the next twelve hours not only were we in the most uncomfortable bus seats ever engineered, we were shivering uncontrollably and trying to sleep. Only when we finally passed out from exhaustion did we get some respite from the cold.

This did not last long. We were woken every two minutes or so by the driver hocking up a wad of red spit from his betel-filled mouth and spitting it out the window a metre from us. Now we understood why he had his window open. Chewing betel is common in India, but it is the last thing you want to envisage when you're queasy from Nepalese roads and trying to sleep. This plus the splats and heaves from our motion-sick travel companions hurling out the window made for a very long night.

Looking over the cliff's edge once the sun rose and we had given up trying to sleep, Luca nudged me.

"*Amo,* look."

The drop we were driving above seemed to be one thousand feet below us, and we seemed to be driving less than thirty centremetres from the edge. Below us lay a white-and-blue bus that must have fallen over the edge, crumpled on the bank of a small river. All the hair on my head stood up.

"Shiiiiit." I looked at Luca. His face mirrored what I was feeling.

Just before our arrival in Gorka a man in his fifties got onto the bus and started to play a stringed instrument that resembled a violin but sounded entirely different. The sounds that came from this instrument were both mystical and calming, his voice was husky and high. The crashed bus below us and the nightmare of the night's ride was forgotten as I listened to the man, entranced by his melodies and voice. I wished I could record him and sell his CDs to the world so that his beautiful sounds would be shared with more than just this small busload of people. It seemed like a waste.

I felt so grateful for that moment in time, on that bus, surrounded by calmness, driving on a mountain's edge, listening to perhaps the most powerful sounds I would ever hear in my life.

The next two days in Gorka were days where my soul just got richer. Luca and I walked up a mountain to check out the temple of Kali that lay at its top. Kali is the god of vengeance. She is the wife of Shiva and is often depicted with her tongue protruding and with two arms on either side of her body, one generally holding the head of the defeated torsos she's standing on. The temple for Kali is where goat sacrifices are made in her name. Luca really wanted to see the sacrifice, while I was totally against it. Luckily for me it wasn't the right day of the week for a goat killing.

On our way up the hill we spotted two girls selling incense and other items of worship to take to the temple as offerings. The youngest of the girls saw us and immediately called out.

"Hello!"

"Hey cutie, how are you?"

"I'm good! You're beautiful!"

"Haha, thank you, so are you!"

An amazing friendship for the next day and a half started between me Luca and Susmita.

"Are you going to the temple?"

"Yep."

"Would you like to look at my sop?" Susmita asked in the cutest of accents.

"Sure, honey."

We walked over and met Susmita's sister. We bought a much-needed bottle of water and some incense. Their shop looked over the top of the mountain. Only when I took a moment to look down into the valley did I realise just how high up we were. We were above the clouds. All I could see for miles was a blanket of cloud between us and the tips of the distant, ice-capped Himalayas. My jaw dropped. Where was I again?

Susmita left her sister with the shop and came with us, asking as many questions as her broken English would allow along the way. She was one of the cutest, sweetest kids I had ever met. Her skin was dark and covered in a layer of dust. Her eyes were big, clear, shiny and black. When she smiled they crinkled at the corners and I could tell she would be stunning when she grew up. We arrived at a small house. Susmita informed us that it was her home.

"Would you like to come in for lunch before we go to the temple? I'm hungry!"

"Sure, sounds great," we answered.

We walked through the straw-walled, dirt-floored home to the backyard, where Susmita's grandma, grandpa and a goat were all sitting waiting for lunch. Her mum was around the corner out of sight, cooking up a storm.

Susmita went inside and came back with two pillows so we didn't have to sit on the floor.

"I'm sorry I don't have any chairs for you. My family is a poor family."

"That is so totally fine, cutie! We always sit on the floor to eat."

My meal and Luca's were served up first. Each consisted of a cup of tea with popcorn inside, a side of green, shredded vegetables and a very dark and very hard piece of bread. I was starving. I took a giant-sized bite out of the bread and regretted doing so instantly. I tried to conceal my horror as my eyes darted to Luca. He had also taken a bite.

The bread tasted just like dirt. It even had the consistency of dried dirt. I had no idea how I was going to go on with this meal. I took a sip from the popcorn tea to try to wash it down. Didn't work. The tea just slid around it and the dirt-like bread stayed in my mouth. I was at a loss as to what to do. I used all my might to make one single strong gulp. Success, the bread went down.

I picked up the small bowl with the dried, shredded vegetables and took a mouthful, praying to all the Hindu gods that this would be edible—not for my sake, but for the sake of the generous family in whose presence I sat. The last thing I wanted to do was insult them.

My prayers weren't answered. Fuck you, Kali. I chewed on that grassy substance for what felt like an eternity.

"Mmmm, so nice this lunch, isn't it?" Susmita prompted, her mouth full of the bread.

"Mmmm ..." I masked my groan as a moan of pleasure. Up until that point I had thought there may have been a chance that the silly white people had been fooled. That the family were about to burst out laughing and tell us we were eating dirt and grass.

I asked Susmita what the bread was made from.

"It's millet husk, the leftover parts of the millet. We used to eat rice but we can't afford it anymore. My family is poor family. My mum is alone and has no money because my dad left town for another woman and has new children now, and she needs to give food to me, my brother, my sisters and my grandparents."

"Oh." My heart dropped at hearing this.

And here we were, unable to eat more than three mouthfuls of our meal. What a predicament. I tried as hard as I could but I knew this stuff was coming up later, and the less the better. We lied and said we had eaten a late lunch and were so full and apologised profusely for not finishing the meal. I felt absolutely dreadful.

"OK, let's go up to the temple, guys."

Susmita walked up to the tap at the front of the house with us in tow. Her mother must have told her to wash herself. She watched over Susmita while she gave her face, legs and arms a quick wash, rinsing off the thin layer of dust. I'm not sure if it was out of respect for the temple of Kali or for us. We thanked the family once more and left for the temple.

By the time we reached the top of the mountain and were inside the temple's walls, I was almost completely out of breath. Susmita called out from a few metres ahead of us.

"Can you see the red, on the floor?"

"Yep," I answered.

"That's blood from the goats that get killed."

"Ahh, OK."

The overwhelming scent of incense, sight of blood, height of the mountain and the aftertaste of the millet made my stomach churn at the thought.

We took plenty of photos together, Susmita being the star photographer. Just as we were about to leave the temple a group of young boys came up to us, stopping about ten metres away. It was obvious Susmita knew them.

"I need to hide my feet," Susmita whispered.

"What?" I asked.

"Just those boys, if they see my broken shoes they will tease me."

I looked down. Susmita's little shoes were a mess.

"OK, come on, let's go." I took her by the hand, and made her walk in front of me so the little shitheads couldn't see her feet. We walked down the hill and back to the village.

First things first, we needed to go shopping for shoes. We found out that Susmita was a pretty fussy shoe shopper. Eventually we found a pair she liked. They didn't look practical enough to me to climb the hill to her house, which was actually a mountain. But she liked them, and I didn't have the heart to be practical at that moment.

After the shoe adventure we went to get our photos developed. While we were waiting for those we bought some fruit for the family. We picked up the photos and handed them over to Susmita with a wad of cash so that her mum could buy rice or whatever she needed. We also gave her my sunglasses because they looked so good on her, along with my jumper and Luca's gloves and beanie. I was starting to feel very unwell so we said our goodbyes to one of the sweetest little girls on earth, who seemed at a loss for words to thank us for our gifts to her and her family.

We walked back to our dodgy room. I went straight to bed, only to wake to the telltale signs of a flippy-floppy stomach sloshing from side to side, and a watering mouth. It was only a matter of time until Susmita's mum's millet would hit the toilet.

For me, vomiting is a traumatic experience. I know everyone hates vomiting but I will literally do anything to try to stop it, even though I know it's going to happen regardless. Five or so minutes after I woke up and three hundred swallows later, I ran to the toilet. The toilet, of course, was a squat toilet. I had no trouble at all gagging and retching. All I could see in the bowl were those stringy grass vegetables.

I went back to bed and slept well into the morning. Good, only one vomit, I can handle that. Next morning I was feeling OK enough to take the bus to our next destination, Chitiwan National Park.

The park was lush, green and welcomingly quiet. We went by elephant on a guided tour through the jungle to find a one-horned rhino in the wild. Next day we paid a man three dollars each to hop on an elephant in the lake bareback and wash him as he sprayed us with water. Although it was an incredible experience, I was shit scared. I felt as though every time I fell off the elephant I was going to get rolled on by its giant heaving body. I later became aware of the fact that these elephants would not have been treated kindly to become domesticated, and since vowed to never support such abuse.

After the elephant bath we went to eat lunch in a deserted restaurant. Big mistake. Next lesson: always eat where there are loads of people, so the turnover of food is high. I spent the entire night vomiting again. This second occurrence happened in a guesthouse that had no electricity at night, so I vomited in the dark. Momo. Even thinking the name of the steamed dumpling that was the cause of my vomiting that night makes my mouth salivate and my tummy tense.

Next morning I was just OK enough to take our bus to Kathmandu, though I was still feeling nauseous when we arrived and checked into our hostel. I was soon to realise that whatever the herb was that was used to make momo was used in all the cooking in Nepal. I could smell it everywhere, it was even wafting into our room.

I lay in my bed and surrounded myself with Susmita's incense to mask the smell of momo and went to sleep. I woke up later that afternoon with Luca lying next to me, waiting. Bless him. He told me that he knew of a restaurant that sold steak. It had been so long since I had eaten the sacred animal of India, my empty stomach rejoiced at the thought. I was feeling a bit better so we rugged up and went out.

On the way to the restaurant we passed a homeless man in his late fifties eating his lunch out of a banana leaf. There was an enormous cow standing right beside him and, before I knew it, the cow started eating out of the same plate while the homeless guy rubbed his cheek against the cow. Yes, the cow is still very sacred here.

At the restaurant I chewed down my sacred cow a little too fast. It was delicious, but as soon as we got back to the hostel, exactly at the point where I had to go either up or down a flight of stairs to reach a bathroom, I needed desperately to empty my stomach. I found the nearest pot plant and vomited up my yummy steak.

Two days later we took a taxi to the airport for our flight back to Delhi, and from there a flight to Bangkok. The country's capital airport looked like the airport for a town of twenty-five people, not two and a half million. Our flight was delayed for a few hours so we were given a packet of chips. We finally arrived in Delhi to find that our next flight was delayed eight hours and that our luggage hadn't made it onto our flight because the plane was too heavy.

We had a short sleep at the airport and then took our delayed flight to Bangkok. Our luggage was supposed to meet us there but actually went to Delhi, and we had no idea when it would arrive in Bangkok. Rather than wait around for it we decided we would keep going and pick it up when we took our flight back to Australia one month later.

We zipped around the islands of Thailand on a scooter, ate one-dollar pad thai and drank plenty of one-dollar fresh juices, having a few five-dollar massages along the way. We went to Phi Phi island, which has one of the most beautiful beaches I have ever seen, and went to visit the long-neck Kayan tribe in the north of Thailand.

These people were among the various tribes who fled from Burma to the Thai border. At the age of five, some of the girls start to wear the heavy brass coils on their neck. Asked the reason for the brass coils, the reply was that they are for cultural identity. The women's faces looked like those of dolls. They sat quietly, making handicrafts, doing their best, it seemed, to ignore the constant flash from the tourists' cameras. I felt extremely uncomfortable and refused to take photos, leaving that up to Luca.

After our stay in Thailand we crossed the border to Laos by boat and made our way down through the country by bus. Which was an interesting experience, to say the least. Later I looked up on the internet whether Asians are more susceptible to motion sickness, and studies show that yes, they are.

Every bus we entered welcomed us with a plastic bag. Around ninety per cent of the people on those buses used those plastic bags until they had to reach for another. The bus was a chorus of retching and splattering. I get motion sickness myself, but because of my fear of vomiting didn't vomit, thank god. But the sound of my fellow passengers heaving their guts up and the thought of those splashy bags all over the bus made my stomach do somersaults for these entire rides. I had to put myself in a very peaceful place mentally not to get off the bus.

Even more interesting were the bathroom stops. We would all pile out of the bus, plastic bags in hand. Our bathroom was the patch of grass on the side of the road beside the bus. Looking around at my peeing partners, I saw that the majority were peeing and throwing up simultaneously—definitely a sight I would never forget. What I didn't understand was why they put themselves through all that. Motion sickness pills are incredibly cheap here, practically free. I thought if they could afford the ticket they could probably afford a tablet for the trip. One little tablet could save nine or so hours of hell.

Laos is an interesting country. Even though it's very much a South East Asian country, it has a strong influence from the French occupation. Streetsellers sold freshly baked baguettes on the side of the road with a slice of laughing cow, long-life cheese and some cucumber. There is even a Champs-Elysées and an Arc de Triomphe in Vientiane, the country's capital, although the style has an Asian twist.

When we arrived in Luang Prabang, we learned from other travellers that we could participate in the religious sunrise ceremony for the four hundred or so monks who resided in the city, giving them their alms for the day along with the local people.

We were so excited to be able to take part in something so special we went to bed early on our first night and woke up at five o'clock next morning. We stepped out into the surprisingly fresh morning air and walked the dark streets. Silhouetted in the mist were women and children carrying long, cane sticks slung over one shoulder. Two baskets hung from either end, filled with fruits, small parcels of rice and flowers. The transactions made between seller and buyer were hardly more than a mere whisper.

We bought some food and flowers and sat in a long line along the side of the road, quiet and calm. As the sun rose the monks appeared in the distance. A long line of over four hundred men were hard to miss with their saffron-coloured robes and freshly shaved heads. They made their way along the road, not touching or looking directly at the people from whom they received offerings. We knelt in front of the monks and were sure not to show our feet. As a woman I had to have my shoulders covered. It was a humbling experience, and surprisingly few tourists used their cameras, for which I was thankful.

Suddenly the same sensation came over me as I had had in Varanasi. Knowing these people went to such lengths every day while I was snoring my head off in Australia, worrying about the smallest things and ignoring the most beautiful things whipped me into an intense state of presence. I had the strongest urge to hug everyone around me. I was grateful to see that there is more to life and humanity than I had thought. All we have to do is seek it. It's there.

To experience life like this is something that can't be written or spoken about, it needs to be felt and done. My mind was finally opening to other possibilities in life. It doesn't have to be stagnant, selfish and boring. Sure I wouldn't be able to go home and get half a city out of their beds to feed others, but I could make a positive change in the way I dealt with people. I think that morning I learned the true meaning of selflessness. Sure I had used that word for years, but I never knew what it meant. It was my new objective to be more selfless when dealing not only with people I knew and loved, but also with people I had never met before and would never see again.

We were sad to say goodbye to that beautiful town that opened my heart and make our way down to the Mekong River. One evening as we were drinking a nice cold Beerlao, watching the sunset over the Mekong at the border between Laos and Thailand, we saw two little girls collecting something from the ground. We went over and asked them what they were doing.

"Escargot," the littlest answered.

With Luca's skills in French he deciphered that they were collecting snails. They had used the French term for the slimy little suckers. We assumed they were for a restaurant or to eat at home, as the girls looked quite serious about their work. If that had been my little sister, she would have been doing it just for fun and to be the little cutie that she is. But not here. Here it is more likely to see a child working than playing, an incredibly hard thing to accept.

After only a week in Laos we crossed the border to Cambodia for four days. We were running out of time. We only had enough time to see the famous Angkor Wat ruins. We did this at sunrise, the recommended hour, and then took a bus back to Bangkok. After finally picking up our backpacks, we did some last-minute shopping and took our flight back to Darwin.

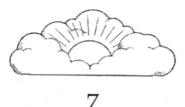

7

Australia, part 2

Once in Darwin we met up with Luca's friend Walter, also from Italy. I had a migraine and had to go straight to bed. Luca and Walter went to the nearby national park to spot crocodiles while I spent two days in bed.

Next big lesson: when you get back to your home country after months overseas, it is essential to let your mother know as soon as possible that you are safe and sound. Not two days later, and especially not when it's her birthday.

My mum was so worried that I hadn't contacted her that she attempted to contact the airline to find out whether or not I had landed in the country. However, due to privacy laws the airline was unable to give her any information to ease her mind. I felt like a terrible daughter.

We spent as much time as we could in the welcome air conditioning of our hostel in Darwin until we could find a lift through the middle of Australia to Melbourne. Luca wanted to see the rest of Australia while he was here. Although I would have preferred to spend the travelling funds in another country doing volunteer work, maybe in India or

Nepal, he had come all the way to the other side of the world for me, and it seemed selfish not to go along with his idea.

We still had our tent; I had left it at a friend's place. All we needed was some wheels. After nine days we were lucky enough to find on the backpacker's noticeboard an advertisement for a lift to Melbourne with a girl by the name of Louise. We met her the next day at our hostel to discuss arrangements. She was a sweet English girl in her early twenties, who planned to drive the three thousand, seven hundred and fifty one kilometres cross-country and wanted some company and help with the costs. We agreed that she would pick us up at six o'clock next morning to start our five-day drive through the desert.

There is nothing quite like lying in a tent at night without the cover, in the middle of the desert with not a sound or person in sight, just thousands and thousands of stars.

Our first tourist stop was at the Devil's Marbles, where Luca and I had yet another pointless fight. All our photos from that day show an obviously unhappy couple with big fake smiles painted on their faces. As usual our fight settled down, and we were back to normal soon enough. But a small voice in my mind told me I didn't want to live my life in an up-and-down state of affairs, fighting one minute and completely fine the next. For some time, though, I was able to ignore that voice and make the most of our love.

The days in the desert were hot and dry, I felt constantly dehydrated. It probably didn't help that we were eating the worst possible food— processed long-life cheese, bread, tinned chicken and tuna. The same thing every day. We stopped at Coober Pedy to see the town where forty per cent of its inhabitants live underground to get away from the heat. The accent out there was strong and the people seemed even stronger. Another outback town we passed through, Cloncurry, had at its entrance a welcome sign, stating:

CLONCURRY
AUSTRALIA'S HIGHEST TEMPERATURE
16th JANUARY 1889
A WARM WELCOME GUARANTEED

At fifty-three degrees Celsius it certainly would be a warm welcome. Thankfully for us it wasn't that day. Being in the outback was a humbling experience. It seemed a world away from the hustle and bustle of even the quietest towns on the coast. I felt as though every Australian should make a trip to the desert, just to see what lies to the east—or west—of us. The red dirt, the dry plains and big open skies are a part of our country the majority of us never see.

When we reached Melbourne, we started to use couch surfing. After exploring a little of the city, we hired a car to drive from Melbourne to Adelaide. We stopped at some wineries along the way, drank some of the best wine I have ever tasted and sampled some delicious cheeses. We camped along the Great Ocean Road, stopping in random places to make love in the warmth of our tiny car. It was a beautiful four days of camping and cuddling against the cold weather. Luca and I got along better in those four days than we had in a very long time.

We arrived at our couch surfing host's house on a sunny afternoon. After only a short drive through the city, I had already begun to like the look of Adelaide. We were met at the door with a welcoming hug by a woman in her forties.

How to describe our host. Eve Alders, the rockstar. She can sing, play guitar, the didgeridoo and the flute. She drinks vodka for breakfast and smokes weed for dinner. Her house was surrounded by grapevines, and her backyard held two fig trees that happened to be in season.

I had never tried figs before. After trying my first one, I couldn't stop. I had figs with honey and figs with cheese, figs for breakfast, with lunch and after dinner. I was starting to feel guilty, the once-full fig tree was starting to look rather bare. But I just could not get enough. We stayed with Eve and her son for the next three days and had a great time. I had never met anyone as hilarious as my mother until I met Eve.

We started researching car-relocation websites. This is a system where, if there is a car in one city that needs to be returned to another, you can pay very little (at times nothing) to rent the car and drive it back to its original city. We found a deal with a campervan and set off for Perth. We had five days to drive the two thousand, six hundred kilometres. After such terrible food during our tip through the desert, we made sure we were better prepared for this trip. We bought six different cheeses and two bottles of good wine. We made bruschetta and bought some fruit and vegetables, which we later discovered was a bit of a mistake.

As we were nearing the border crossing between South and Western Australia we read in Luca's guidebook that we couldn't take fruit, raw vegetables or *cheese* into Western Australia. How were we going to eat five blocks of cheese in two days? We actually managed to do it, only to find at the border that the guidebook was incorrect and cheese was totally fine!

The drive was long and pretty barren. One of the roads we drove along didn't have a single curve for over two hundred kilometres. Once we got to the southern coast of Western Australia, we stopped briefly in a beautiful town called Denmark, and later in another by the name of Esperance. It was the first time I had seen the Indian Ocean. The crystal green waters seemed to be brighter and clearer than on the east coast. The brilliant-white sandy beaches in both towns were practically deserted. If only we had had more time. I could see myself soaking up the sun on those beaches for days on end.

We were about an hour away from Perth and had a couple of hours to kill so we decided to pull into a garage for a break. Luca spotted a park in some shade under a tin-roofed carport.

"I'm a genius. I'm a genie in a bottle, like Christina Aguilira." And PUM! We crashed. We had forgotten just how tall the campervan was, and we scraped the top of the roof.

"Fuck, *amo*, fuck, now what am I gonna do? They are going to take my thousand dollars." Luca had paid a one-thousand-dollar bond for the van to get it back in one piece.

We were in a panic as we would be charged extra if we got the van back late, so we drove to a panel beater's garage nearby, who polished most of the scratch marks out for us, free of charge. It looked almost as good as new. We arrived at the car return place just in time. Luckily the guy who was to inspect our car was Italian. He and Luca instantly built a rapport, and the guy barely looked at the vehicle upon inspection.

We stayed in Perth with a fun couple we'd met through couch surfing until we found our own place. I was out of money and needed a job. We lived in Perth for the next month in a share house with seven other people, all of whom, coincidentally, were Irish.

Luca and I spent our first-year anniversary on a Swan Valley wine tour, getting wasted and eating delicious food. It was perfect.

Perfect as it was, Luca and I had probably the biggest fights of our lives in the Irish house. It was hard for us to keep any enthusiasm about our relationship, but we were as intense in love as we were in our fights, so it was impossible for us to give up easily.

After a month we had saved enough money to make a small trip up the coast to Sydney for Luca's flight back to Europe and my flight to the Gold Coast to see my mum. We hired a car and went up as far as Exmouth. We stopped along the way at a surreal pink lake at Port Gregory and the yellow pinnacle desert, which consists of hundreds of strange rock formations. We also stopped at Monkey Mia, fed wild dolphins and marvelled over the green of the Indian Ocean at Denham, eventually arriving at Coral Bay, then onto Exmouth and finally Turquoise Bay. Concealed within these three places were beaches that literally took my breath away. Glowing white sand, still ocean with colours of green, turquoise, and shades of blue. At Coral Bay we spent hours floating above the coral reefs, our goggle-masked eyes feasting on a constantly changing underwater world of plentiful marine life. It was paradise.

On our return we drove directly down to Perth, our flight to Sydney being the next morning. We stayed one week in Sydney, enjoying the delights that the city has to offer. All too soon it was time for us to say yet another tearful goodbye at the airport. Luca had to go back to work in Europe and I couldn't afford to come with him. I moved to the Gold Coast and started working in a bar to save for our next adventure together. We were still in love and decided to attempt the long distance thing again and see each other as soon as we could.

Three months later my feelings about our relationship started to change. I was happy not to be fighting almost all the time. I was getting used to being without a partner, and I was frustrated at having a boyfriend on the other side of the world without a single embrace for three months. The first time had been hard enough. I also felt I had lost myself a little in the relationship. I decided that this was the year I would do the voluntary work I had been so wanting to do, but putting off to do what Luca wanted instead.

It took all my strength to call him and say the words that had been flooding my thoughts in the past weeks, "I can't be with you anymore."

Within a day or so he had bought a flight to the Gold Coast. And within a week he was due to arrive. Meeting him at the airport flooded my soul with love and nostalgia. All negative emotions and rational thoughts evaporated almost immediately.

We moved into a room together in a house owned by a lovely guy named Barry and stayed there for the next eight months, working to save some more. Luca wanted me to come back to Italy with him. After the incredibly sweet gesture he had made in flying to Australia to save our relationship, I felt it was the least I could do. My dreams of volunteering would have to be put off yet again, although another dream I'd had a long time ago that I'd actually forgotten about was about to become true. This was to become an English teacher in Italy.

Along with my bar job I got a second job in the Japanese restaurant that Luca worked at called O-Sushi. It was such a nice atmosphere at O-Sushi, everyone was so friendly. One of the young girls who worked there was friends with the owner's sons Yogi and Almog. There are three O-Sushi restaurants, all owned by these boys' parents, and they worked at the store in a town south of the Gold Coast called Byron Bay. The names of these boys intrigued me. I felt I should meet them, although I had no idea why.

Shortly before we left for overseas, an O-Sushi Christmas party was held, and the staff from all three stores attended. Throughout the night my young friend hung with two boys. I knew they were Yogi and Almog and I wanted to meet them. At some point during the night I thought I could feel one of them looking at me. I resisted the temptation to meet his gaze out of loyalty to Luca. It was hard but I knew it was the right thing to do; I had a boyfriend. Also the boy watching me was sixteen, some seven years my junior.

My other job at a bar down the street from O-Sushi was horrible. My boss was a jerk, and anyone who works in bars or nightclubs knows that drunk people aren't always fun when you're sober, although drunk people do tip well. Luca and I had decided to go to Asia again on our way back to Europe as we had a stopover there. We were also going to New Zealand, considering it was so close.

With eight month's tips from the over-friendly drunk patrons I managed to buy flights to and from New Zealand, a tour of New Zealand, a flight to Asia, flights around Asia and then a flight from Asia on to Europe. This made those tedious late nights worth the effort.

8

On the road

The morning of our flight we got a lift to the airport from my darling girlfriend Nicola. While waiting at the gate, we noticed a guy with spiky blond hair and a lot of facial piercings. He was wearing a black leather vest with nothing underneath, revealing a square object as big as three matchboxes submerged under his skin. I also noticed a girl, who was a regular customer at O-Sushi.

"Hey, how are you?" I asked her.

"I'm really good, thank you! Hey, do you remember the petition I got you to sign so I could win a sponsorship surfing?"

"Yeah," I answered.

"I won it!" she replied, smiling from ear to ear.

"Wow! Congratulations! Are you Australian?" I asked out of curiosity.

"No way!" she replied with a slightly disgusted look. "I'm a Kiwi."

A New Zealander. "Ahh, OK," I answered, not so up for a conversation anymore.

The girl went on to tell us that there was a street performing festival in Auckland over the next few days and that the spiky blond guy would be performing. That was perfect; we would be in Auckland for those days.

"He'll be performing at the festival. He swallows swords and does all sorts of crazy stuff with his body. You should check him out," the girl said. "He had that magnet inserted into his chest so the swords stick to it as he swallows them, to prevent damage to his oesophagus."

"Oh, wow." That would be interesting to see.

We landed in the freezing cold, mid-summer night of Auckland and waited out the front of the airport, trying to find someone to share an airport transfer van with. And who were we to share with other than our spiky blond friend. His name was Shane, The Space Cowboy. For the next week I had that song stuck in my head.

Before we got into the van he bought two bottles of Sprite, poured vodka into both of them and passed one to us to share. Before we went our separate ways and headed up at the apartment we would be staying at for our time in Auckland, he told us where he would be performing the next day, and the website where we could find him for the rest of the festival. We were to stay at the home of Luca's friend from university and his girlfriend. They were both from Mexico. They owned a Latin-American restaurant in the heart of Auckland and were incredibly sweet.

We spent the next few days enjoying what Auckland and its surrounding areas has to offer. One evening we went for dinner and salsa at our hosts' restaurant. It was probably one of the most delicious meals I have ever had. The name of the restaurant is Besos Latinos, meaning Latin kisses. It is situated in an old stable, refurbished and filled with numerous restaurants offering international cuisine, including a French patisserie, an Italian bruschetta bar and a Mexican restaurant. Our friends couldn't open another Mexican restaurant, which is why theirs is a Latin cuisine restaurant providing a culinary experience not to be missed.

We started our tour from Auckland, went north to the beautiful Bay of Islands, then down, stopping along the way until we got to the south of the North Island. Then we then took a ferry to the South Island and enjoyed the treasure waiting there. New Zealand is a magical place with beaches, islands, glaciers, mountains, thermal springs, rivers, waterfalls, snow, amazing slopes, rainforest, culture and more. We could understand why so many movies are filmed there. It really does look like a place where fairies and hobbits might live.

One of the most memorable experiences was when Luca and I went on a blackwater rafting tour to see glowworms. Each person on the tour was given a rubber tube in which to float through the caves containing the glowworms, plus a helmet with a torch attached. We all jumped into the cold water, forming one straight line. Almost instantly we were greeted by a long dark tunnel lit up by thousands of tiny glowworms. Our guide told us to turn off our torches. What followed was breathtaking. In the complete darkness the rows of glowworms lining the tunnels seemed to go on as far as the eye could see. In fact it wasn't that far, but because of the illusion the glowworms created, the effect seemed never to end.

Just one more reason why the possibility of fairies living in this magical country fitted so well.

We took our flight out of New Zealand back to the Gold Coast two days before an earthquake of 6.3 magnitude hit Christchurch, killing one hundred and eighty-five people, destroying the city along with the church we had only days before admired.

The day after our return to Australia we had a flight from the Gold Coast to Kuala Lumpur, Malaysia. Getting off the plane, I was again engulfed by the smells of South East Asia, a tantalising sensation. But something was very different about this South East Asian country—the religion. Malaysia is a Muslim country, and it was interesting to see

Malay women wearing burkas, although I remembered that Islam was also a main religion in Indonesia. No surprise, considering how close the two countries are to each other. Their languages are also incredibly similar. It was a nice twist on the usual Buddhist theme in South East Asia.

We stayed only two days in the country's capital; there was not too much to see. We went to the north-east of Malaysia and took a boat across to Parenthian Island, where all the restaurants and bungalows were situated. It was a little polluted and not the prettiest of island beaches by any means, although we found unspoiled crystal waters and white sandy beaches further away from the main tourist area.

We stayed in a small bungalow practically on the beach. The strand was lined with seafood restaurants, their tables set so close to the sea that small waves crashed around our ankles as we ate. The restaurants all competed, with practically the same food on offer. In the evenings they lay their fresh produce out on display beside a smoking barbecue, and we would pick from the many options they had. It came grilled, with rice and salad, for around seven dollars. It was a deliciously satisfying meal, and we had it for dinner every night.

We stayed there for eight days, living like that. The main reason we had come to this island was to take a PADI diving course, the price of the courses and cost of living being considerably cheaper than elsewhere. Our diving instructor, whose name was Spike, was in his fifties, short, stocky and pretty highly strung.

The feeling diving gives is one of complete freedom—once you get the hang of it. The first time I tried I panicked at the surface and didn't think I could go down; it just felt so unnatural. But because I didn't want to look as if I couldn't do what everyone else seemed to be doing with ease, and because I didn't want to put a stop to the dive, I found every ounce of courage I had and made myself do it. And I am so happy that I did.

There is a life under the surface that we just never see. It is an amazing thing to witness, let alone while breathing and floating among the marine inhabitants. On top of that is the incredible sensation of weightlessness and peace, with the only sounds being the bubbles from your own breath. And then to suddenly see out of the corner of your eye something sizeable coming towards you, something you have never seen before. After hours of diving we worked up incredible appetites and would eat fresh seafood on the shore to our hearts' content.

During our diving course we had the option to do a night dive. My inner voice told me not to do it, that I wouldn't like it, but I hadn't learnt to listen to her yet and, because Luca decided to do it, I did as well. I have never been as scared in my entire life as I was that night. That one-hour dive seemed closer to ten hours long. I could only see where I pointed the torch—how could that possibly be fun, especially with the knowledge that there were numerous deadly fish in this area and I had seen them just hours before? Shining the torch on the sea urchins, their shadows made the length of their spikes seem a metre long. For the entire dive I found myself avoiding their shadows rather than avoiding their spikes.

Night diving is something I will never do again.

After we got our diving certificates we were ready to move on. We went back to mainland Malaysia, then back to Kuala Lumpur to take a flight to Manila, the capital city of the Philippines. On arriving we took a taxi downtown and were greeted with poverty-stricken people. My heart beat against my chest as we passed a mother and her children asleep in the street, I couldn't help but feel guilty for my indulgent touring. At our hostel we found signs plastered all over the walls, warning us against locals who offer drinks to tourists while in actual fact drugging them and then stealing all their possessions. Other signs which were my main concern read, in large capital letters:

STOP
SEX TRAFFICKING
OF CHILDREN AND YOUNG PEOPLE

Holy fuck, where were we? There were other signs informing travellers to report any kind of misconduct with children. I soon found out that the child prostitution rate in Manila is phenomenally high. Child traffickers prey on poor families, who sell their child, usually to feed the rest of the family. Most of the time this transaction is made between locals and foreigners, many of whom are Australian.

Walking the streets, I was certainly on the lookout. I didn't see anything suspicious, although I saw numerous ancient white men with girls who looked to be a quarter of their age. I was embarrassed and disgusted. I had seen a little of this kind of thing on our last trip in Asia but it seemed the norm here in Manila.

After a day in Manila we had seen enough and took a bus out of there down to Donsol. The reason we came to Donsol was to swim with whale sharks. It was incredible, to say the least. It only cost twenty dollars and we had hours on a boat, searching for and swimming with these harmless gigantic creatures.

There were ten of us on the small boat, all perched upon its edge with our snorkels, masks and fins at the ready. A guy high up on the mast watched for the whale sharks. When he spotted one he would scream to us, "Masks!" We would all clumsily and hurriedly follow suit. Then, "Fins!!" And we would scramble around trying to get our fins on as fast as we could. Then, "JUMP!" And we would all jump into the warm waters looking from person to person and then to our guide, who would be searching frantically for the whale shark. Suddenly the lookout would scream, "LOOK DOWN!" and we would all plant our faces in the water.

There are no words to describe the feeling of submerging your eyes just beneath the water's surface and finding a twelve-metre whale shark with its wide, long slit of a mouth open and coming at you. I knew already that it couldn't hurt me, so I wasn't afraid exactly, it was just ... surreal, and one of the most beautiful things I have ever experienced. On the whale shark's back were hundreds of green and blue spots that seem to glow. He came so close to me that I had to hold my legs with my hands not to hit him in the head or step on him in my flippers.

We spent the afternoon diving in and out of the water like this until we were all completely spent. After that we moved on from Donsol to some of the hot dive spots in the Philippines to try out our new diving certificates. We stopped along the way to rent a motorbike and rode out to a reserve that housed tarsiers. These incredible little creatures are the smallest primates on earth, weighing between eighty and one hundred and sixty-five grams. They are so fragile that touching them can break their bones. Their eyes, in proportion to their bodies, are larger than any other mammal and, because their eyes are fixed, tarsiers have the ability to move their heads one hundred and eighty degrees. These tiny creatures are adorable and extraordinary to witness.

We arrived at our dive destination of Balicasag late in the afternoon and booked into the cheapest hostel we could find. Next morning we arranged our dives for the forty-eight hours. To this day I haven't seen anything underwater as magical as the dive sites we visited just off the coast of Balicasag. The walls of coral were spectacular and the marine life was diverse. This was the land of miniatures. Everything was tiny, from the clown fish to the crabs. They were so cute and small, and the corals they lived in, both soft and hard, were a delightful array of both bright and soft colours. One coral bed in particular was covered in a whitish-pink soft coral that had millions of coral flowers which opened and closed. It looked like a live sea carpet blinking at me. Incredible.

Next we arranged a dive near Apo Island. We had to take a small boat for an hour or so to reach it.

That boat. That boat ride.

The boat was about eight metres long and three wide. On the way to the dive site we flew along the water, and the water flew into us. There is no other way to describe it. Every two seconds as we went over each bump, we landed with a thud and a splash that felt like an entire bucket of water landing straight in our faces. We hardly had a chance to breathe before the next load hit us. And it was freezing! This went on for over an hour. Needless to say, we were all laughing. By the time we arrived my stomach was aching from holding onto the boat and laughter. We certainly weren't looking forward to the trip back. The dive, though, was worth it. It was yet another other-worldly, underworld paradise.

We were floating along together peacefully when suddenly my regulator was knocked out of my mouth. I tried hard not to panic and acted out the manoeuvre for retrieval that Spike had taught us. Once I was finally sorted, I looked for Luca, who I assumed was responsible for this sudden removal of my only life-giving device. I found him right beside me with his eyes big in his mask and his hands in a prayer position which in Italian in this instance meant, "I am so sorry!" As soon as he saw that I was OK, he pointed to what had induced his frenzy.

There, only a couple of metres away, lay a big old turtle having a nap among a rainbow of coral. Half a metre above him lay a purple-and-black banded snake around two metres long. We floated towards them for a few seconds until the turtle woke up and swam away. *Unbelievable.* How lucky we were to witness something so beautiful! I tucked the mental image away in my mind and hoped that I would never forget it. After our dive the instructor told us that we had been crazy for getting so close to the snake. Apparently it was venomous. Oops.

The trip back was even worse than the trip to the site. The boat broke down almost as soon as we took off. Well, we hadn't broken down exactly, our captain had accidentally put water instead of fuel into the engine. We had to get help from one of the boats that passed us. When we finally got back to shore we were soaked through and frozen, but on a high from laughing so much, yet again.

We finished our diving in the Philippines and took a bus then a bumpy ferry to an island named Siquijor to find a witchdoctor to try to fix my migraines. We arrived late, so we checked into the nearest cheap hostel and went to sleep with the sound of the sea lapping the shore. We woke to find we were only six or so metres from the ocean. We had breakfast and hired a motorbike to visit the beaches around the island, stopping to have lunch in an organic cafe. Our lunch consisted of an assortment of colourful flowers with chicken and dressing, plus a herb pasta and cold lemon grass tea, all of which was grown where we were, and all organic. We went to a gorgeous, almost-deserted beach with white sand and clear blue waters. No one was there but an old man in his homemade speedos, searching for sea urchins with a pair of ancient goggles.

We stopped by to have a chat with no words. He gave us some of his fresh sea urchin eggs and some bread. I skipped the bread as it looked a bit past its use-by date and took a chance on the sea urchin eggs alone, and they were delicious. They tasted just like the sea, not fishy at all. Just like tiny orange balls of sea. We had a nude swim, made love in the sun and left before it got too cloudy and rainy to find my witchdoctor.

Our search for the famous witchdoctor San Juan proved harder than we expected. Everyone we asked told us not to go to see him, that witchdoctors were dangerous. We finally found a helpful local who wasn't opposed to the doctor's magic and arrived at his house a little before dark. I was met at the entrance to the humble house by San Juan's son and six tiny, gorgeous puppies.

"Can I help you?" he asked in broken English, raising his eyebrows with every word. Philipinos had this amazing gesture, made by shooting their eyebrows up and down. It could mean a variety of things from agreeing with what I was saying, to showing interest on a topic, to greeting me.

"Yes, I'm looking for Dr San Juan?"

"Ahh, I see. My father is very sick, what is it that you need?" He pulled back a curtain to the next room long enough for me to catch a glimpse of the famous San Juan.

There in the dark sat a man whose age was indecipherable. I don't think I have ever seen anyone that old before. He looked as though he was blind, his eyes had a thick glaze over them.

"I get headache very bad," I told the son in broken English, pointing to my head with a pained expression on my face.

The witchdoctor went into another room and returned with a bag full of what seemed to be woodchips. He told me to make a tea out of them and drink it until the wood was finished.

"OK. Thank you," I mumbled, trying to keep the disappointment from my voice. My high hopes were completely shattered. I couldn't see this tea doing much for my problem.

We walked back to where we had parked our motorbike. Suddenly out of nowhere the sky started to bucket down what seemed to be a mini flash flood. We attempted to drive through it but had to stop when Luca got a bug in his eye.

"*Amo!* Blow on it, blow on it, quick! There's an animal in my eye!"

It was so hard to keep a serious look on my face while trying to explain the method of pulling his top lash over his bottom to get "the animal" out of his eye. He insisted that it didn't work and that I would have to blow on it. At long last it seemed "the animal" was out of his eye.

We took shelter out the front of the school we had stopped near. Three teachers were also waiting out the rain undercover and, upon seeing us, called us over to them. There were two spare seats. We sat with the two men and one woman. It wasn't long before they offered us a banana. I took one bite, looking forward to the smooth, sweet taste of banana. Instead my tastebuds were greeted with the strangest, driest taste sensation. From what I could understand, the banana had been boiled green. I forced down the rest and expressed my gratitude.

Eventually the rain eased. We waved our friends goodbye and rode back to town. We made it in one piece and stopped at a barbecue on the side of the road. Anyone who has been to the Philippines will know that on the menu for almost every meal is pork, pork and pork—except of course in the Muslim areas of the country. But this barbecued pork was really something else. It had been coated in a kind of tomato sauce before being put over the smoking coals. What resulted was caramelized, juicy pork. It was so delicious and the sole reason I would buy one of those coal barbecues as soon as I got home.

The next day we took a tuk tuk back to the ferry. We had our ticket checked three times before boarding. Once on board, I was rocking from side to side, when I realized I had forgotten to take a motion sickness tablet and it was now too late. If I took one now, it would start to work shortly before we arrived, if not when we arrived; it was useless. I lay down and waited for the unavoidable queasiness to come.

The boat rocked from port to starboard, I really thought we were going to go under. Even though I don't usually vomit from motion sickness, if it weren't for my phobia of vomiting I think that day would have been an exception. I was sure my face was a pale shade of green. As we were mercifully approaching shore, a crew member came to hassle me for my ticket. Yet again! I could barely open my eyes, let alone search among my belongings for a ticket for the fourth time.

"Luca!" I yelled for my security. "The guy wants my ticket and I'm going to vomit all over him if I have to try to find it, but he won't leave me alone."

Luca came to the rescue, and after several minutes of searching he found my ticket.

"Thank you," I managed through my desert-dry mouth.

We finally got to land where I lay down on a park bench for some time. When I was finally starting to feel normal again, we took two buses up to the north of the Philippines to the Banaue Rice Terraces and organised a three-hour trekking tour for the next day.

We took an old, brightly painted bus to the top of the terraces and piled out, cameras in hand. The bright green terraces were a delight, cascading down the valley with little huts spotted along the edges. It looked a lot like Machu Picchu and was an impressive site, to say the least. While on the trek we visited some of the locals, who had tiny stalls selling small handicrafts. I bought some recycled plastic purses and handbags. It was nice to buy souvenirs from people who really needed the money. This was the way I wanted to do souvenir shopping from now on.

Our stay in the mountains was a short one. We had to get back to Manila for our flight back to Kuala Lumpur, from where our flight left for Vietnam. (Flights in and out of Kuala Lumpur to other parts of South East Asia with Air Asia were substantially cheaper than direct flights.)

We didn't have very much time in Vietnam. We arrived in Ho Chi Minh and made our way down to the Mekong River. Being in the city where Christina Noble first came to start her charity was an empowering experience. We decided to spend the rest of our trip in places where we could help people. We went to a restaurant in Ho Chi Minh City called Huang Lai. Its waitstaff are children from the street given the opportunity to gain work skills in the hospitality field and so get off the streets. The food was delicious and the kids were sweet. We left the biggest tip we could afford to every one of the waiters and rejoiced in seeing the smiles of gratitude on their faces. I was beginning to feel torn when giving money to children in developing countries, but in this case I knew that this was the best and only thing I could do.

We also decided to visit a massage centre that trains blind people in massage, giving them the opportunity for employment. Although there are many blind massage institutes varying in price, the one we visited only charged one dollar for a one-hour massage. When the masseuses had finished, we slipped each one the biggest bill that we had as we thanked them. Feeling their notes, their faces dropped in shock.

"Thank you," they whispered to us.

"You are so welcome," we replied. It was a good feeling helping people while travelling. I was starting to think of a way to help other travellers take the time out to help people during their journeys.

After our massage we took a stroll through the night market. Both our tummies were grumbling with hunger. Looking at the menu at one of the stalls, I had to stifle a giggle. The menu read things like: Real Estate Fat Fried In Fat, Buildings Fat Baked All, and Software Seafood Fried Noodle. By the time we read the six-page menu we couldn't hold our laughter in any longer. Tears were rolling down our cheeks, there was nothing we could do to stop them. We walked away ashamed of ourselves. The stall whose owner we had just upset looked to be the tastiest of all of the stalls—even if he did claim to cook up real estate.

Our next good deed was to do a home-stay. We paid a family to stay in their home with them and they cooked for us. It was a nice experience and it felt good to be helping out a family that lived in such a remote area.

This was our last stint in South East Asia. We both knew we would miss it. After our very small contributions to the public I started to get a feeling that South East Asia could possibly be where I could, like Christina Noble, start something to help those in need.

9

The *vita* of an Italian

S adly the time came around to leave behind South East Asia. We took our flight from Kuala Lumpur to London, and stayed on there for a couple of days with Luca's friend Antonio. He was the guy who almost two years earlier had flown back from Italy to put me up in his bed for the night when I had spent all my money and couldn't afford somewhere to sleep.

On one of our days in London we went to visit the famous market of Portobello in Notting Hill. I was looking for a Mother's Day present when I came across a small stall selling cards. The cards looked beautiful and were made out of recycled paper. I looked further around this little stall. There were two young and pretty girls both sporting big sweet smiles. I found some information about the cards in a pamphlet that sat on the girls' small desk where they made transactions. They were made in South America by women living in rubbish dumps. The profits from these cards helped to stimulate business prospects and skills for the people living in those areas.

I bought one straightaway. I knew my mum would love it, and I had fallen in love with the concept.

Thinking back to all of those poverty-stricken countries that I had been to and all the adults and children I had seen begging in the streets, I felt that familiar urge of wanting to change the lives of others for the better. Seeing the good of humanity in action by these two young girls spreading goodwill made me realise that this dream is very much achievable, one way or another. Little did I know then, the experience in this small stall would serendipitously play a part in my destiny.

We flew from London to Italy and were greeted by Luca's mum at the airport. She whisked us back to her home with that incredible view. This was to be our new home; Luca's mum now lived with her boyfriend.

After a short one-week trip to Malta for our two-year anniversary only a week and a half after we had arrived in Italy, Luca and I were back to living in reality, although the experience of moving my life to Italy didn't seem at all like reality. Although I had travelled some, actually living in another country was something else. Especially a country whose language I didn't speak. My new city Castellammare di Stabia had about sixty thousand people, and it seemed that everyone I encountered could not speak English. It was very strange. Every single person around me spoke an entirely different language. No matter how hard I tried sometimes my message just did not get across. And even when I thought it had, chances were that it probably hadn't.

We started looking for work and were both lucky to get jobs fairly quickly, Luca as a tour manager and, as destiny would have it, I as an English teacher. It had been five years since I had decided that I wanted to move to Italy to teach English and learn the language and, although I had almost forgotten that dream, it had been already written. Here I was, doing it without even meaning to. This realisation made me believe that if you truly want to manifest something, sooner or later it will happen.

The days I spent in Italy were some of the best of my life, and not just because I, along with the whole of Italy, was on an espresso high. I was living a long awaited dream that I had almost forgotten in a land where lemons grew as big as melons, and melons were sold for ten cents a kilo from the backs of overflowing trucks. Fresh seafood and homemade pasta were cheap and plentiful, and the whole region believed in *carpe diem*.

When I say that I was on an espresso high, I am not exaggerating. Not only was I hooked on the caffeine, but also the custom and tradition of going out for a coffee. If you order a coffee in Italy, it comes as an espresso unless you ask otherwise. It is cheaper to drink the coffee standing at the bar rather than sitting down. The barmen wear ties or bow ties, and the coffee is as thick as honey. When you put your spoonful of sugar into the little cup, the sugar slowly sinks down through the thick, liquid gold.

No wonder the Italians talk with their hands. I don't know how many coffees I had in one day on my craziest social day, but my poor heart told me that it was a little too much. And this was normal for them. On more than one occasion we would go out to post a parcel, for example, only to turn the corner and run into a guy that Luca went to preschool or college with. Even though we might have already had a coffee, it would be rude to say no to just one quick espresso. We would finish the coffee, post the parcel and on the way out of the post office he would bump into his best friend's ex-girlfriend, and what do you know? Just one more quick coffee—and it would go on like this.

Learning the language while I was living in Italy was a long and difficult process—especially in the region I was in, as the people cut off the last syllable of most words. For example, *wait* in Italian is *aspetta* and in Napolitano, *aspe*. Another example: where I was living, *Castellammare di Stabia;* in Napolitano, *Castellama* will do.

The teaching job I had gotten was cruisey. Because the students got the course for free, they would only show up half the time. Another reason there was a high number of no-shows was because the lessons were held in the middle of summer. It was so sweltering hot that I could barely blame them for not wanting to turn up. Those who did come, though, were an extremely sweet group who would soon become very good friends.

Although I enjoyed my job immensely and made several good friends, learned a lot of Italian and gained valuable experience in teaching, I didn't see my first paycheck until over a year later! And the next pay, for the last half of the time I worked there came six months after that. Apparently that was normal procedure for government-funded projects in Napoli. There were lots of things that I had to learn about the way of life in Castellama, but it was amazing just how fast I became accustomed to the differences. I had thought when we first arrived in Italy that I would need two Valiums every time I got into the car with Luca (or his family or friends, for that matter), because of all the near-crashes and car-bumping methods of parking that I had experienced. But soon enough I got used to all of that, along with many other different ways of life.

The thing I loved most about where I was living were the small *festas* thrown during the summer for a few days at a time in the little villages surrounding Napoli. These festivals were held for whatever type of produce was ample at the time, the farmers having ended up with too much. What better way to sell the produce than at a festival full of those food-loving Italians. There were festivals for eggplants, mozzarella, wine and cheese, chickens, jazz and so much more. The food was ridiculously cheap and quite often free at these festivals, and there would usually be local music to dance to while drinking what tasted like fine wine for sometimes as little as fifty cents a glass. Driving to one of these festivals one afternoon I turned to Luca.

"I've never seen so many car accidents in all my life as I have so far in Italy," I said as we sped past small stores selling hubcaps. Looking around at the cars surrounding us, I noticed that half of them were missing at least one hubcap. Luca had explained to me when we first arrived that people stole hubcaps and then sold them back to the people who had "lost" theirs.

"But what are you talking about, *amo?* We never crash here in Italy."

"What are *you* talking about, Luca? I have seen at least three crashes in just a couple of weeks!"

"Tell me exactly wh—"

We were interrupted by his crashing into a Vespa.

Both riders went flying off the scooter and at first sight it looked like a desperate affair. My stomach dropped. But after a few seconds, before we could even register what had happened, both slowly got up as Luca and I climbed with weak knees out of the car. We exchanged details with the police, who arrived on the scene in no time.

The crazy thing about the whole situation was that we were in the right. Just luck. Pure luck had it that they were facing a fine and not us.

No one followed the road rules there. At a roundabout the usual situation was that whoever was the gamest, went. At intersections it was another story. The concentrated driver made eye contact with the opposing driver. They had an exchange of looks, then off would go the winner of the glances. It was crazy. And obviously it didn't always work.

"You never crash here, hey, Luca?" I said as we got back into the car.

He just gave me a look of disbelief.

The streets of Napoli and its surrounding suburbs began to fill with garbage. Most of the people in Castellama live in apartment complexes and throw their rubbish into the nearest dumpster in the street. This was something I wasn't used to; many people live in houses in Australia and have their own garbage bins.

These dumpsters lined the streets of my new region and were emptied frequently, although the emptying would stop when the council ran out of room for the rubbish—the Mafia often sold the region's dump sites to the north of Italy. This meant that the inhabitants of a particular region would have to wait until more space was found to put their rubbish in, resulting in the dumpsters overflowing and rubbish being strewn along the streets.

The first time it happened, the piled-up garbage lasted less than a week. The next time it happened, though, it was really something else. The rubbish heaps lining the streets grew so high that they reached above the windows of the first-floor apartments in some streets. As ample amounts of seafood were consumed daily in this region, you can only imagine the smell that began to rise from the mess. One street in particular for the entirety of its length was piled high with rubbish on either side. The gypsies who frequently sorted through the town's rubbish seemed to stop their searches with hoes and trolleys. I'm not sure if this was due to the smell or because they had found enough objects for the time being. At one beauty salon in particular, the owner had to climb over a metre or so of rubbish just to get into her shop. And this was in the middle of summer.

Eventually the welcome sound of garbage trucks filled the streets. I don't think any of the Neapolitans had been happier to hear them.

My students and I went out for frequent pizza nights. In some places we ordered pizza by the metre. All in all, though, I didn't make very many friends during my stay in Italy, and Luca and I seemed to be fighting far too frequently. One special friend I did make was Rosario, Luca's grandmother, whom I had met on my first visit to Italy and who lived downstairs from us.

When I first arrived in Italy to live I didn't have the most amazing clothing in my backpack, especially in comparison with the fashionable men and women that surrounded me on the streets in my new town. Luca's mum and grandmother soon solved that problem for me. Both went through their closets and outfitted me with a completely new wardrobe, handbag and all. Luca's grandmother sure had style for an old bird.

I'd always wondered why women in the streets were looking at each others' bags until Luca informed me that a handbag is an important status symbol there. He told me that some girls would not eat for a week, instead using their wages to buy a ridiculously expensive bag. I could not get my mind around that one. I was still that girl who came from the small sleepy town of Forster, where the most expensive clothing and accessory brands people bought were usually from the surf shop.

One day we were at the beach. I had my things all over the place, as usual. One of Luca's girlfriends looked at me in shock.

"What are you doing!"

I looked down in horror. What was I doing now?

"That's a Louis Vuitton bag! It's covered in sand!"

"Oh. Wow... I didn't know ..." I quickly started to brush the sand off.

The girl just looked at me in disbelief.

Luca turned to me looking excited. He was holding a hairband he had found on the ground.

"*Amo*, here, look what I found!"

"Eww, how disgusting!" one of Luca's male friends exclaimed.

My eyes told Luca to drop it and not to say anything. He was trying to be sweet, really: I always pick up hairbands and use them. Maybe that is disgusting, thinking about it. But I'm still alive so it can't be too bad.

I had quite a lot of adjusting to do in Italy, especially when trying to speak the language. I was in a constant state of panic at the thought of having to have a conversation with someone. By the time I would remember how to say something, the conversation would have passed the point. So I was feeling pretty lonely for a while.

One of the two castles in my new city gave the name to the city, although different people had different stories of which castle was the one responsible for the name of Castellammare di Stabia, which means Castle by the Sea. One of the castles was built on a small island in the sea and the other on a cliff face by the sea. The entire coastline from Napoli to the next big city Salerno was formed of rugged limestone cliffs that fell into crystal-clear, blue and green Mediterranean waters.

It was a fairy tale.

One day when the usually busy streets of Castellammare were almost completely bare due to the heat, we decided to go for a day trip to the famous island of Capri. We took a small canoe steered by a gondolier into the *Grotto Azzura,* the Blue Grotto. As we entered through the cave's small entrance to the song "Cantare" sung by our gondolier, all the tourists seemed dumbstruck by the bright, clear-blue glowing waters inside. It looked artificial.

There was a pathway that led to the grotto from above, where the Roman emperor Tiberius had once lived. That was the thing about Italy—well, Europe in general. The history was just incomprehensible. One beach in particular that impressed me was the one that Luca and I used to go to, close by Castellammare di Stabia. It was made up of ancient Roman ruins meeting the sea.

I was starting to really fall in love with this country. I made a few short trips around Italy over the next few months. One trip we went on was to the region of Puglia, the heel of the boot. We went to this region to attend the wedding of one of Luca's college friends.

We stopped at a roadside stall for an espresso along the way. Luca told me even he couldn't understand what the people behind the counter were saying to each other, they were speaking in their dialect of the Puglia region and it was completely different from the dialect of Napoli. When ordering, both Luca and the guy working at the cafe spoke to each other in Italian, so we were able to get our coffee.

The style of pasta typical in this region is called orecchini, which means little ears, because that's the shape of the pasta. The pasta that we call bow ties in Australia is called *farfalle* in Italy, which means butterflies, while the smaller bow ties are called *farfalline*, meaning little butterflies. Another typical dish from this region is a cheese called *burrata* (meaning buttered, in Italian) which is a big, boob-shaped blob of mozzarella filled with mozzarella and cream, which gives it an incredibly soft texture—making it seem even more like a boob. This cheese is served with the delicious crunchy bread of Italy, freshly sliced tomato, basil, olive oil and salt. It is pretty much heaven in your mouth.

Luca and I, along with one of Luca's friends and his girlfriend who were also attending the wedding, were to stay together in a small apartment by the sea that Luca had organised for us. It was a cute little beach-style apartment with two bedrooms, a kitchen and a dining area. Luca's friend and girlfriend weren't due to arrive until the next day, so we dropped our things and headed straight to the beach we had passed along the way. This one had actual sand! All the beaches I had been to in Italy so far had been made up of rocks or pebbles, I was looking forward to lazing around on the sand all afternoon. The water was clear and turquoise-blue and the sand a brilliant white. We visited the surrounding beaches, and each one was just as beautiful as the last.

The next day Luca's friend and girlfriend arrived. We spent the week leading up to the wedding lazing in the Mediterranean sun at the beautiful beaches and eating delicious fresh seafood. We went to a fish market in the town of Gallipoli (not to be confused with the Gallipoli in Turkey), a beautiful little seaside town close to where we were staying.

For the first time I tried razor clams, which are long, flat shellfish you squeeze lemon on and use one of its shells to scrape the flesh off the other side.

We bought kilos and kilos of fresh fish and some fresh sea urchin eggs like the ones we had eaten on the beach in the Philippines. Later that evening we barbequed all the fresh fish; next day we made pasta with sea urchin eggs, olive oil, tomatoes and a little parsley. That would have to be in the top five pastas that I have ever eaten.

I had never been to any weddings other than Australian ones, all of which but one were fairly unreligious events. This wedding was the complete opposite of that. The church was a rather grand affair, with leadlight windows and carved wooden doors. The entire inside of the church was made of marble, including the numerous statues surrounding the seating area. Although I'm not religious by any means, churches always provoke in me a deep peace, no matter the religion, and I always feel humbled when I am inside the church and when I leave. I always feel so small and insignificant, like all my silly problems mean nothing. Maybe it's the history that goes along with religion that makes me feel so small. I get the feeling that many other people may also feel this way in a church, whether they are religious or not.

Afterwards we drove for what seemed like hours to get to the reception. We got lost along the way and all I could think of was the food I would be missing out on. Luckily for my rumbling tummy we arrived just in time. The place where the reception was held looked like something out of *Vogue,* something only a millionaire could afford to rent, let alone own. It was incredible. The bride and groom appeared from inside the building and walked down two separate sets of stairs to meet in the middle. There was an eruption of camera flashes as the newlyweds kissed.

I found myself trying to imagine Luca and I walking down those stairs towards each other, towards a life together forever, but it just didn't feel like it was going to happen. Suddenly I had the urge to tell him that we were wasting our time, that if, after two years together, I couldn't even imagine marrying him (although I really wanted to), that it was obviously not meant to be. I consoled myself with thoughts of other couples I knew who had been together for much longer than Luca and I before knowing they were ready for marriage. What was my rush anyway—right?

We made our way over to three enormous lamplit tables covered in an abundance of gourmet foods. Men stood at each of the tables, wearing suits and bow ties, cutting the meats and serving the lobster. Luca and I said goodbye to each other and hello to our plates for the next hour. After we had finished the starters, it was time for the main course! Big mistake: we had thought that our entrees were our main meals.

We were told to change eating locations to a beautifully decorated gazebo. There we pushed down the food the waiter brought to the table and then moved yet again for dessert. By this time my stomach was sticking out unnaturally far, but the sight of the dessert made me forget how full I was for a brief moment. The dessert table was exploding with cakes, small tarts with colourful fruits and glazed jelly, tiny glasses filled with scrumptiously sweet creations ... and then some.

The bride and groom lit sky lanterns and we watched as they travelled through the sky together. Luca held me close and the unsettled feeling I had experienced earlier about our relationship started to return. We danced the night away until the early hours of the morning. Only when all of us seemed too exhausted to go on did we head back to the apartment.

Next day we were to drive back to Castellammare. We said goodbye to the couple we had stayed with and picked up two of Luca's other friends and one of their girlfriends for a lift back home. Just as we were about to leave, one of the boys locked the keys in Luca's mum's car. They had to break open the lock and pull all of the bags out of the boot to find them.

Two hours into the drive we received a call from the groom's father, who owned the house where we had locked the keys in the car. I couldn't quite decipher the conversation, but I had a feeling that it had to do with me.

"*Amo*, we accidentally forgot to pack your bags back into the car."

Shit!

We decided not drive the two hours back but to have them sent to me instead. We stopped along the way to see the tiny town of Alberobello, which translates as *beautiful tree*. The entire town consisted of *trulli*, which were the type of buildings erected in Alberobello in the 14th century. The architecture of these buildings is unique. They are made of limestone and shaped like cones. The outer and inner walls are white, the roof is grey and comes to a point. Many of the roofs had a faint Christian symbol painted on them and, although they are very old, they are in incredible condition, with people still inhabiting the tiny seven-hundred-year-old homes.

When we got back to Castellammare we found we could no longer enter our little home as there had been asbestos in the ceiling. While we were away there had been work done to make a new ceiling; the area was now unsafe for some time. Not only did I not have my essentials that had been left behind in Lecce, I couldn't get the rest of my things either. After a short discussion of what our options were, we decided to move in with Luca's dad, as neither of us had a lot of money.

I went back to work and finished my last week at the school before it closed for a two-week break over the hottest time of the year. I had done a lot of thinking and, after one too many arguments with Luca, I decided that I wanted to go to Spain and Portugal for a few weeks alone. Things weren't working. I knew I needed to change something.

I was hoping that the time away would help me to see what I needed to do. I knew that I loved Luca and that all of our fighting was senseless, but I wasn't sure that I could stay in that relationship much longer. The bad was starting to outweigh the good, and I knew that neither of us was living our best life. Sure I was doing something that I had planned to do long ago, but I just wasn't happy doing it.

I felt that I was wasting time here in Italy. I wasn't making any positive changes in the world, and that was all I really wanted to do. I knew that I would feel a deeper sense of satisfaction if I was putting the good fortune that I had been dealt in life to good use. Like those girls at the market stall in London. Even something as small as selling those cards would have made me feel more content with my life. I hoped that this trip to Spain and Portugal would give me some answers—and the courage to do whatever it was that I had to do.

10

On the road again

I packed a backpack small enough to meet the carry-on requirements of the low-budget European airlines, taking only the things I needed. Luca took me to the train station and we said goodbye to each other through the windows of the train. I felt incredibly confused about our relationship, as though Luca was another part of my body. It was like I was leaving behind part of myself. As I watched him disappear in the distance I didn't know whether I even knew the part of myself that I was left with.

That feeling didn't last for long. As I sat looking out the window of the train at the city flashing by, the nerves that had been wreaking havoc in my stomach started to turn into incredibly strong feelings of excitement. I reached into my bag and as calmly as I could pulled out my guidebook of Spain.

It was going to be OK. *I* was going to be OK. Better than OK.

All the stress and the tension and the said (and unsaid) words between Luca and me started to fade. Sure I knew that if it had been me left at home and Luca sitting here, I would have felt entirely different. I knew that the excitement of my little adventure was probably distracting me rather than relieving me of our problems, but it was a welcome distraction and one I really needed.

I looked through my guidebook to see if there was anywhere in Spain that I could volunteer. I couldn't find anything. It seemed crazy that there was as much information available as I could ever need about places to spoil myself, but no information if I wanted to do some good in the country. I remembered my idea to make a website for this kind of thing and decided that it could be something worth looking into.

I arrived in Rome and bought a panini with prosciutto crudo (cured raw ham), rocket and mozzarella for the trip. I took my flight from Rome and landed in Valencia, Spain, brimming with excitement. The feeling of freedom was strong in my being. I had only been to Spain for three days on the tour that Luca and I had met on, and I knew it was a country I was going to love.

I had arranged to stay with the father of Luca's friend while I was in Valencia for the next four days. I bought a sim card and called him. His name was Juan and we barely understood a word each of us said, what with with him rolling his rs in a hurry and I speaking in broken Italian. He picked me up from the subway and we made our way to his house, where I felt very comfortable. Juan was sweet and told me to make myself at home.

It was two o'clock in the afternoon. I left my things and decided to go and explore the city by foot. I passed a temperature gauge on the side of the road which read forty-two degrees Celsius! No wonder Juan had told me to take a bus. I stopped in at a bar and ordered the last of the paella; it was ridiculously delicious. Paella is typical of Valencia, so I guess it had to be.

The next few days I wandered the streets, went to the beach, ate toast with pureed tomato and olive oil for breakfast and started to fall in love with Spain. I met a girl from Holland, and we went out one night for paella and sangria. There was no other size for the sangria but a one-litre carafe, so we got a little tipsy and started to talk about men. I told her about my problems with Luca.

"I think I should just go home, move to Byron Bay, a beautiful town on the coast of Australia, where there are lots of open-minded men, who are much more in touch with their feminine side, and are so sweet and alternate," I said.

The girl seemed suddenly more interested in what I was saying. "Oh, where is that?" she asked me. "I'll join you!" We both had a giggle and I didn't think much more of it.

Just how on the mark I was when I'd said that, I had no idea then.

Next day a very hungover Kristin took a bus down to a small town called Almeria, which lies in the Andalusian region in the south of Spain. I stayed with a girl from Columbia and her boyfriend, who was from Granada, along with their dry-humping dog.

His humping efforts were quite aggressive. When he dug his claws in to get a good hold of me, it would almost draw blood! I wanted to kick him off my leg as he humped away, but there was nothing I could do but push as inconspicuously as I could. I love dogs but this was just too much. At one stage he jumped onto the lounge and started humping my back! Needless to say I spent most of the time in my room.

I was taken for a short tour of the city by my host. The streets were filled with people preparing the town for the festival that would start the next day and go on for the next weeks or so. We passed by a bullfighting ring. I stopped, interested.

"I hate this," my host Diana told me.

"Why?" I asked, completely clueless about the severity of the bullfights.

She went on to explain the cruelty of this famous tradition. She told me that if I wanted to go to one, I was more than welcome, but I was not to expect her to accompany me.

"Don't worry, Diana, there is no way I would want to see that."

Diana was an incredible person and one of the first people I had met so far on my trip that I had properly connected with. Although the girl from Holland was lovely, she was a little cold, and also a little ... rigid? I loved the openness and warmth that southern Europeans and Latin Americans possessed. Diana was not only warm and open. When I told her that my dream was to make a difference in the world, she told me of the voluntary work that she did.

Just outside the city of Almeria lay an enormous refugee camp housing countless people who had migrated from Africa. Diana informed me that many of the women were "owned" so to speak by the Spanish mafia, who had gotten them to Spain. In return for their migration the women had to pay back the mafia by selling their bodies until the price was met. These women could barely speak Spanish and, as you can imagine, needed help when going to the doctor etc. That's where Diana came in. She would volunteer her time to take the women to doctors and other appointments, helping them with their language and other problems along the way.

I told her that I would love to help and wanted to know if there was anything that I could do in the short time that I was there. Unfortunately Diana was on holidays during my stay and it was too dangerous for me to do it alone. It wasn't as though three days would give me enough time to make much of a difference anyway. Although I felt disheartened being so close to people in need without the means to give any help, and guilty because of how much fun I was having, I was happy to meet someone doing something good. I felt like I was on the right track and that I had met Diana for a reason.

All of the south of Spain holds festivals over the summer like the one that Almeria was now preparing for. On my first afternoon we went to a small outdoor restaurant by the sea. We ordered a vino tinto for two euros, and were asked what we would like for our tapas plate. I let the guys choose for me as I had no idea what anything was. When my plate arrived I was shocked. It was practically a meal. For free! We ordered another drink and were brought another plate. Both plates contained different types of meat and a small salad. It was delicious and I felt I could stay here forever.

The stifling heat saw most of the people at the restaurant diving into the water close by before heading home for a well-earned siesta. Two glasses of vino tinto and two big tapas plates had me yawning and understanding the need for siestas in Spain. We went for a quick swim before heading home to crash for the afternoon.

Next day Diana and I got ready early and headed out to the streets to see what the festival of Almeria had to offer. It was amazing. Flamenco dancers dressed in ruffled colourful dresses roamed the streets, their hips swaying to the flamenco music that could be heard on every corner. The women looking on were dressed in their absolute best, their dark eyes visible from behind their colourful fans, which fluttered in front of their faces like the wings of butterflies.

The streets were closed off and lined with countless tapas bars. Their aromas caused my mouth to salivate instantly. I had one of the most enjoyable days of my life, eating mouth-watering tapas. Just as at the restaurant the day before, they came free with every drink. The melodious, passion-filled cries that came from the flamenco singers gave me goosebumps and swelled my heart with some unknown emotion. What was this place? Gee, did the Spanish know how to party. I was starting to understand my old flatmates and their lust for life.

My host told me that I should go to Columbia, that I would love it there. I asked her if it was dangerous, and she said it wasn't if you knew where to go. All I could picture were jungles, guns and drug traffickers. I would later find out how wrong I was.

Although I didn't want to leave I had already pre-booked my bus for the next day to one of the most beautiful towns in the entire world— Granada. Along with being one of the most beautiful and special towns, another of Granada's lures is that it also has the amazing tapas situation, where food comes free with drinks.

I visited a lookout in Granada where I could see the Alhambra, which is a Moorish palace standing beautifully before the backdrop of the countryside that lies beyond. Beside the palace is an impressive cathedral built directly over the palace's mosque, a statement popular during the Spanish Inquisition.

The afternoon that I walked through the narrow cobblestone streets to the lookout I had been lucky enough to sit with two men playing and singing flamenco so passionately that it bought a tear to my eye. The sun set in a hazy pink sky as I sipped the plastic cup of sangria I had bought from a street vendor close by. As I let the music fill my soul I tried to imagine this town when the Moors had lived here.

Most of the buildings in the town were white and of Arabic design. As I walked back through the city to where I was staying I noticed just how prominent the Moorish influence was, from the architecture to the Turkish baths, to tea houses. Granada, I would have to say, is a place every single traveller would want to experience.

I said goodbye to that jewel of a town and took my next bus to Málaga. I was supposed to stay with the cousin of the girl I had stayed with in Granada, but he'd cancelled at the last minute. So I arrived in Malaga fairly late in the evening with no place organised to stay. Although I felt completely safe I was starting to panic as the memories from our first night in India began to flood my mind. I walked to two hostels, but both were fully booked. The girl at the first hostel was less than helpful and the guy at the next was too helpful, offering me a place at his house and promising he would sleep in his hammock.

Yeah, right.

He was sweet enough, though, to call the hostel around the corner for me. Luckily there was space there. I thanked him and made my way to the hostel, using the map that the receptionist had highlighted for me. I turned the last corner to my street and walked to the number scribbled on the map. I looked up to find a dark and gloomy building with colourful flamenco dresses hanging from the upstairs balcony. The guy had said it was a little creepy.

I pressed the buzzer and the door clicked open almost instantly. I was greeted at the door by a toddler, who took one look at me before running off to get his mum. I was shown to my own private room for the same price as a dorm at the last hostel. That was something, at least.

I went out that night with two girls I met from Canada, one of whom could speak Italian, so we practised our Italian together whenever it wasn't too rude to exclude the other girl from our conversation. My Italian had improved dramatically since arriving in Spain. I think it was because I knew the Spanish wouldn't pick up on my mistakes, which in turn loosened me up, resulting in my making less mistakes. When I arrived back in Italy, everyone commented on just how good my Italian was.

We didn't go out until one o'clock the next morning, the nightlife doesn't start in Spain until around two o'clock. This meant that I didn't get home until after five o'clock. That was just out of this world for me. In Australia, the latest I usually get home from a night out is three o'clock in the morning.

I was feeling pretty drunk from a few too many *chupitos* (shots), and the girls had told me that there were flamenco dresses in one of the rooms in my hostel. Tipsy me went investigating and, after walking through a long, dark strangely-decorated hallway, I came across a dark and eerie room that I thought could be the right one. I flicked on the switch and bathed the room in light. It looked like a dressing room with two racks of flamenco dresses in various colours and styles, a mirror and a couple of couches. I tried on a few and took some photos of myself. I was happy because I knew of people who had paid a lot of money to do exactly the same thing in Malaga and Granada.

As I was only in Malaga to meet Laura's (the girl I had stayed with in Granada) cousin, I didn't really have any plans for this city. After reading through my guidebook, I decided to go for a day trip to Mijas where, it was said, all the buildings were white, they used donkeys for taxis, and the town was really pretty. On my way to the bus stop I met a boy called Emilio, who was originally from Spain but lived in Brussels and could speak Spanish, French, Dutch, and a touch of English. He decided to follow me on my day trip. I don't know how we did it, but we managed to spend the entire day together in deep conversation with no common language. It was a great experience.

The town was as beautiful as expected, and, of course, there was a flamenco show. Emilio explained to me how flamenco made him feel. He said when he heard it he could feel it deep in his soul. I don't know how I understood this from our mix of languages—maybe my soul did. We stayed until the sun set and took the last bus back to Malaga. We had something to eat in a small dodgy restaurant, then he walked me back to my hostel. We exchanged our Facebook details and I hoped that he wanted nothing more than to be friends.

Next day I took the bus to a pretty little town called Rhonda. It was famous for its three bridges, which dated from three different occupations, although there had been more than three occupations during the history of Rhonda. As the bus drove down its streets I could see just why so many people had wanted to call this land theirs. The town was split in two by a deep ravine, and connected at three different levels by its three famous bridges. The town itself looked like something from a fairy tale. I looked around for as long as my tired, hot and sweaty self could handle, then collapsed in a heap at a restaurant that had a cheap set menu. Surprisingly, though, that lunch was to die for.

I stayed for just the day in Ronda, then took a bus to Cordoba, stayed for two days there and then moved on to Seville. Both these towns were magical. And hot. After Seville it was time for me to say goodbye to Spain and hello to Portugal.

On the long bus ride from Spain I began to feel a deep sadness come over me. I had never felt that way when leaving a country; it was strange. I guess I had just loved Spain and I wasn't ready to leave. I'd tried to think about what I was going to do about my relationship with Luca but for some reason I never seemed to be able to bring myself to think seriously about it. That bus ride was the first time I had felt like crying on my whole trip, and as the thoughts about Luca and me came the tears began to flow.

We had done and seen so much. We had spent more time together than I had spent with anyone in my life, apart from my mum and brother and my two gorgeous little sisters. I knew that he loved me, but the fights and frustration were just too much. That was not what I wanted for either of us. I had moved to Italy to start a life together. I had assumed that everything would be fine and that life would be amazing. But it wasn't. I found myself wanting more, just wanting to be happy, and for things to be easy. How would I leave? Where would I go? Maybe I could move to Almeria and help Diana with the refugees. I could learn Spanish and teach English for money. Or should I just go back to Australia and study something that would allow me to work with charities and get paid?

I had met one of Luca's friends in Italy who worked for UNICEF. Her name was Myriam and she was the sweetest little thing I had ever met. Her mum was from Morocco and her dad was French. She had spiral-brown hair, dark skin, big brown eyes and an adorable smile. When I met her she had told me that her job was to try to get big organisations to donate money to places that were in need. She had also done fieldwork in those places as well. I'd told her that I would love to be able to do what she was doing, and she told me that she had a Bachelor of International Studies and that I could probably start there.

Since then those words had been playing on my mind. International Studies, I liked the sound of it although I had no idea what it entailed. Maybe it was time that I studied something. I had seen much of the world and knew what I wanted to do to help it. I knew what was going on in the world from a traveller's point of view. Maybe now it was time to understand it from a more academic point of view.

I arrived in Lisbon at around nine o'clock that night and met a sweet girl in the tube, who was kind enough to walk me to my hostel after I had asked her if she knew of its whereabouts. I had a crazy first night in the hostel with my welcome drink and a bar-hopping party that the hostel had organised. It was just what I needed after my sad journey there. Next day I went sightseeing with four guys from Holland. They were lovely—even though we had met because I heard them referring to me as Jennifer Lopez because of my oversized backside.

The next day I called Luca to tell him what I had been thinking. His reply was that he would book a plane ticket directly to Lisbon. He arrived the next day and we met in a park close to my hostel. As soon as I was in his arms I felt the same familiarity that I had felt when he'd arrived in Australia. That same love and appreciation I always felt when

I was with him flooded my veins and I knew that it might be impossible for me ever to leave him. He gave me a beautiful card with words from the heart that made mine melt.

I had told him that he might have to catch a flight straight back to Italy, but once I saw him, I felt so happy that all our problems disappeared and were replaced by excitement at the thought of travelling together again. I walked back to my hostel, grabbed my backpack and the bag that held the presents I had bought for everyone and walked into the city to hire a car. Then we drove to the nearest camping store and bought a tent and other essentials for camping. We took out my map of Portugal and placed dots and drew lines across the country's roads, marking our planned route to Porto.

We were back camping again, like we were in Australia. It was such a beautiful week together. We were both on a high from the fact that we hadn't broken up and were making a big effort not to fight or argue over the little things we usually argued over. That week I couldn't possibly imagine my life without him.

When we eventually arrived in the magical city of Porto, we were more than ready for a real bed. How had we done this for three months in Australia? Next day we went on a port-tasting frenzy and passed out in the park at the river, which was lined on the opposite bank by a rainbow of colourful buildings.

We took our flight back to Italy in mid-September and two weeks later we took a flight to Athens for one night on our way to Egypt, staying in Athens with a couch surfing host. We found the economy in Greece so, so bad. The wages for a bar job were half that of Italy, while the prices for things like coffee or a drink in a bar were double. I felt bad staying with our hosts for free, knowing what a terrible state the country was in. We made an effort to be sure to pay their way whenever we could. Our hosts took us out for a gyro, which was a dream come true, as I found out what a real kebab, or gyro, should taste like, and next day we went to see the Pantheon. It was impressive, even under the scorching Mediterranean sun.

We took our flight to Cairo that night to join our tour group two days later. The situation in Egypt had only just started to calm down a little after the revolution caused by the overthrowing of President Mubarak's regime. Nevertheless, we decided it would be much safer to see the country and the places we wanted to go as part of a tour.

Before we joined the tour we had two days to spare in Cairo. On one of those nights we went to the city's largest night market. While I was busy looking at something, Luca disappeared into an indoor stall. He came out five seconds later and told me to have a look inside because it was more my type of thing in there, and he left again to check out something else. We usually did that at markets and would meet up somewhere in the middle when we were done looking. This time, though, we decided to stay closer. I was getting more stares than either of us were comfortable with, so I knew that he wouldn't wander too far.

The store owner introduced himself to me. He was about sixty years old and seemed to be sweet. He shook my hand and asked for a kiss on the cheek. I had only been in Egypt for a day but had the feeling that this was not the way people performed introductions in this Islamic country. I went against my instinct and went to give him a kiss on the cheek. The next thing I knew I was being grabbed by the back of my head and pushed against his sloppy lips, and he was slobbering all over my mouth as I was trying to push against his firm hold.

Luckily Luca came in at that exact moment. If there is one thing I learned about Luca in the time we shared together it's not to kiss his girlfriend. He was white with rage; every single part of his body was shaking. I didn't know how to treat the situation and let it unfold before me. Luca began to scream all the names under the sun at the old man in both English and Italian. Then he began to push him. I was already imagining our names in the newspaper under missing people and motivated myself somehow to pull him away from the store. News had spread through the market and all the surrounding store owners were asking for Luca's forgiveness. One man in particular empathised with Luca.

"That is your woman," he was almost shouting. "No one else can touch her."

He went on to say that if a man did this to an Egyptian man's woman, no one would question him if he were to kill the man.

What had I started?

Just as I thought we were getting out of the place we ran into a group of policemen. Luca found an officer who spoke English and made it his mission to get the store owner into as much trouble as possible, but the policemen told me that it really came down to me and what I wanted to do. If I were to make a statement against the man, he would go directly to jail, no questions asked. If not I had to write a statement saying that I forgave the man for the "misunderstanding".

I went with option two. I was not going to be responsible for this man's fate, no way. Apart from this incident, Egypt was more incredible than I could possibly imagine—especially the tombs of the kings, which still had colour in their paintings after five thousand years.

There is one temple called Abu Simbel that completely blew my mind. It was a long ride into the desert. Our tour bus took a convoy of eight police cars as the area was said to be dangerous at the time. The whole temple was originally carved into the mountain. It had been moved brick by brick as the surrounding Lake Nasser was flooding around it due to the building of the artificial Aswan High Dam on the Nile River. This was impressive alone; some of those bricks weighed as much as twenty tons.

The Great Temple was dedicated to the gods, Amun, Ra-Horakhty and Ptah. Four statues of Rameses II make up the facade. The smaller temple is dedicated to the goddess Hathor, the most beloved of Rameses's many wives. It took twenty years to build at around 1265 BCE. The temple is believed to be situated in such a way that on October the 22nd and February the 22nd, the sun will pass through the facade and hit three of the four gods' faces. The fourth god, left untouched by the sun's rays, was the god connected with the underworld and therefore was to be left in darkness. It was hard to believe this was possible to achieve five thousand or so years ago.

In the land of henna, Arabic music, hommus, bearded men and mosques, I couldn't get the story of Aladdin out of my mind. It had always been a favourite childhood story of mine, especially the Popeye version that my brother and I would die laughing over.

We took a magical two-night boat trip along the Nile on an open-air raft. Sleeping out in the open on a boat on the Nile was such a peaceful experience it almost seemed surreal. Afterwards Luca and I took a quick one-day tour to Jerusalem and the Dead Sea in Israel and another one-day tour to Petra in Jordan, then we returned to Cairo with our group. I couldn't help but feel a bit of relief. Egypt was the first dangerous country I had ever been to.

Our next stop was Morocco. Our flight from Italy to Morocco left from Milan, and I was yet to visit Italy's fashion capital. We stayed with Luca's aunt, which would have been great if Luca and I hadn't had so many fights since our camping trip in Portugal. The honeymoon period after the break up scare was over. Again I started to doubt how long we would last.

After two days in Milan we took our flight to Morocco and landed mid-morning in Tangier. Morocco proved to be a colourful, delicious and delightful country. In Tangier (and from what I understood most of the north of Morocco), almost all the men smoked marijuana, or kif as they called it. Even the waiters smoked kif in between table service, using their awesome-looking long, thin pipes.

Both the men and the women wore wizard-like gowns called jalabas. These came in various colours, their long hoods coming to a point at the bottom of the wearer's back. We got around the country with ease as Luca spoke French (along with four other languages). For three days of the two weeks that we were Morocco we decided to lose ourselves in the Sahara, which was an experience out of this world. Literally.

The story of Aladdin was strong in my mind when we had first arrived in Morocco and were walking through the tiny twisting streets of Tangier, but even more so as we rode through the desert on our camels. We stopped for lunch at the house of a nomadic family. The mother-of-five cooked for us while we played with her gorgeous, smiley kids. After lunch our guide prepared the small dining table where we had just dined, placing on it a typical silver Moroccan tea set and small glasses, and filling each cup with the sweet minty tea found around the country. It was considered rude not to accept this tea offering from stall owners and such, and we had become quite accustomed to the ritual.

After we had finished our tea, we bade our hosts goodbye and headed off again into the desert. The children who ran beside us quickly fell behind as our camels picked up the pace, leaving a trail of sand in our wake.

A few hours of camel-riding later and we arrived at our small campsite in the middle of the larger sand dunes. It was just before sunset. We sat with another couple to eat the dinner already prepared for us by our guide as we watched the sun sink below the horizon, surrounded by sand dunes spotted with date palms. I thought of Aladdin again. We spoke with the Berbers as the night crept on. I was trying to fathom their way of life as I glanced around me at the stars. They were countless and utterly wonderful. And for who knows how many kilometres around, there was nothing but more of this.

Next morning, although harder than imaginable, we got out of bed well before the sun rose to climb to the top of the mini mountains of sand. The dunes were deceiving in the dark. I kept plummeting off and into the sides of them. And just as we'd think we had arrived at the top, another looming dune would slowly be revealed. It seemed never-ending and I feared we would miss the sunrise.

We didn't though, and what a sunrise it was. All we could hear were our breaths as we watched the colours and the patterns of the sand changing continuously before our eyes, while the breeze picked up and the sun crept higher in the sky. We took a heap of photos, then had some fun running and rolling in the sand. Luca stood on one side of a dune some distance away and I on the other. Somehow we figured out that even at incredibly long distances we could hear each other speaking in the softest of whispers.

"I love you, *amo!*" Luca whispered.

"I love you too, Luca," I whispered back.

Although I knew what I was saying was true, my heart sank as I said these words. Not only did I feel off-track with life and what I wanted from it, I felt that it wasn't going to be long before our relationship came to an end. It was a scary thought. As quick as it came I flushed it from my mind.

The most memorable cities from our time in Morocco were Chefchaouen, where the entire walls of the old town were painted blue, and Marrakech. Marrakech is a world-heritage site and the intangible experience of being there is something you just have to see and feel.

The main square of Marrakech was filled with all types of street performers. One evening a little person came up to us, grabbed his small violin, played it frantically for something like three seconds, then held out his hand and said in an incredibly fast voice, "Money money money money!" As soon as he saw that he wasn't getting a dime, he ran off. The entire ordeal took around five seconds but our laughter stayed with us all evening.

There must be something with violins in Marrakech. There was also a semi-blind man sitting on the ground with his violin. He would play his out-of-tune instrument until he sensed somebody passing by, then he would stop playing and, quick as a flash, hold out a plastic cup. I gave him some cash. He grabbed it, looked from left to right out of his huge, eye-enhancing glasses, then stuffed it down his shirt, ready to play again.

There were also men with monkeys on chains, men who wore traditional outfits, who rang bells and sold water, along with many women who had small stalls side by side sporting henna book after henna book. To this day this main square is the loudest and most colourful I have ever seen. If I concentrate hard enough I can still hear the clangs and chatter that made up the atmosphere of this special city.

Just off the main square and somewhere in the winding streets, we found a hole-in-the-wall restaurant with red plastic chairs and seven or so small blue gas bottles heating small portions of tarjine. We had eaten tarjine all over the country but nothing had tasted as good as this. It was filled with perfect combinations of flavours and the meats melted in our mouths.

The nights in the main square saw many competing restaurants set up, the hosts trying their hardest to steal our gaze and usher us to their restaurant. We made our way one night to the stall that was famous for its lambs' brains and tongues and shared a plate of body parts. (Luca always the adventurous one.) Although the taste was surprisingly good, the texture was almost enough to bring it right back up again.

Our two weeks in this magical country flew by. Before we knew it we were back on the plane to Milan. Luca had been hired as a tour guide for Oktoberfest from Milano to Munich, which would go for three days. Being Luca's girlfriend meant I was lucky enough to join the tour for free.

After our three days of sightseeing and beer drinking it was time to head back to an unimaginably cold Castellammare di Stabia, where Luca and I began to fight more than ever. On numerous occasions I found myself close to booking a flight back to Australia, but I could not bring myself to do it. My options were to stay in Italy, cold, a little depressed by the weather, fighting daily with Luca and probably starting work back at the school where I'd worked during the summer, or to fly to the south of Spain, where I had completely fallen in love with the culture, and maybe work with the girl in Almeria who helped refugees, or even find teaching work, or fly back home and see my mum, whom I hadn't seen for over a year and was missing terribly. Especially when I called her from the other side of the world, crying about my dysfunctional relationship.

"I don't know what to do, Mum," I sobbed to her one afternoon over Skype. "I know that I care for him so much and that I don't want him out of my life. If we break up, it's not like I can just catch up with him for a coffee. I'll probably come home and possibly never see him again." This thought made me feel sick. It certainly wouldn't be the easiest of break-ups—especially if it was the wrong choice.

"You have to do what makes you happy, Kristin."

My mum's words made me cry even harder.

"He makes you cry. You shouldn't be with someone who makes you cry. Even if they don't mean to, you're not living your best life."

Something in what my mum said in that moment empowered me. I wasn't living my best life at all. I knew that I had to leave. I wanted to be happy. And for some reason, Luca and I no longer made each other happy enough.

Somehow a deep strength from inside me helped me to do the inevitable. I went onto the website I had visited so many times before and clicked on the button I hadn't be able to click on before. Confirm payment. After I purchased my ticket, my soul seemed to break along with my heart with the knowledge that it was over. Almost three years of living side by side with this man with many ups and downs was soon to come to an end. I cried myself to sleep that night and many more during the month I still had in Italy.

During that month Luca and I spent our time in denial and possibly in hope that I would cancel my flight. We practically lived in each others' pockets, eating ample amounts of delicious food and drinking even more delicious wine.

It was coming up to Christmas. The streets began to fill with small nativity scenes made up of figurines of religious figures and famous icons, both alive and passed on, such as Barack Obama and Amy Winehouse. People have these nativities in their homes as well as in the streets to represent the birth of Jesus, who does not appear in the scenes until Christmas Eve. Presents are not given on Christmas Day in Italy. Instead, stockings are hung out for a witch who comes and puts candy that looks like coal if you have been naughty, or a gift if you have been nice. At four o'clock in the morning, the streets of Castellammare di Stabia would come to life as the city's most devoted men and women walked them, singing an eerie yet beautiful song to the Madonna.

During the days leading up to Christmas, the streets were a constant bustle even in the harsh weather. I could hardly leave the house. All I wanted to do was watch movies and eat pizza. I was too cold even to go to the grocery store or to cook.

11

The boy who fits me better than my sweater

My seventy-two-hour journey from Napoli to Australia was one I will never forget. It started with Luca and I having an espresso as usual for breakfast. Then I realized that I was far too upset at the aspect of our goodbye to be on my espresso high so I took a Valium—which didn't seem to have any effect whatsoever.

On the first flight from Napoli to London I decided to have a glass of white wine. I spilled half of it all over me and tried to hide my discomfort from my new lovely British friends, who had seen how upset I was by my departure and had tried to keep my mind off the situation with some small talk about the Neapolitan mafia and so on. I didn't mind that I had lost almost all my complimentary wine. Although it might have helped to numb my sadness, it wouldn't have helped with the migraine that I felt coming on.

I arrived at London airport at nine o'clock that night. My flight from there to Kuala Lumpur wasn't until ten o'clock the next morning. I said goodbye to my new friends and made my way to the part of the airport

I needed to be at in the morning. I found a quiet place to set up camp and attempted to sleep. I took a migraine tablet. Only some time after swallowing it did I realise it contained caffeine, which was not what I needed, facing a night of sleep at the airport.

I spent the entire night rolling around on my bed of three plastic chairs waiting the hours away and briefly drifting off every so often. Next morning I took myself to the bathroom and washed my face. I walked to the mini mart, bought some milk and a muffin and sat down at a cafe to eat my breakfast, only to be interrupted, as girls travelling alone always are, by a man. After some small talk he started to act suspiciously and as always my paranoia didn't take long to kick in.

"What do you do for work?" he asked me.

I had read in a blog for females travelling alone to tell strange men that you are a policewoman. I hesitated just a moment before answering.

"I'm a policewoman," I lied.

"Wow! So you get to drive fast cars and arrest people."

"Of course I do," I answered, trying my hardest to keep a straight face, "I'm a policewoman," I finished with an air of superiority that I hoped would come across as convincing.

The man seemed to feel uncomfortable and took off, which only fed my paranoia more; I was happy with the decision to tell a white lie. I checked in, boarded my flight, took a sleeping pill, which I really don't think I needed, and passed out for twelve hours of the fourteen-hour trip, only waking for the in-flight meals and non-alcoholic drinks; after my cocktail of medication over the past twenty-four hours, alcohol was the last thing I needed.

I arrived in Kuala Lumpur with very limited funds and a one-night stopover. I collected my bags and went to leave them at the storage as I was carrying (unknowingly to my airline) fifty-four kilos of luggage, disguised as thirty. I found that it was ridiculously expensive to leave my baggage in storage so I decided to leave just one. At that moment I realized that I was missing one of my bags. I ran back through customs and thankfully found it at the lost baggage office. After proving that it was mine, I heaved it along with the rest of my baggage onto a trolley and headed to a cheap restaurant I knew of just outside the airport.

Although I was on a tight budget, I ordered two dishes. Halfway through my first plate I realized that I could probably only eat one. I took the rest in a takeaway container to eat for dinner or breakfast the next day. I took the bus into the city centre and lugged my bags around, trying to find a taxi that wouldn't rip me off. I found one that semi ripped me off, but I was desperate by that time and it left me enough money for my room and to get back to the airport.

I finally found a hostel that I wasn't actually looking for, thanks to my friend helping me on the uneven streets with my gigantic suitcase, the wheels of which were being held together by a bobby pin. I was met by the lady of the house who was Chinese, lucky to be five foot tall. She spoke with such exclamation and enthusiasm that even with my dull headache I couldn't help but laugh.

"Ooooo, look at your handwriting, verrrry nice handwriting, verrrry neeeeat!" she half-screamed at me as she showed me to my room. My fellow roommates all looked up in surprise, the blond European-looking guy in particular, trying hard not to burst into laughter. I later discovered that he was the only normal person occupying my room for the night. There were four of us in total, including a Japanese guy that for the next five or so hours that I was in the room chatting to the blond British guy, spent his time lying on his back with one arm in the air, sporadically chiming in on the conversation.

The suspense was killing me. I had to ask. "Why do you have your arm in the air like that?"

The Japanese guy opened his eyes for the first time and looked directly at me. "You will find out tonight," he said. "The air conditioner will start talking and then you will find out, won't you? If I put my arm down I'm a dead man. Yeah, you will find out tonight."

Oh, shit, what can of worms had I just opened with this obviously schizophrenic guy.

The last of the four of us was a man from Finland, who lived in South East Asia. He seemed normal in the beginning and we all decided to go for something to eat together, minus the Japanese guy. We asked if he would like anything from the street. He replied, "Yeah, a fucking fat bitch," and then fell into a fit of laughter.

We went to an Indian restaurant that I couldn't afford even though it was incredibly cheap, but because it was the British guy's birthday and he wanted my company, he was generous enough to shout me. The Finnish guy started to get louder and louder the more vodka he drank, and refused to leave when the Indian owners realized he was pouring vodka into his chai tea. We finished our meal and all left together, the Britisher and I both awfully embarrassed.

Back at the hostel the Japanese guy seemed to be asleep. Not for long though, thanks to the Finn, who was on the bunk-bed underneath me. He decided to start kicking my mattress over and over, each foot planted into various parts of my body.

"Ouch!" I exclaimed as his foot connected with my hip.

"I'm sorry, but I feel like you're my sister," was the reason he gave for his behaviour. Eventually he stopped when I didn't answer him after he asked me if I forgave him.

As strange as the current situation was, I passed out quickly, only to wake the next morning with a monstrous a headache. My British friend, upon hearing this, kindly took me to the bus stop and carried my bags for me.

My flight to Australia took eleven hours. I didn't sleep for one minute, I couldn't, the thought of a hug from my mum was so exciting, I just kept thinking of all of the things we were going to do together and talk about. Surprisingly I was starting to feel OK about being away from Luca, and because of this I knew that I had made the right decision.

My mind wandered to what I was going to do next. I could only think of one thing: to help people in need. I wanted to start a foundation like my hero Christina Noble had done. I was coming home penniless and with no clue how I would be able to help anyone. First thing would be to get a job.

The plane landed with a thud and my heart jumped into my throat. I was so excited! Seeing my mum dressed in her brightly coloured clothes and with her hair longer than ever, was a sight for sore eyes. After a long embrace we piled into the car and made our way to the supermarket to grab a few things and quickly meet up with my best friend in the entire universe—Alicia.

Alicia is tall, thin, now brunette and has the face of a *Vogue* model. Her eyes are big and green; she has a tiny, perfect nose and she doesn't know just how gorgeous she is, which makes her all the more beautiful. Alicia and I have been through the best of times and the worst of times together and there have been times in my life when I don't know what I would have done without her. Alicia is the type of person who doesn't say a bad word about anyone, no matter what the situation.

It was so incredible to see her, although I was fading quickly. The jet lag and lack of sleep was taking its toll so it was a very quick hello and goodbye to Alicia, a quick run around the grocery shop and then back to my mum's little tree house in Ocean Shores, a small town about forty-five minutes south of the Gold Coast. She had only just moved to this place and it was was decorated beautifully, as usual.

Once back in Australia, becoming invisible was hard to get used to. In Italy I couldn't walk three blocks without someone whistling at me, calling out to me or even in some cases singing a song to me! Here it was as though I had thrown Harry Potter's invisibility cloak over me the minute I stepped off the plane. I spent the rest of December with my mum, spending Christmas with her and my brother, whom I also hadn't seen for over a year.

My brother is the epitome of tall, dark and handsome. He models for the best modelling company in Australia and frequents catwalks and the pages of popular magazines. Needless to say, I am just a tad proud of him. When he was seventeen or so, he decided to move to Sydney and become a model. And he did just that. He is the sweetest boy in the world with an enormous heart and an amazing sense of humour. It is never hard to have fun with him. His boyfriend is also just as sweet and handsome, with incredibly spotless and smooth skin, gorgeous, big almond eyes and an even bigger smile.

At the end of December I was ready to start looking seriously for work. I decided in the meantime to volunteer at a community kitchen that provided warm meals to the homeless in Byron Bay. Byron Bay is a hot spot for backpackers and alternate-living Australians alike, the perfect combination for me as there were plenty of people from abroad to hang out with, making coming back home less dull than it had been in the past. I was feeling torn about where to live as my best friend still lived on the Gold Coast. But I was so close to living in Byron Bay, where the lifestyle suited me more, as well as already having my volunteer work there.

After much contemplation and advice from my mum I decided to move to Byron Bay, the town where only months before I had told the girl from Holland, over many a glasses of sangria, that it was easy to find a sweet and sensitive man, although of course this wasn't on my mind at that time. I would work hard for the next six months or so, save as much money as I could to go to Africa to help where I could and possibly to start my own foundation. I was dreaming big but I couldn't see why not to.

I was hoping to maybe meet up with Luca in Africa while I was there. I didn't want to go too long without seeing him, even if it did look like things were over. I wanted to stay the best of friends, I still cared for him dearly.

I knew there was an O-Sushi in Byron Bay, another branch of the Japanese restaurant I had worked for on the Gold Coast a year or so earlier. It was a short walk from where I was volunteering and, one day after I had done the lunchtime shift, I walked over to O-Sushi, told them I was a former employee at the other restaurant and asked if they were hiring. My hopes were a little too high. They had just hired somebody.

I left feeling a bit down, but I had already been offered a job at another bar. I just needed to get the certificate to serve alcohol in the state of New South Wales. This involved six long and tedious hours in a classroom, learning about responsible service of alcohol. After that the job was mine.

I drove the twenty-five minutes back to my mum's house and woke the next morning with a severe migraine, which forced me to stay in bed for three days over New Year's Eve. Once I felt better I went to the library to use the internet; there was no reception in my mum's little tree house. In my inbox I found messages from the manager at O-Sushi telling me they needed me and to call them as soon as I could. I rushed out of the library, gave them a call and organised with the manager to have a meeting the next day with him and the part-owner, who was also part owner of the O-Sushi where I had worked in Coolangatta.

I felt confident about the interview as I had already worked for the company. I was surprised however at the amount per hour that I was offered. It was lower than my wage at the age of fourteen. Also I was told that I would have to stay a minimum of one year. I had been hoping to be somewhere in the world helping people by then. I had spent many years thinking about doing that and the thought of putting it off any longer seemed impossible. However, I felt a little put on the spot and I accepted the job, but after arriving home and a little bit of calculation, I decided to go with the bar job. My aim was to make money and leave as soon as possible, so I sent the manager of O-Sushi a message letting him know of this.

I received a message back almost straightaway asking for another meeting. Both Joel and the part-owner Dan had gotten a good feeling about me. They were open to paying me more and letting me stay a shorter time, and, after yet another meeting, I was hired. It seemed the universe was almost forcing me to work at O-Sushi in Byron Bay. Only in hindsight did I see why.

I was feeling a bit nervous on my first shift. It had been a long time since I worked in customer service. I was still finding it hard to speak English normally and still thinking a lot of my sentences first in Italian, then English and vice versa. I was still settling in and wanted to make a good impression. I hadn't worked very long at the other O-Sushi and, although I had waited on tables for almost my entire working life, sushi restaurant work has a completely different style of waitressing. I was also feeling nervous because I knew there was a chance that a boy who used to work there might still be there. The boy whose name I couldn't quite get used to was a friend of a friend. He was the same boy I had avoided eye contact with at the O-Sushi Christmas party two years before.

Yogi was his name. Yogi. What kind of name was that anyway? I shook my head; he probably didn't work there anymore. I walked inside, and who was there to train me?

"Hi, I'm Yogi, nice to meet you," said a tall, handsome and polite young man.

His eyes were a golden brown, his skin smooth and light, his face heart-shaped. His lashes were soft and plenty. His shoulders were broad and his waist was small, like an upside down triangle. He had one of those pretty man noses. Oh my goodness ...

This was Yogi.

"Hi, I'm Kristin," I replied, trying to hide my nervousness.

Yogi began to show me the ropes. Soon we were interrupted by Joel, who told Yogi to do something else and to let me just show them what I knew of waitressing in that type of restaurant. After that first day things were much smoother and more flowing between Yogi and me, although every time he was around I couldn't help but be excited. Not only was he gorgeous, he was incredibly sweet. I found myself absent-mindedly scanning the roster to see when he and I would be working together next. We flirted lightheartedly, and I always told him that if only he was older he would be the perfect man for me—Yogi was only eighteen at the time, and I was twenty-five.

I went on various dates; it's impossible not to do so living in Byron Bay, a town filled with young backpackers looking for some fun. But having a man was the last thing in my plans and all my dates eventually led to nothing.

I started to fall in love with my new home. Byron Bay is an interesting place. The local indigenous people the Arakwal, are of the Bundjalung nation and traditionally once spoke Nyangbul, one of the seventeen dialects spoken by the Bundjalung people. Their name for Byron Bay was Cavvanbah, which means meeting place. Which indeed it is.

The surrounding region, lying beneath the remnants of an extinct volcano now known as Mount Warning, is rich with minerals, making for good soil that grows fruit, vegetables and coffee. Lake Ainsworth, about half an hour's drive from Byron, used to be an Aboriginal women's waterhole. It was and still is sacred to women, as it was once an Aboriginal women's birthing place. It is surrounded by tea trees, whose roots seep wonderful antiseptic qualities into the lake. The women were said to wash in the tea-tree infused water after giving birth, with the lake traditionally not frequented by men.

After a few months of working and realising that Luca and I were probably not going to meet up in Africa, I decided to go to South America instead. That was where I had wanted to go rather than Europe the last time I had travelled. I decided to contact the charity that worked with women in rubbish dumps (the ones who'd made the card I bought in London for my mum) and to try to do some volunteer work there. It seemed like the best place to start. I could learn first-hand what it took to start a foundation, and at the same time help an existing charity.

Try as I might, though, I could not find the organisation. I couldn't remember its name, despite researching all the big rubbish dumps in South America. I was just going to have to pick one and go there. I decided on one in Trujillo, Peru. It was the country's largest rubbish dump, with men women and children living and working there. I would lend my hand if possible.

In the meantime Yogi went overseas for four months, which I was more than disappointed about. We worked well together. He worked hard, and it always felt light in the room whenever he was there.

I had decided not long after Yogi had left that I wanted to take salsa classes. I kept meaning to go with Yogi's friend, another colleague of mine called Almog. Almog was the other young mysterious boy at the

O-Sushi Christmas party two years prior and was the son of one of the part-owners, while Yogi was the son of the other. But the salsa lesson times never seemed to work out, and Almog had told me I should go with Yogi when he got back, because he was the one who could dance.

I found it impossible to get the thought of being held in Yogi's arms on the dance floor out of my mind. What if I started dancing with Almog, and then Yogi got back and I couldn't be his partner? I had no idea why I was thinking this way. We were just friends, he was only eighteen. Still I couldn't get it off my mind.

Yogi came back and everyone, myself included, was more than happy to see him. He looked a little older and as if he had grown taller and broader in the four months that he had been overseas. He looked … hot.

Not long after he returned something happened between us that I cannot describe. Every time we gazed at each other something inside me stirred and, unless I was imagining it, it was the same for him. We would brush past each other during the busiest hours and I would feel my skin prickle and the world melt away. If this wasn't all in my imagination, I wondered, how on earth were we going to progress from workmates to anything more? Could we? He was my boss's son—and he had only just turned nineteen.

Not surprisingly I had a dream about him and decided that I had to let him know, to see if he was feeling what I was feeling. It turned out he felt the chemistry as well, and we started to see each other outside work—nothing big to start off with: dinner with friends, a coffee here and there. One night he came to my house. We sat under the stars and listened to music until he had to go. I walked him to his car and, just as he was about to leave, he reached out of the window, took my hand and pulled me into the car for the softest kiss I have ever felt in my life. Although brief, it seemed to last for an eternity, after which I somehow made my way back inside and to my room. That night I was barely able to sleep at the thought of working together next day.

After two weeks of texting and seeing each other only at work, we finally had a day off together. It turned out to be cold and rainy. We checked the cinema and with nothing good on to see I suggested we go to my house and watch a movie.

"That could be dangerous, though," he replied.

Hmm ... I knew that he was trying to be a gentleman, but it had been a very long time since I had made love and everything about him made me want to kiss him from then into eternity.

We walked into my room, which was a little bit cold. It was the middle of winter and the thought of snuggling up to this beautiful man made me giddy. I set up my TV, which I had never used before. At that moment I wished that I had—not only would it have made concentrating on the task at hand much easier, but I would also already be snuggled in tight to Yogi. We started to watch a Spanish movie called *Nine Queens,* a movie that we didn't successfully watch all the way through until the fifth attempt.

We were about halfway through the first time when he started to kiss me. His hand was gently brushing against my skin. From the tips of my hair to the tips of my toes I was completely on fire. He took off his shirt and I saw his gorgeous body for the first time. He was so big! We would later joke about him being lumpy. His arms and hands were the biggest I had ever been held by and I fell willingly into them. I felt small and all his. He kissed me all over my body and at last we made love. The entire experience felt completely surreal. I had no idea how long we were entwined in each other's bodies.

Afterwards we went for a drive to the supermarket to buy something to cook. Living in a small town, we ran into a few people we knew.

Everyone we met must have thought we were high on drugs that night. We just couldn't wipe the smiles off our faces.

Our lovemaking continued like this. Each time we discovered each other's bodies and souls more and more. Our relationship was nothing like I had experienced before. What was this? It was both beautiful and terrifying at the same time. There were countless occasions where it seemed as if it was only our souls connecting and we weren't even present as people. One night we were making love and the entire room seemed to be trembling.

"Can you feel that?" I whispered into his ear.

"Yes."

Another night Yogi was planning on coming to my house after he finished work. I was going to cook dinner as I had the night off. I wasn't sure if he liked white wine. We had only talked about our mutual love for red wine before that night, and the dish that I was going to prepare was much better with white wine. I walked into O-Sushi to ask him. He met me at the door. We were both so mesmerised at the sight of each other that we just stood staring into each other's eyes for what seemed like forever.

"Umm, do you like white wine?" I finally managed to ask.

"Yeah."

"OK, bye!"

After the whole interaction, I still wasn't sure if he really liked white wine or not, but I knew that it didn't matter. Nothing mattered. The electrifying energy we felt around each other absorbed any feelings of doubt, uncertainty, unhappiness. It was a feeling that I had never had before in my life.

Months went by like this, and Yogi still hadn't told me that he loved me. I was starting to get worried. I was falling helplessly in love like I had never been before. I began asking my guy friends if something was wrong, if I should be worried, but they just told me to be patient, it was normal. I felt so much love for Yogi I didn't know how patient I could be. I was far too scared, though, to go out on a limb and tell him that.

On Halloween night we were invited to a party. Before the party we had our first salsa class, where we showed up in matching Halloween sailor costumes. Being Byron Bay, an incredibly alternate town, no one seemed to notice, although we couldn't have cared less if they did; we were too happy for anything to affect us. After the class we went to the party and spent the entire evening just wanting to be in each other's arms like that typical gross couple who annoy everybody, and went home early.

We were lying in bed naked, wrapped in each other's arms when Yogi said something softly behind me.

"I love you," he half-whispered.

"Pardon?" I asked, not sure if I had heard right.

"I love you," he repeated, more than clear the second time.

"I love you tooooo!" I half-screamed back at him.

So it was officially official. We were madly in love.

Later he explained his tardiness by telling me something that was quite obvious: the fact that I was planning on going to South America had scared him and, even though he was in love with me before he told me, he felt too scared to feel that way.

As always, love won.

It was hard to stick to my plan of going to volunteer in South America, but I knew I had to do it. Yogi and I were still very much in the honeymoon phase of our relationship. By the time I left we would have only been together for seven months. I did make one big change, though. Rather than going for a year, as I had intended, I decided to go for only four and a half months, that way I would be home in time for Yogi's birthday—the day before, to be exact. Considering that I was not going to be in South America long enough to start my own foundation and that three of my girlfriends were coming with me, I decided to do some sightseeing as well as volunteering.

Although I was incredibly content in my relationship, I couldn't help but feel a little unproductive. It had been almost a year since I had moved to Byron Bay and, although I had saved a lot of money, I knew I wasn't going to make any big changes in the world any time soon. The thought came back to me of my friend who had studied International Studies and was getting paid to help. That's what I needed to be doing.

I was now working in a restaurant and a bar to speed up the process of saving money to help people, but my customers didn't know that. And many a time these customers could be downright bastards, putting it nicely. It was exhausting and I couldn't help but wonder if I was doing the right thing. I just wished that I could win Lotto and make a charity from that. Working my arse off for ungrateful people certainly didn't seem to be the way.

One afternoon after I had been to the travel agency, Yogi came over to my house,

"I booked my flights, Yogi," I splurted, with nowhere near as much enthusiasm as I usually had when I spoke about travelling.

And I wasn't enthusiastic at all. The only thing I wanted was to be with Yogi. All the time. I felt in that moment as though I couldn't care less about volunteering, or seeing Machu Picchu or Iguazu Falls. Nothing compared to being with him.

"How long are you going for?" Yogi asked, anxiety etched into his face.

"Four and a half months," I replied.

"That's long."

"I know."

Silence.

I suspected that Yogi might have thought that I would make the trip shorter than that, while at the same time he'd worried that it would be longer.

"You know when I told you that I wanted you to go and that I didn't want to hold you back from what you had to do?" he asked me, his beautiful brow furrowed.

"Yes?"

"I was lying."

We lay together for the entire afternoon, trying to cheer each other up. What else to do but buy a nice bottle of wine, eat some takeout and watch a movie. Our favourite past time.

I spent the summer working a lot, going to the beach, making love with my heart-throb in the sand, eating home-cooked meals, discovering each other more and more, and loving what we discovered.

The year I spent in Byron Bay was one of the richest and fun years of my life so far. I was in pure love. Most of my days were filled with morning yoga, followed by naked swims at a deserted beach and fresh sushi for lunch before starting work. I was painting, surfing and meeting new and interesting people all the time.

On New Year's Eve I worked in the bar until just past midnight. At the end of my shift, while everyone was stumbling over each other spilling their drinks along the way, I collected my things and headed towards the front door, only to be stopped by one of our regular customers.

"Thank you so much for your service tonight. I do realise that the last thing you wanted to be doing on New Year's Eve was working, but you always had a smile and made it a very pleasurable night."

"Why not?" I replied.

He looked at me with such seriousness that I felt a bit uncomfortable.

"You've already met your husband, haven't you?" he asked, taking me aback.

"Yep!" I answered, although much more lightheartedly. I always called Yogi my husband, and he always called me his wife. I don't know how it started, or how we felt so comfortable doing so, but it just seemed to fit.

"But you're not married yet," he continued.

"No, not yet," I replied. Where was this going?

"He is going to ask you next year."

I stared at the customer blankly.

"You don't know who I am, do you?" he asked me mysteriously.

"No," I answered.

"I'm actually a very famous psychic. Would you like me to do a more in-depth reading for you? I don't normally do this, but I'm being told that I should."

"Sure," I answered. "Why not?"

I had expected to be working another two hours or so before before knocking off early, and I had never had my fortune told before. We took a seat at one of the benches in the bar that used to be a train station. I had actually taken a train with my mum just over ten years earlier to this exact spot for a week's holiday and had watched a band play here. How strange life can be.

"OK, do you want to know about children?" He asked me.

"OK," I answered, a little warily.

He sat for a couple of seconds, as if listening to someone. "You will only have one child. It will be a girl." he almost blurted out.

Strange, I thought, I had only ever wanted one child. To hear it come from someone else with no judgement was nice. Everyone usually had something to say about the fact that I only wanted one child, and I couldn't help but feel guilty about it.

"You know what, I'm going to read your cards," he went on. "I really don't usually do it like this, but they are telling me there is something that you need to see rather than hear."

"OK," I said, "let's do it." I couldn't help but wonder who *they* were.

He drew three cards. One was for my past, the other for my present and the last for my future. The card for the past was the one that interested me the most. It was a picture of a tree. The tree was gold and had bright green leaves. Its deep roots were exposed.

"You want to do something big," he said.

"Yes," I confirmed warily.

"You feel as though you have been walking around in circles, when in actual fact you have been planting deep roots that will later support something very beautiful."

My fruitless work in hospitality sprang to mind. That night more than ever I had felt like I was wasting my life. While everyone was with their loved ones celebrating the new year, I was there getting shit from customers and missing out on New Year's Eve with my love.

I started grinning. This isn't for nothing. I have a dream. And I'm doing what I can to fulfil it. I *am* doing it. I'm planting roots for a foundation where I will one day look back at those bastard customers and laugh!

I started to feel a shift of positive energy inside me. I am going to make a difference. The fruit will come.

The present and future cards I didn't quite understand, so my psychic friend took my email address and told me he would email me the details later on in the week.

I felt like I was floating. I suddenly remembered the words from the book *The Alchemist,* about having a personal legend. I knew that mine was to help people, and I knew that I was on the right track. Working New Year's Eve had turned out to be a blessing in disguise.

I was so happy walking out of that place filled with people drunk out of their minds. Somehow that reading had made me feel a little more connected to my destiny.

By the end of the summer I had finished up at work and was staying with Yogi at his house in Mullumbimby, a town in the hills outside Byron Bay, where I had coincidentally told the girl from Holland where I wanted to find a lover.

After a week in Mullumbimby Yogi and I flew to Sydney to stay near my family for a week before my flight. I felt no excitement whatsoever about the trip looming in front of me.

My mum had given us her apartment for the week and gone to stay with my brother. One day I was looking through a box of letters and cards to my mum from me and my brother. I saw in the pile something made out of recycled paper! It was the card I had bought from the foundation in London a year and a half earlier, the foundation whose name I had been unable to remember. I pulled it out excitedly and searched for a brand or name.

The Earth Education Project, Nicaragua.

I had heard of Nicaragua before but wasn't sure where it was exactly; I thought it was in Central America. I took out my *Lonely Planet* and had a look at the map. I found Nicaragua was nestled above Costa Rica and below Honduras.

"Ahoovi, look!" *Ahoovi* was my new nickname for Yogi. It meant *my love* in Hebrew. "It's in Nicaragua! The foundation, the Earth Education Project, the one that I was searching for!"

Here I was, just two days before my flight out of Australia and I'd found the name and place of where I wanted to go. As Yogi would say, "Coincidence? I think not!"

I sent a message to the Earth Education Project via Facebook, telling them of my serendipitous experience and how I wanted to volunteer and learn how to start a charity, so that maybe one day I could do something similar in my neighbouring South East Asian countries.

Now all I had to do was wait—and re-plan my trip so that I would end up in Nicaragua. Looking at my itinerary and funds, I could see that I wouldn't be able to spend as much time volunteering as I had wanted. Nicaragua was far from Peru, and flights were very expensive. It didn't matter, as long as I got there. That was all I could think about.

My mum took us both to the airport as Yogi was flying back to Byron. My stomach was in one thousand knots. I was finding it impossible to swallow.

"It's only four and a half months," we repeatedly assured each other.

When the moment came to say goodbye, I could no longer hold back the tears.

"I love you, Yogi! I wish I wasn't going!"

"It's OK," he soothed. "You're doing what you have to do. I'll be here waiting for you."

"Really?" I asked through my tears.

"Of course."

And with that, I forced myself to turn around and walk to Immigration .

12

Latin America: Brazil

I had been travelling around Latin America for almost four months. From Brazil to Argentina, Chile, Bolivia, Peru, Ecuador, Columbia, Panama. Now I was in Nicaragua. My favourite country by far had been the one we first landed in—Brazil.

Ohh Brazil.

After I left Yogi at the departure lounge I walked through Immigration and on to the boarding gate, where I met up with one of the girls I was to travel with. Her name was Yukiko. She was thirty-one and from Japan. We were living together in Byron Bay and, one night, over a large glass of red wine and cheese, we were talking about how I wanted to go to South America. So Yuki, along another two housemates Yurie and Grace, decided that they also wanted to come with me.

We had planned for the start of our trip to meet up with another old flatmate Maria, who was Brazilian and living back in Rio de Janeiro. Maria was about five-foot-four, but her personality was twice the size. When she smiled, her dimples caved in incredibly and her positivity could pull anyone out of a dark mood. And that Brazilian bum of hers was as round and perky as a bubble.

Yuki looked much younger than she was. She had dark skin and long, dark hair, and was always happy when someone thought that she wasn't from Japan. She was generally always happy and listened to everything that everyone had to say. She loved to dance, eat, and drink red wine, and we made good partners in this.

Yurie was a wolf in sheep's clothing. She was the cutest-looking girl in the world and, although at first glance she seemed innocent, once you got to know her, she was incredibly funny, and swore like a trooper. It's not often you find a Japanese girl who swears. She was quite frequently inclined to stick her finger up at me, as well.

Grace was an individual—an artist, a dancing queen, a writer and an eccentric, all rolled into one. She had crazy curly hair she flipped around the dance floor, and a figure to die for. She was covered in freckles and could never tan, so she always smelled like sunscreen. She was probably the bossiest person I knew, but she had a heart of gold.

Together we made the perfect combination as housemates. We were yet to see how we would be as travelling companions. Yuki and I were flying to Brazil together and were to meet Grace in Rio; she had left for Brazil a week before us. A week later, Yurie was going to meet us all.

Our flight, like most international flights from Australia, was long and exhausting. Our total travel time was over forty hours, including stopovers in the airport, and bus trips. We arrived in Rio De Janeiro at ten o'clock in the morning, completely spent. When we got off the plane, I started to feel a little more excited at the Arrivals gate. We were greeted by two Afro-Brazilian women dressed in costume, dancing samba! I had a feeling that my departure from Australia, although extremely difficult, would be easier for me than for Yogi. At least I had the distraction of organising my travels and experiencing new things to keep occupied.

We had planned to stay either at Maria's house, the four of us in one bed and paying her landlord quite a bit for the night, or to stay at a couch surfing host's house. I had both addresses written down in my book, but wasn't too sure which one was which. Obviously, I am incredibly good at unorganisation. We took a bus into Copacabana, as both of the addresses were in that area of the city, and got off at the stop close to the first address. My Italian helped out a lot in communicating with the locals and we found the street we were looking for. We had just started walking up the street to the house when a tall bouncy blonde came up to us.

"Are you Australian?"

"Yes," I answered, having no idea how she knew.

"I'm Nora," she introduced herself.

Then it clicked: we would be couch surfing with a girl from Germany named Nora. Now I at least knew which house we were on our way to. Nora had been just about to go out as we were two hours late. We were lucky to run into her just in time.

She showed us into the apartment. It was a small studio with a double bed, a double mattress on the floor and a fluro-pink, blow-up mattress for the pool. We put our things down, made a sandwich, figured out how to use the house phone and called Maria and Grace.

"Amor!" came that sweet-toned, exotic, Brazilian accent. She told us to meet her at the metro, where we would all take a van together to the beach one suburb along, where her boyfriend was.

As Yuki and I waited for about ten minutes at the metro station, we had our first taste of the attention females received when in Latin America—the men were acting as though they had never seen a woman in their lives. It was worse than Italy! I began to regret wearing a short skirt and midriff top—practically all I had taken with me in my small, carry-on bag.

"Kristin! Yuki!" we heard two girls scream.

The four of us jumped all over each other, tears coming to our eyes. We spent the afternoon at the beach, surrounded by supermodels. We had to stop ourselves from staring at all the beautiful Brazilians. We didn't want to look like perverts.

On our way home from the beach we stopped at a small stall that sold brigadeiro, a sweet made of condensed milk and cocoa. I had already been prepared this dessert by a Brazilian friend in Australia, and I was excited to sample some here. It was as delectable as I knew it would be. After our snack we said goodbye to Maria and went back to the couch surfing house to meet our host. He was a nice Brazilian guy who was ready to party as next day was the first day of Carnival.

Imagine an entire city in fancy dress. That is Carnival. There were cats, Mario Bros and Carmen Mirandas everywhere I looked. In the metro, in the stores, out to lunch, on the bus—EVERYWHERE was a party!

We started the morning of our first day at Carnival by taking a bus to an area with a massive bloco. A bloco is a street party with loud music, live or not, blasting from speakers. It was mainly samba. Everyone was drinking, dancing and wearing their most beautiful Brazilian smiles.

We took a taxi to the top of a hill and partied in the morning sun alongside the over-excited Brazilians. We spent the rest of our first day going to blocos, drinking low-alcohol beer, jiggling our butts to the samba beat and eating the refreshingly sweet dessert acai, a superfood berry mixed with strawberries, bananas and sugar, topped with slices of banana and muesli. Brazil was proving to be every bit as enticing as I'd thought it would be.

The next four days were each one like the next, changing only in our costumes and type of bloco. There was a gay bloco, where men were dressed as rabbits, one of whom was a mobile bar, although the only thing on offer were shots of tequila. He had a bottle of tequila, a salt shaker and a container with limes, and sold shots for three dollars a pop. There was also a Beatles bloco which played samba remixes of Beatles songs, a bath bloco, where everyone had to look as though they had just come out of the shower, and oh, so many more. We met so many free-loving lasses and lads, who were more than happy to show us the basic steps of samba. After a lot of butt-swirling, foot-kicking practice, our dancing somehow ended up worse than our initial attempts.

One day Maria took us to a favela, an area where the poor of Brazil live. A lot of the houses were made simply of plastic or whatever materials the people could find. Gradually, as the owners found an income they were able to build on top of their site, making small makeshift homes, one on top of the other. Favelas can be dangerous, although that was not how I felt at all, walking the tiny, winding streets filled with smiling children and parents curious about these tourists who were walking in their part of the city. We stopped for an ice cream, then an acai, happy to give some business to the poorer community.

At the front of the favela was an old woman selling small, handmade souvenirs. I bought a purse from her, which seemed to make her day. Maria translated what the woman was saying.

"No one ever buys things from her, and she feels so lucky that she sold something. She is hoping that this change in luck will bring more customers."

When I heard that, I went back and bought another wallet for my brother. The woman almost fainted as I handed over the bills. What a gift it is to help people in need, I thought. Why is our world so upside down? To many people my bank account would seem like nothing. Yet I would love to share that nothing to make someone's day. What are the rich people of the world doing? Holding on to their money like it's their last breath. I read a beautiful quote somewhere, and it suddenly sprang to mind: "Nobody ever became poor from giving."

I decided to stick to my plan to go to Peru, unless I heard something back from the Earth Education Project. I didn't want to come all this way and not do something good. After all, I wouldn't have come here otherwise. Sure, so far my experience had been fun, and South America would certainly be filled with interesting places and things to see. But I had done enough of that already. Although excited to be at a festival I had heard so much about, I couldn't help but feel that I would rather be at home with Yogi. I was hoping that once I started volunteering, things would be different and I would be happy that I was spending my year's earnings on this trip.

One afternoon we were invited to a barbecue by Maria's friends. No barbecue in the world can compare to a Brazilian barbecue—and not only for the food. The guys who were hosting the barbecue, were not only barbecue meat kings, but also bossa nova and samba musicians. They sang late into the night, the big-bummed Brazilian girls sambaing their way around the terrace, taking their turn in bringing around to everyone a tray of succulent meat.

After the barbecue we took a van back to our house a few blocks away. Brazil has buses and also vans as means of transport. Vans are easier to find as they are plentiful and don't only stop at bus stops. A group of people got into the van with us, including three guys, one of whom was so high on god knows what. He turned to us, and said in the strangest, high-pitched voice. *"We* are *sooo joyousss!!"*

After almost a week of barely anyone being able to speak a word in English, it took us a while to realise that he had indeed just said what we thought he did. We all roared with laughter, which really got our new friend's attention for the rest of the ride.

For Carnival, in Rio at least—I'm not sure about the rest of Brazil or the other countries that host Carnival—the celebrators (men mostly) participate in a competition with their friends to see who can get the most kisses. Rather, who can force the most kisses on unsuspecting victims. We were no exception.

"Just one kiss!!" our new friend exclaimed. He was acting as if we were denying his divine right.

"No!"

"Just one kiss! *Solo um beijo!*" He reverted to Portuguese, as if this approach might work.

"No!" we all replied.

I think he got confused with our *no*'s and their *nao*'s. He grabbed my friend by the back of her head and stuck his tongue into her mouth. To my surprise, she accepted his tongue and gave him hers as well. After the kiss was over, his three friends were screaming and wolf whistling in celebration. Then they realized they didn't get it on film. By this time he had changed victims, having his sights on me.

At this, Grace and Yuki and I all screamed *no,* each sporting a serious face, trying to convey the fact that there was no way he was getting a kiss from me. I sat there with both my hands over my mouth. He was forcibly trying to kiss me, while both the girls were trying their hardest to pull him off. He ended up backing off a little, but kept insisting.

"Vai tomar no coo!" I told him as loudly as I could over the roars of his friends.

The entire van erupted with laughter, hoots and whistles: I had just told our new friend to get fucked. I had learned this phrase from Luca for my nasty Brazilian boss, though I had never had the courage to use it. Our new friend was not too impressed at all, and said a few words under his breath that I felt weren't too friendly.

After Carnival, Yurie flew over to meet us in Rio, where she, Yuki and I went to an island called Ilha Grande near Rio and stayed for two nights, while Grace went to another nearby town by the name of Paraty. It was magical—golden beaches surrounded by lush forests and blue-green waters. One night we decided to splash out at an expensive seafood restaurant with a huge meal and a bottle of white wine— Chilean, of course, as the super sweet Brazilian wine was close to undrinkable for us.

"You know," I turned to Yurie, "I never see westerners travelling with Asians."

"You're weird then, aren't you?" she replied.

Ah Yurie. Only she could say that and get away with it.

We returned to Rio and met back up with Grace to see the Champion's Parade, a parade with all the winners from that year's Carnival. Next day Yurie, Yuki and I took a bus to the north of Brazil, while Grace took a bus to another part of the country. We planned to all meet up again at the waterfalls that bordered Brazil, Argentina and Paraguay.

In Brazil there were restaurants where you paid for your food by weight. It was around two dollars per one hundred grams of pre-prepared food, which was generally very tasty. We visited at roadside stops with this style of restaurant for pee-stops frequently as there was no toilet on the bus.

Ten hours into the bus ride, Yurie started to get bad motion sickness and Yuki suddenly had problems sleeping, when she was usually the one who could almost fall asleep standing up. I was the only lucky one on that trip, sleeping almost the entire way, after taking motion sickness pills, which always knock me out.

After thirty long and trying hours for the girls, we were expecting only two more to go. But when the driver made an announcement, I overheard the word *sete* in the mix. *Sete* in Italian means seven ... Seven hours.

"*Sete horas?*" I asked the guy in front of me in my mix of Italian and Spanish, hoping that I had misunderstood.

"Sim," he replied.

We looked at each other with the saddest faces. Especially Yurie, her face almost green from feeling so unwell. An extra seven hours on this bus was not what we had wanted to hear.

Finally, we arrived in Salvador de Bahia in the night. I had organised to couch surf at a guy's house, and had his address scribbled on a piece of paper; I was trying to keep my iPhone hidden as much as possible. I went from taxi to taxi, but no one seemed to know where the hell that address was. Finally, one taxidriver got out his smart phone and looked it up. We pushed our bags into his boot and piled into the taxi, feeling more than a little worse for wear.

We drove through the city with the streets getting dimmer, less populated and less paved. We started slowing down in a street that I was sure was in the middle of a favela. The car stopped outside a building that seemed to be semi-built, with quite a lot of rubbish on the surrounding paths, along with a few dodgy-looking men looming nearby.

"Here?" I asked

"Sim," the taxidriver replied.

"Is it dangerous?" I asked in Italian, hoping that it would translate well into Portuguese, and happy that the girls couldn't understand; I could feel their uncertainty of the area.

"Mais or menos." More or less, he replied.

Shit.

"OK girls, I'm just going to find his house and come back and get you. Wait here, OK?"

I really felt that one of them should have come with me, but as it was my responsibility for this accommodation, I didn't want to ask them. I roamed the small alleyway marked seventy-five until a woman called out to me.

"Are you looking for Angelo?" I guessed she asked me; I only understood the word *Angelo*.

"*Sim,*" I replied.

She motioned towards an apartment a little further down the alley.

"*Obrigada.*" I thanked her, and called out to Angelo. To my relief he responded and told me that the gate was open. I walked into a house that was one big room with a separate bathroom and laundry. There were two hammocks hanging inside across three mattresses taking up most of the space on the floor. I was greeted by Angelo and three other couch surfers.

I told him that I had to go and get my friends from the taxi. I walked out through the alleyway, paid the driver and led them inside. I could sense their relief when we entered the house. We were all exhausted after our thirty-seven hour bus ride so we went straight to bed, all seven of us in the one room.

That week in Bahia I fell completely in love with Brazil. In Salvador, the old colonial part of the city is called The Pelourinho. Its buildings are painted various colours ranging from pastel to vibrant, its church a pastel purple. In the cobblestone streets, men and women carted around large ice boxes selling fresh cold coconuts. I couldn't go a day without drinking the contents of at least one. When I had finished my coconut I would take it to one of the stores for them to cut it in half, so I could scoop out the meat.

In the evening, drummers would walk slowly while playing, making their way through the streets, spreading music that I couldn't help but jiggle my butt to. There was one restaurant in particular that we could never go past without getting our fill. It was practically a bar, serving also as a restaurant.

There were only three dishes to choose from, and they were always superb. We either got a takeaway meal, or ate it standing at the bar with a bowl of farofa (a dry condiment, similar to flour but tasty) and a bowl of spicy salad, consisting of tomato, coriander and chilli, which we could help ourselves to, as much as we pleased. They also had an interesting alcohol selection. From one barrel (and I still don't know how), it was possible to choose an assortment of different beverages, which came from one of the many taps on the barrel. Two of these I will never forget. One was a type of wine that tasted like a more serious version of lolly, grape-flavoured juice—it was even purple. The other was a spirit of some sort, which was meant to be sipped. It tasted of alcohol and cloves. So delicious! I frequented this bar as often as I could.

We decided to go to a beach town a little further north of Salvador by the name of Praia do Forte. We were also couch surfing there with a guy who had seen that I was looking for a place to stay in Bahia and had sent me an invitation if I ever wanted to go to his town. The main reason he was interested in me was because I was Australian and he just so happened to make didgeridoos and boomerangs. He said in his message that he felt like he was an indigenous Australian on the inside.

The four days we spent with our Argentinian host consisted of beach, guitar and good meals. One day we decided to go to a small beach town close by, named Imbassai. We were going to meet up with Angelo there, and left our house just on time. We didn't know yet that if you want to get anywhere on time in Bahia it's necessary to leave an hour or so before you normally would. We got into the van and sat there for twenty minutes, while the driver screamed the name of the destination town at everyone walking past.

"Imbassai!"

Yurie started to join in. *"Imbassai!!"* came from my cute little friend.

Everyone started laughing at this. And she didn't give up. We were going to be late and miss our friend, by just how long we had no idea.

Eventually the bus filled and we got there twenty-five minutes after we'd said we would. Not surprisingly, there was no Angelo to be found.

Next day we relaxed at the beach and took the last bus back to Salvador. Both the girls wanted to stay, mainly because of our cute host, I believe, although they insisted otherwise. I was ready, though, to see more of the delights Salvador had to offer.

Our flight to São Paolo from Salvador left at five o'clock in the morning, two days after we returned. This meant we had to be at the airport by three am. Which meant we had to wake up at two o'clock in the morning. Yuki didn't sleep, which was her usual thing, lately. Yurie was smart enough to get to bed early, whereas I went to sleep an hour before we had to wake up. Before I knew it, our alarms were all going off. I felt as though I had been drugged. I grabbed my backpack and started making my way out the door. An over-smiley, well-slept Yurie called out to me.

"Kristin, do you still want the miso soup paste?"

I had been travelling with miso soup paste for the entire trip since Australia. My mum had read that it was good for your body while flying, helping to eradicate toxins or free radicals, so Yuki and I had drunk it for the entire flight. I was too tired to figure whether I had the strength to add the one hundred grams to my luggage; I just stared at her.

She turned to Yuki. "Yuki?"

Yuki wasn't any more helpful than I, so we left the miso soup behind and took our taxi to the airport. I slept for the entire flight and, once we arrived in São Paolo, I set up a bed along three chairs and passed out for three hours. The girls couldn't sleep, they were worried someone would steal our backpacks. I woke up from my rest still exhausted and feeling very greedy and guilty for my nap.

We took a bus to the metro to take the metro to another bus stop. A guy who had seen we were a bit confused got off with us and helped us the entire way to the main bus terminal. At this point in time, even though I was suspicious of him, he was like an angel sent from God. I was too tired to be doing the organising (I was the only one with some Latin-speaking skills) and couldn't have been more grateful for his help.

We got to the bus station early and had a picnic of tuna, bread and olives. Our usual cheap meal. We boarded our twelve-hour, overnight bus to Foz do Iguaçu, the town situated near the massive waterfall in the south of Brazil. We arrived early in the morning. Yurie took a taxi to her couch surfing host, while Yuki and I took a taxi to our host's house.

Our host was from Peru and lived with a guy from Ecuador, a guy from Paraguay, a guy from Brazil and a girl from Argentina. She met us at the door in her pyjamas and still half-asleep. She was about five-foot-four, dark-skinned and Latin-eyed. She was adorably sweet and showed us into the house and to our room. We were in desperate need of a shower. It had been two days since we had left Salvador and we hadn't showered during that time. Usually I would never ask, but we are always changing, aren't we?

"Is it OK if we have a shower?" I dared.

"*Si, si, claro!*" she replied.

She gave us both a towel and we took turns in washing off the layers of dirt. Afterwards we called Grace, who was already staying in a hostel in town, and planned to meet at the falls.

Our couch surfing host, even though she had already seen the falls many times, came with us. We took a bus to the falls and were surprised by two familiar faces getting on at one of the stops. Grace and Yurie! They had by chance taken the same bus, out of I-don't-know-how-many. We were all reunited again, and it felt good. We started to swap stories along the way. Realising that my couch surfing host couldn't really understand our speedy English, we decided to practise our caveman Spanish on her. It sounded terrible! But at least we were trying—right?

After we entered the park, we found that each person was hungrier than the next. It can be hard travelling with multiple people, so we would tell each other how we felt on a scale of one to ten. Then we would know how serious the situation was, and what we should do. For example, we would be out dancing, and one girl would say she was tired. If on the scale the girl was only a six, we could push the limits and stay an hour or so more. The same would go for if we were hungry, thirsty, needed to go to the bathroom, etc. That day, we found we were all above ten on the hunger scale, but hadn't wanted to say anything because we knew that we all wanted to see the waterfalls.

Yurie hesitated before stating what number she was at: twelve. The pronunciation of this number Yurie was yet to master.

"Twe-liv," she tried with all her might.

I began with my coaching of the pronunciation of the dreaded number. "Elv."

"Elv."

"Twelve."

"Twel-iv." She just couldn't get her cute little mouth around the word. And for some reason, maybe to teach her how to say it, Yurie was doomed to having to say this number every day. Whether it be the time, her room number, the date, the number of our bus, it was always the same. Twelve.

We stopped at a small bar and bought an empanada each. There were lots of coatis around (small, racoon-like animals). They seemed a little too interested in our lunch. Suddenly one ran up to Yuki and snatched her empanada out of her hand before she could take one bite. The look on her face was absolute devastation. I paid for half of her next one, so it wasn't as heartbreaking forking out another five dollars for a pretty shitty empanada.

Foz do Iguaçu are really, something else. The view of the Argentinian side from the Brazilian was breathtaking enough. But the next day when we went to the Argentinian side and saw the view of the Brazilian side, it was even more spectacular.

We got to the other falls the next afternoon by first taking a bus to the border, Yuki and I on one bus, Yurie and Grace on another. I had started to sleep when suddenly Grace and Yurie got onto our bus.

"You guys have to get off, don't you?"

"What?" I answered, half-asleep.

"This is the border, girls! You have to take your bags, get off, get your passport stamped, get on another bus and get off again at the Argentinian border to get an entry stamp."

The bus started to leave with us still on it and no exit stamp in our passport.

"*Para!*" I yelled at the bus driver. This was first time that I had nearly passed over a border without being told of the routine involved.

We rushed off the bus and waited in line to get our bags checked and, finally, our passports stamped.

13

Argentina

We took the next bus to the Brazilian border and met Yurie and Grace there. They waited for us to get through Immigration, then we all took a bus to the town at the Argentinian side of the falls. It took us just a few hours and we had only crossed a little bit of land, but already I could feel the difference in the culture. Initially it was just due to the language, but it was also about how the people dressed, which was more conservatively than their neighbours in Brazil. Even the buildings' architecture seemed to differ. And they pronounced *sh* everywhere! For example, *ella,* which means *she,* is pronounced *esha* here.

We looked for a bus going straight to the falls as the day was getting on and we didn't have much time to lose. We took a private van, along with one other guy who happened to be from Argentina, and started on our way to the falls. Halfway there, though, we were stopped by the police and the driver was asked to get out of the van. He walked over to where the other police were standing. I thought that it might have been a checkpoint for the waterfalls for tours and tour guides, etc.

After a very long wait, I asked our new Argentinian companion in broken Spanish what was going on. From what I could understand, it seemed as though the driver didn't have a licence. We realized it might be a very long time before we would get to the falls, so we all decided to get out and try our luck hitch-hiking. At this, the driver ran over to us and told us that he would only be five minutes longer and to get back into the van. We piled back in and waited another ten minutes. Again we decided to hitch-hike to the falls. When he saw this, the police officer must have felt some sympathy, either for us or for the driver, and escorted us to the falls. We asked the driver what had happened, and he told us that he had been fifteen kilometres over the speed limit.

We sat in silence until we arrived, then we organised a pick-up time with the driver and hurried off to the the falls. First off, we decided to see what we had heard was the most impressive waterfall. This was called the Devil's Throat, or *Garganta del Diablo* in Spanish. It is one hundred and fifty metres wide and eighty metres high. Incredible.

We walked out onto the platform and were met by swarms of butterflies. We saw a rainbow over the waterfall before we saw the fall itself and, as we got closer, we slowly lost our ability to hear as the crashing noise of the water drowned out all our voices.

Seeing that much water fall consistently was mind-boggling. Earlier that day we had been told that an Argentinian teacher had thrown herself over the waterfall's edge. I stood in silence for a long time, imagining what it would be like to die like that. I had seen the James Bond movie with Yogi before I left at the cinema, the one where he gets shot and falls off the top of a train into a huge waterfall. I don't think it would be my choice of suicide, that's for sure.

We walked from waterfall to waterfall, taking hundreds of photos, along with our new Argentinian friend. We got back from the falls with an hour to spare before our first full cama-bus experience. We washed our faces and put some warm clothes on to be prepared, in case there were the usual penguins and snow happening on the public transport;

we had a twenty-hour bus trip ahead of us to Buenos Aires. While we waited for the bus, we walked across the street to a small supermarket and bought a bottle of red wine, some blue cheese and some crackers for the journey.

As we were boarding the bus I started to freak out. "Fuck! Fuck! I can't find my bus ticket anywhere!"

"It's all right, I'm sure you will find it. Just relax," Grace reasoned.

I ran up to the bus driver and asked him in broken Spanish what I could do. He told me that I would probably have to buy another. I was definitely not up to spending another one hundred dollars on a bus ticket I had already purchased, so I walked over to the office to try to reason with the clerk.

Although he was extremely friendly, it was already past the time of departure and he could not issue me another ticket. He informed me that I would indeed have to buy a new one, and if I wanted to get a refund with my insurance I would have to go to the police station there to report it missing, which I obviously had no time to do.

I ran out of the office and joined the girls, who were ripping my bag apart.

"What about in the guidebook?" Yuki said suddenly.

Lights went on in my mind. It was in there, I knew it already. I ripped through the bag that held my guidebook while a very impatient bus driver leered over our shoulders.

"I FOUND IT!" I screamed.

We were all overwhelmed with relief and piled onto the bus. We were greeted aboard with a glass of whisky on the rocks by the bus's host. His role was similar to that of an air hostess although he was a bus host. I was the only person on the bus who could speak both English and a little Spanish, so he made friends with me and assigned me the task of being his translator for the English-speaking people on the bus.

This bus was high class! Our seats folded almost all the way back, there was self-service clean water available, and we were to be served a hot meal for both dinner and breakfast. We opened our bottle of wine almost as soon as we had taken off and, before I knew it, the mixture of motion sickness tablets, whisky and wine had gone straight to my head. I turned around in my seat to face the people behind us and decided to make friends with as many of them as I could. By the time our meal came, I was very drunk and very dry in the mouth and found it almost impossible to swallow any of it. I quickly grabbed Yuki's bottle of water (I had forgotten to bring one), my sleeping bag and pillow and passed out cold until we arrived in Buenos Aires the next morning, a lot more hungover than I had planned.

We took the subway to the station, where we were to meet a guy who had the keys to an apartment belonging to one of Grace's friends. She was letting us stay there free of charge for practically as long as we liked. We were all exhausted and couldn't hold a conversation with the guy, who luckily had to go to work. We took another subway close to our new home and walked the remaining few blocks through beautiful big streets until we came to the address Grace had saved on her phone. It was a large cream, colonial-style building with a huge, dark wooden door. The door had large brass circular door knockers and looked every bit the part.

We walked through the foyer and up one flight of stairs to a quaint, two-storey apartment. It had a red staircase and polished wooden floors, while the kitchen had a black-and-white checkered floor. It had a very Argentinian feel. The water glasses in the cupboard were old jam jars and the high-ceilinged space was filled with alternate-chic style furniture.

We spent a week in Buenos Aires dancing the tango and eating juicy steaks, accompanied of course by full glasses of deep, red-coloured gold, otherwise known as Malbec, one of Argentina's best known wines—for a very good reason.

One night we were out to dinner at La Cabrera (with possibly the most tantalising steak ever to be served), where we met two women and a man from the States. One of the women had a black eye. Our conversation came to which area we were staying at in the city. When we told them, their faces dropped.

"You have to be careful there, guys. Have you seen my eye? That happened to me while I was walking from one hostel to another in the middle of the day on a Sunday. Two guys and a girl drove up behind me. Two of them got out of the car, hit me and tried to take my backpack, which wouldn't come off me before they got back into the car, so they pulled me to the car and sped off with me outside dragging behind them until finally it ripped off."

All four of us girls sat there open-mouthed in disbelief. It was hard not to shake off the feeling of vulnerability when walking home from the metro that night.

After we got home and showered, I checked my email before going to bed. And there in my inbox was an email from the Earth Education Project!

> *Dear Kristin,*
>
> *I hope this finds you well.*
>
> *Firstly I would like to apologize for the delayed response - your message got lost in the Inbox. For future correspondence please email me directly.*
>
> *Secondly thank you very much for your interest in our work. It's wonderful that you got to know about us in London and would now like to come and visit the project in Nicaragua.*

I think it is very noble that you would like to start a project recycling paper in Asia as well.

Insofar as you coming to Nicaragua we can accommodate you as a volunteer as part of our volunteer program. This entails you working as part of the EEP team to assist on specific projects and in areas in which we require a volunteer corresponding to what we are working on at the time. Before we go further, do you speak Spanish?

I look forward to hearing from you.

Best wishes,

Andrea

My heart seemed to skip a lot of beats. *"Girls! Girls!"* I screamed. "I got an email from the charity I want to work with! They've offered me a position as a volunteer!"

"That is so good, Kristin!" My friends congratulated me, their smiles oozing delight at my happiness.

Hmmm … did I speak Spanish? Kind of.

From that day onward, I made it my goal to learn as much Spanish as I could before arriving in Nicaragua. It was time to look at flights to my new destination.

We spent the days of the following week and half in Buenos Aries, roaming its streets, and the nights in our favourite tango bar La Catedral. La Catedral was a dimly-lit, high-ceilinged warehouse style of building. At the main entrance, there sat the same overweight, impolite man night after night, selling tickets for the evening's dance lessons and show. Entrance was half the price if we didn't want to join the dance lessons.

A wide and worn staircase led up to the venue itself. The dark rooms were decorated sporadically with what seemed to be once-loved wall art and furniture. The lights hung low, lighting up the dance floor only, which was surrounded by rows of tables and chairs. The bartenders were young and funky, the women exceptionally gorgeous, all dark hair and eyes, with plump red lips. We always joined the tango classes, accompanied by a glass or two of the house red. The lessons were dynamic and particularly hard to follow in Spanish.

"What the fuck are we doing here?" I whispered in exasperation as we were striding in a line behind our teacher, feet flopping like horses as our ears strained to make out as much as we could of the fast-paced language.

"I have no idea, let's just go with it?" Grace replied with a flick of her curls, flashing a flirtatious smile.

"Si, señorita," I couldn't help but beam back at her. And it was worth it. By the end of the night we had gotten the basic steps down to a tee.

One night I was partnered with an Italian guy. At last, I thought, someone I can interact with while dancing, maybe even learn a few more steps. But every time I would try to say something in Italian, the Spanish word for whatever I was trying to say would come to mind, or I was left completely blank. This had happened in less than two weeks. How? It was incredible. Less than two weeks ago I was speaking Italian and, while it was definitely a far cry from perfect, I could at least hold a conversation. The last time I had visited a Spanish-speaking country my Italian had improved. I guess that was because I hadn't tried to learn Spanish; I had just spoken in Italian the entire time. It seemed that the language had taken a vacation from my brain.

After a week in the city we decided it was time to move on. Yuki, Yurie and I had decided to take the bus to a city north of Argentina called Mendoza, the wine capitol, while Grace was going to stay on for a few more days and then meet us up there. The morning we were to leave for Mendoza I could not shake the strongest feeling of anxiety. I packed, repacked and then re-repacked my bag over and over.

"I must be getting my period soon, chicas, I feel so … weird," I told the girls, who weren't really paying attention to what was going on.

Absentmindedly I decided to put my credit cards in my shorts' pockets, along with my iPhone, my camera and my passport. We took a cab to the bus station, and Yurie and I went about trying to find the best-priced bus tickets for yet another first-class Argentinian bus experience to Mendoza. Just as we were purchasing the tickets, Yurie realized that her passport wasn't in her backpack. We purchased them anyway and then started looking for it frantically. I went to find somewhere with internet to ask Grace whether or not it was still in the apartment. When I got back I realized something very odd. My backpack was nowhere to be seen.

I am great at misplacing my belongings, so my mind was racing, trying to think whether I had just happened to "misplace" my ten-kilo backpack. Of course I hadn't, but routine in the past with my lost items had always seen them showing up when least expected. Soon the reality of the situation began to come clear to us: my backpack was definitely not misplaced. I had previously noticed many police around the bus station. I ran up to the closest one and frantically told him that my backpack was stolen. I knew that I was probably coming off rude and bitchy, but I couldn't find the words in Spanish at the same time as my etiquette. In the end he got the picture and took me to the police station, which was down one flight of stairs.

I entered the front room of the station and was greeted by around fifteen pairs of eyes, all of which seemed to be very interested in the young, distraught blonde lady. I'm guessing it was pretty obvious what had happened and that the officers belonging to the eyes had seen it all too many times before. They were wearing olive-green, full-length uniforms and cute little black berets.

The officer motioned towards one of the two black metal chairs in the foyer and told me that he was going to find someone who could speak English. The rest of the men went about their business, trying not to look my way too often. But officer or not, a Latino man is a Latino man, uniform or no uniform. It seemed as though something pretty serious was going on with the police. I wondered why all fifteen officers could possibly need to be in this small office. I couldn't help but indulge the thought that someone had caught the person who'd taken my bag and that they were all waiting for him to be brought in.

Instead, though, two men were half-dragged into the room by a group of officers. Another followed, carrying a black backpack. One of the officers had seen that I was watching through my sobs and came over to tell me that the men had been caught with cocaine in their backpack. It seemed as though the officer was trying to cheer me up somehow with this piece of gossip. I gave him a half-smile to let him know that I appreciated the inside information.

After what seemed like several hours, and my tears had died down to small sobs, the first officer came out of the second room with another officer in tow, who must have been the English-speaking officer.

"Hi." I tested my waters. After a lot of experience with "English-speaking" people in Latin America, I had a feeling that he wasn't going to be as English-speaking as I had hoped.

"Err, hel lo ... I ... you ... what ... can help?"

"Oh." My instinct had been a little too on the money. As slowly and clearly as I could, I started to describe what had happened. Once I could see that the message was getting lost in translation, I reverted to my terrible Spanish, which the officer seemed to understand a little better.

He took me into his office and told me that he would make a phone call to his boss, who could speak English. After a few attempts, he got through to his English-speaking boss. I literally crossed my fingers when I took the receiver.

"Hello?" I half-questioned.

"Ah, hello. You have had something stolen?"

"Yes," I sighed into the phone, utterly relieved by the boss's command of English.

"OK. I can't hear you very well over the phone. You can use my office and my computer to send me an email of exactly what happened and what has been taken, with all of your details. Then, once I have received the statement, I will translate it into Spanish and get my colleague to print it out for you."

"Thank you so so much," I answered.

I handed the phone back to the officer. When he had finished on the phone, he motioned me over to the desk and told me that I could use his boss's computer, while scribbling down his boss's email address on a piece of paper.

I sat and started to write what had happened and the list of things that were in my backpack. Each new realisation of what had been inside worked knots into my stomach that made me want to vomit. It was like the incident in Darwin all over again. Each time I thought I had completed the list, I would remember another item. I think what I was most upset about losing were my migraine tablets. They were incredibly hard to find, and I usually had to get Luca to send them to me from Italy. Finally I finished the report, sent it through and waited for the officer to bring me my copy.

I desperately needed to go to the toilet. I showed myself out of the office and found the toilet. On the way I passed some policemen and for a moment thought that I might get into trouble for roaming unaccompanied around the station, but they didn't seem to mind. I walked into the toilets, half-crying again, when suddenly the song, "Don't cry for me, Argentina" came to mind, and I found myself in an uncontrollable fit of laughter. I had to stifle the giggles so that the policemen didn't think I was crazy or making the entire story up to get an insurance claim. For the last week I had been singing that song in the craziest tones to the girls, driving them absolutely mad. I couldn't help but be amused by the irony.

I walked out of the toilets and back into the office, where the officer was waiting with the statement. I looked over it, deciphering what I could and with a light heart and smile I signed the bottom of the page stating the items I had lost. I thanked the police officer and made my way back up to two very sad-looking Japanese girls. I ran up to them and hugged them both, half-laughing. They could not believe it.

"I'm so sorry," they both said.

"It's OK. It's so *so* OK! We are OK. We have each other! Who cares! Let's go home."

"What is going on, why aren't you upset?" Yurie asked me, completely confused.

"Dooon't crry forr me, Arrgentina!!!!" I exclaimed at them as dramatically as I possibly could.

I think in that moment the girls thought their friend had gone completely mad.

The three of us walked out of the bus station, the girls lugging their backpacks, me sporting my black shorts, black singlet and sneakers only. That was it. Sucks for the robbers, though, because I had all four credit cards on me, two of which I always left in my backpack. Note to oneself: it certainly pays to listen to that inner voice.

I hailed a taxi and jumped into the front as the two girls hopped in behind. Suddenly I was surging with energy and could not stop talking to the taxidriver—in Spanish. I have no idea how, but the words were just flowing, and I was so funny! The taxidriver was laughing a lot, but of course, a Latino being Latino, the conversation came back to me having a boyfriend or not, and if so, why wasn't he here, and that I should try a man from Argentina.

I was happy when we pulled up out the front of our big building. I no longer wanted to talk to the sleazy taxidriver. A taxi was parked in front of us, and who should clamber out but Grace! She had just arrived at La Catedral for yet another night of tango, when one of our friends had seen on Facebook what had happened and told her, just as she was ordering her wine. She drank it down and came home just in the nick of time. The girls and I were not too keen on being stuck out in the street with the remaining two backpacks that we did have.

"Ohh darling, I am so sorry!" Grace exclaimed as she draped her arms around me, eyes full of pity.

"It's fine! I'm totally fine! I don't know why but I'm so happy! I'm over it!"

"What?"

"Yes, I am, I don't know why. Maybe because we are all safe? I just feel so ... good?"

"Wow girl, you are one positive being."

"Why, thank you." And that was it.

The next two days we spent in Buenos Aires were pretty uneventful. Yurie sorted out her passport; it wasn't on the table, though I could have sworn it was. Who knows, maybe it was in my backpack. I re-bought all the necessities, like a toothbrush and toothpaste, etc. And before we knew it, we were packing again to take the bus to Mendoza when ...

"FUCK!" came from Yuki.

"What?" I called out.

"My wallet, I can't find it anywhere. I think I left it at the restaurant last night. I have to go find it."

And with that she left.

We had two hours to get to the bus station, and we had already bought our tickets. Grace had bought a bottle of whisky when she had heard about my backpack, thinking that I would need it. It turned out that now was a better time than any. We sat waiting anxiously for Yuki to buzz the intercom. The minutes turned to hours and, just when it looked as though we would miss our bus to Mendoza yet again, the *bzzzzz* came from the intercom.

"I got it," Yuki puffed into the speaker. She came up and grabbed her pack.

We finished off our glasses of whiskey and made it to our bus just in time. The trip to Mendoza was another long leg, although we were again spoiled with wine and a warm meal for dinner. I had an amazing night's sleep next to Yurie, the seat going down almost completely horizontal, while Yuki slept next to Grace. Next morning we made friends with a chatty, middle-aged woman sitting close by, who was on her way to meet a chico she had met on the internet. She shared some of her cake with us and then gave Yuki and me a lift to my couch surfing host's house, while Yuki and Grace went to their hostel.

Mendoza was freezing, and the city itself didn't have too much to offer apart from the wine. For one of our days in Mendoza we took a bus out to the wine region and hired bikes to ride to the surrounding vineyards. The tastings were as big as a full glass of wine, meaning that we didn't feel the cold or the push of our pedals on the ride back.

That afternoon I decided to stay in the hostel that Grace was staying in. I checked in and sat down at a computer to do some organising for the next part of my trip. A girl who had randomly given Yurie and me biscuits earlier that day came up to me.

"You are friends with Yuki, right?" she said in a cute accent that I couldn't quite pick. French maybe, or German?

"Yes," I replied.

"Our bus to Salta is leaving soon and I have been waiting for her, we have arranged to share a cab to the bus station. She still isn't here, and I really need to go now or I'll miss it. If you see her, can you please tell her that she needs to go to the bus station straightaway, otherwise she will lose her ticket."

"OK, sure, I will tell her. Thank you so much."

And off she went.

I turned back to the computer, thinking, "Come on, Yuki! You have a bus to catch. What are you doing? Where are you?"

My couch surfing host came online. I told him that I would stay in a hostel for that night. Then he asked me, "Don't you have a flight from Buenos Aires tomorrow?"

Suddenly I realized that I had the dates wrong and that the last bus to Buenos Aires left in less than two hours. Just as I was getting up Yuki in my mind, I had done almost exactly the same thing, but worse!

I thanked him for the wake-up call (with a few fucks thrown into the conversation in my panic), threw the bowl of pasta that a group of young British boys had shared with me into the sink, grabbed my bag, which thankfully I had not unpacked—it was only the size of a child's schoolbag, I didn't really have anything to put in it yet—and told the receptionist that I had made a mistake and could I please cancel my reservation.

"Sure, cancelled, not a problem."

"Oh, but I paid."

"Sorry, no refund," he said as he pointed to a sign that didn't actually imply that there was a no-refund policy.

"But it was literally ten minutes ago. I haven't even stepped one foot into the room yet."

"Sorry, there's nothing I can do."

"OK, fine," I said, trying not to huff.

Just as I turned to leave, Yuki ran through the door.

"Kristin!"

"Yuki!"

"Let's go!"

We grabbed her backpack and hailed the first taxi we could find. Yuki got to her bus just in the nick of time. I still had a couple of hours left, so I went to look for the best-priced ticket I could find. I bought some cheap biscuits that tasted almost like dirt and then took a motion sickness tablet, knowing that the wave of sleep would take me over soon enough. Some hours later, after a night of tossing and turning and numb hips and feet, I woke up to the unmistakable signs that we had entered the city of Buenos Aires.

As soon as I stepped off the bus, I again felt that liberating feeling that I had felt over the years: that feeling of freedom when traveling alone; the thought of things to come, unexpected and unplanned, the feeling of only being responsible for myself, my backpack and where I was going to sleep that night. Better still, my backpack weighed no more than five kilos, and I was on my way to a new country. As much as I'd loved Argentina, I hadn't exactly had the best luck there.

I had some time to kill before my flight and had seen, while pulling into the bus station, a large colourful market close by. There is nothing better than a good market to fill in time. It's even better solo, not having to feel you're taking up someone else's time by looking at objects you really don't want or need, just simply enjoying the pleasure of contemplating the purchase. It was a warm day, although I knew that it would be cold where I was headed next. La Paz, Bolivia's capital, was a dizzying height, almost four thousand feet above sea level. I would need to find something a little more heavy duty than I had in my pack, and I hoped to find something at the markets.

On my walk to the markets I found many an empty and worn backpack hanging from various posts around the place. Arriving at the market, I came up with the reason. Almost everything at the market was old and used. It looked as though backpack snatching was the fashion at the bus station and this was the way of getting rid of the stolen goods. I started getting excited at the thought of possibly finding some of my things that had been stolen.

I found a stall that sold matte cups—new ones. Matte is a tea that is drunk in South America, mainly in Argentina and Paraguay. You could pick an Argentinian or Paraguayan from a mile away when travelling. Many of them carried with them a small bag for their thermoses of hot water and the unmistakable matte cup and straw that filters the tea. The tea is prepared in the cup itself. The cup is usually made of wood. The greener the wood, the sweeter the tea and the less sugar needed. I bought matte cups for my mum and my brother; the ones I had already bought for them had been stolen along with my backpack.

"You shouldn't be here," the old toothless store lady told me in Spanish.

"Por que?" I asked her why.

"It is too dangerous for you. I have been watching, and there are many people with their eyes on you."

"Do you think I can go a little further?" I asked. I still hadn't found a jacket for Bolivia.

"No, you should leave straightaway." The lady motioned back to where I had come from.

I started to walk in the opposite direction further into the market. My intuition was that the lady was being a little paranoid and not used to so many people watching someone, something that I had become accustomed to, being a white female traveller. But then I started to feel paranoid myself and decided it wasn't worth the risk. I walked back to the bus station, and made my way to the shuttle for the airport.

"One ticket for the shuttle to the airport, please."

The man behind the counter said, "One hundred pesos, thank you."

"Oh, really?" I had no idea it was going to be that expensive. "How much is the public bus?"

"Six pesos, but it takes three hours, and it is dangerous."

"Oh."

"OK, don't tell anyone, but I will give you a staff discount," he told me in English.

As I stood at the counter making up my mind, he continued to charge each Argentinian in front of me full price. I decided to accept the offer.

"OK, I'll take it. Thank you so much!"

"Not a problem. Just remember not to tell anyone."

"My lips are sealed."

I took the shuttle to the airport, checked in and went to my gate. I had a short nap and woke up with a migraine coming on. After I boarded the plane, my migraine started to worsen, and I had nothing to take for it but some medicine I had bought from a chemist in Buenos Aires; my original medicine was in my stolen backpack. I was dreading the seventeen-hour journey of a two-legged flight with long stopovers. I popped the substitute pills with my fingers crossed. The same journey with a direct flight from Buenos Aires to LaPaz would have been around two hours.

On arrival, I found in Santiago de Chile that, although I was only in transit on my way to La Paz, because my forwarding ticket was first to Iquique, another city in Chile, I had to pay Immigration almost one hundred dollars. There went my budget again. I had to laugh about my few dollars of savings from earlier on that day.

While I was making my way to Immigration, I became caught up among a group of middle-aged Americans whose flight had been delayed and had to stay the night in Chile, meaning that they didn't have to pay the fee. One of the airport staff who was looking after these passengers tried his hardest to get me on the list of people who didn't have to pay the crazy fee. But once I arrived at the Immigration desk, I found that I did indeed have to pay. I made my way to check-in, where I was told that check-in wasn't open for another two hours. So I found a place to have a nap and set an alarm for two hours' time, which would be three o'clock in the morning.

At a quarter past three I exhaustedly made my way back to check-in, only to find that I didn't actually need to check-in and could just make my way to the gate. I could have done this in the first place and not broken my sleep. I was starting to feel pretty under the weather. I passed out on the chairs at the gate without setting an alarm. Every ten minutes or so I would wake up and look around me to ensure that I wasn't going to miss my flight. The room started to fill, and I knew that I would soon have to wake up properly as it must be close to boarding time. I went back for one more nap.

"Iquique? Iquique? Is the plane still here?" I asked the staff crew at the boarding gate in terrible Spanish.

"Si, it's still here," the smiling Chilean woman told me.

"Gracias! Muchissimas gracias!" I ran as fast as I could back to my bags and down the runway onto the plane. If my head hadn't been throbbing, the looks I was given by the passengers, who had obviously been waiting for me, might have bothered me. But the way I was feeling I could not have cared less. This was going to be hard: my first migraine while travelling alone.

We landed in Iquique just after sunrise. The view from the plane was unimaginable with an endless barren desert meeting the sea, and the city of Iquique nestled in between. It was only going to be a stopover, but with the way my head was feeling and the fact that I hadn't seen the sea for around three weeks, I began to contemplate staying in Iquique for a few days until my migraine passed, and taking a bus the remainder of the way to La Paz, which was close enough and very cheap.

I had until three o'clock that afternoon to be back at the airport, so I took a taxi into town and left my bags at a hostel while I took the day to consider whether or not I would stay. I met a girl who was going to a nearby town to check it out. It was an old town built beside railway tracks and was one of the only tourist sites in the area. I decided to join her. The migraine had dulled a little from the medication, and I still hadn't made up my mind whether or not I would take my flight later that day.

After a lovely day of taking photos of the old town, we walked back to the highway and hailed a bus. Just like our bus ride to the old town, we were the only travellers on the bus and were greeted by the same stares from many of the people on it. I felt uncomfortable and out of place and couldn't wait to get back to town. About halfway back, the bus made a strange noise and, shortly after, we pulled over to the side of the road. The air conditioner was shut off, and the bus started to get very warm. One by one, people were getting off the bus, and we followed suit soon after. The bus driver told me we had broken down and wouldn't be moving any time soon.

I looked around at what the others were doing and noticed that they were all beginning to hitch-hike. I asked the driver for our money back, which he was surprisingly happy to part with, and joined our fellow travellers in trying to hitch a ride back to town. We were soon to find, though, that nobody was going to take us travellers over the Latinos.

We decided to try to outsmart them and walked further up the road. A small collectivo van pulled over and picked us up. We were sure he was going to charge us, but we didn't mind at all. I had decided I would take my flight that afternoon, and my friend was more than eager to get out of the sweltering heat—she looked very hot and bothered as she hopped into the back of the van.

There was no more space in the back, so I hopped in the front beside a teenage boy and the very overweight driver. His fingers looked like fat sausages as they took the wheel, and he hardly paused for breath, talking to the obviously uninterested boy the entire twenty minutes or so back to the city. Each time he got out of the car to let a passenger out, the kid would turn down the horrible music blaring from the car's speakers, only to have it turned up again by the driver when he got back in. We made it back to the city in one piece and, as foreseen, the driver tried to rip us off. We gave him the amount we had paid the last bus and told him that we were sorry but this was all we had. He accepted, knowing that we knew what he was up to.

I walked back to the hostel, where I picked up my bags, said a quick goodbye to my new friend and arranged a taxi to the airport, along with a brother and sister from Holland. Saying goodbye to them at the airport's entrance, I walked over to my check-in counter, my migraine still a dull ache, making it hard for me to find my passport. After some rummaging I found it and handed it over along with my boarding pass.

"I'm so sorry, miss, but your plane left three hours ago."

"I'm sorry?"

"Your flight was for three-fifteen this afternoon. It is now six-thirty."

What? Somehow in my sleep deprived, fuzzy-migraine state I had confused my flight times and thought that my flight was at nine o'clock that night; I had even thought I was two and a half hours early.

"Oh," I said as the tears begin to swell. I looked up at the girl behind the desk without a clue as to what to say. "I'm just really tired," I told her. "I've been in transit for days and I have a bad headache." I trailed off, trying to think what I should do next.

The taxi back into town was really expensive and, after contemplating the bus ride to La Paz and finding that it was going to be far too much time on a low-quality bus with the possibility of having a migraine the whole way, I came to the conclusion that I really wanted to take that flight.

"Just hold on a moment, I will talk to my supervisor," the woman told me. She seemed very sweet and concerned about my situation.

Two minutes later the girl appeared with a man in his early forties. He could speak English, so I explained to him in more detail what had happened, all the while holding back the tears; I am always more emotional and sensitive when I have a migraine.

"It's OK, ma'am, don't worry. I have booked a seat for you for the same flight tomorrow, free of charge. Go back to town, have a nice big sleep and we will see you back here tomorrow."

"Oh my goodness, I don't know what to say. Thank you so so much. *Muchissimas gracias!*" I said, flashing them my biggest, most grateful smile. I could not believe my luck. I turned on my heels, hailed the first shuttle I could find and went back to the hostel I had just came from. Even though I felt like getting straight into bed, I knew I would kick myself later if I didn't go to the sea, if only to watch the sunset.

I took another migraine pill and walked over to the sea. The beach was met by the rolling, barren hills that surrounded us. I nestled into the cooling sand to witness the magnificent daily event of the sun setting over the ocean. This city seemed like an oasis in its surrounding desert, although its architecture was somewhat out of place, with malls and high-rises silhouetted against its desolate backdrop.

A man selling ceviche, fish marinated in lime juice and coriander (which, after some time, cooks the fish), walked up to me for a chat. Even though I was concerned about food poisoning, I just couldn't give up the chance to sit on the beach and eat ceviche while the sun set.

"I won't vomit from this?" I asked the man.

"No, of course not. This fish was caught today," he assured me.

I bought a small container and watched the people around me watching the sunset. I felt like calling out to everyone, making us all introduce ourselves, so we could share this beautiful experience together. Instead I just sat quietly as the big fiery ball slipped beneath the horizon, leaving behind hues of pink and orange against the darkening blue sky.

I walked back to the hostel. My medicine was kicking in, making me feel incredibly tired. I called my mum and gave her a quick update on my travels and then took myself to bed. Thankfully there was no one else in my room and I had a deep recuperating night's sleep.

Next day, after a shower, I headed down for the included breakfast, only to realise that in my migraine-medicated haze I had gotten the time for the included breakfast wrong. I set about making some bread with olive oil and tomatoes from the communal food pile that everyone shared. As I was just about to eat my breakfast, I realized that I hadn't booked a shuttle to the airport and there was a chance that I would have to get a taxi alone which would cost a fortune. I went to reception, who thankfully organised one for me. I finished my breakfast, packed my bag and took my shuttle to the airport.

I got on the plane relieved that I hadn't spent the night on an uncomfortable bus for twenty hours or so to La Paz, and grateful for the restful stopover I'd had, thanks to the lovely staff at the airport.

14

Bolivia

Just before landing, we ran into some turbulence, and it was horrible. As my face turned pink I had to do all I could not to take that dreaded paper bag from the seat pocket in front of me and hurl my tomato-and-bread breakfast into it. Thanks to the rough landing and the sudden adjustment to the high altitude, I was left barely able to walk. I managed to find an ATM, a map and a collectivo into the city, along with ten or so Bolivians jumping on and off along the way.

I started to feel a little better and also to absorb the new culture I had just landed in. The first thing I noticed was that nobody was staring at me. Not only that, no one seemed the slightest bit interested in me. Even in my peripheral vision I could see that no one was looking my way; rather, they seemed to be looking in any direction but mine. That was a first since I had left Australia. Both in Argentina and Brazil, maybe a little less during my short stay in Chile, I could be assured that if there was anyone around, their attention would be on me.

In some parts of Brazil, we had found the men much more forward than in other places, but it was a small scale. In Argentina the men were less direct and would mumble something sexual under their breath, whereas in Brazil they were not in the slightest bit afraid to express themselves. Two of the funniest things I experienced from these approaches were first, some men in a car in the north of Brazil driving around with a sign that said *Voce linda,* meaning "You're beautiful" in Portuguese. They would drive past women, honk their horn and then hold up the sign. The other comical way the men approached women was in Argentina. While passing a woman, either in a car, on foot or on a bicycle, the men would make an incredibly loud kissing noise. It sounded like it was being made by a machine, it was so loud. I was eager to learn this kissing trick and, after much practice, I got it down to an art myself, if only to make the noises when no one could hear me.

Years ago I had read a novel called *Marching Powder* about Bolivia and had always wanted to go there. I had read up on some facts about the country. There was a very small population of non-Indigenous people, something that was new on my travels in South America. In Brazil and Argentina there were many more Caucasian or mixed races than Amerindians, but in Bolivia Caucasians amounted to a mere fifteen percent. Driving through the streets, it was very easy to see this. It wasn't until later when I had to take Yuki to the bank that I saw one of the only Caucasians I would see in my two-week stay in Bolivia. The rest of the population was made up of thirty per cent Mestizo and fifty-five per cent Amerindian, along with a small population of Americans, Europeans, Africans and Asians.

There is a population of roughly ten million people in Bolivia and, even though twice as many newborn babies survive than twenty years ago, still more die here than almost any other country outside sub-Sahara Africa. Bolivia has the highest child mortality rate in South America, and is second only to Haiti in all of Latin America. This is due to the unclean water available to the families in Bolivia. This alone made me want to stay in Bolivia to try to figure out a way to start a foundation to get that statistic down. Of course at that point in time it was only an idea. Still, I stored it in the back of my mind hopefully for one day.

I asked the lady beside me if she knew the area my guidebook's map said was the best place for accommodation. She told me that it was still some distance away and, when she got off at her stop, she asked our fellow travellers if they could let me know when to hop off. I thanked her and she smiled back at me warmly. I had a feeling that I was going to love Bolivia.

We passed streets spotted with women in traditional dress, who caught my eye. Most of the older generation and Quechua women from both Ecuador and Bolivia dressed this way, including the women in my van. Their attire was so interesting. They wore a felt bowler hat, rounded at the crown. The women in this part of the world began wearing these hats in the nineteen twenties; British railway workers had made them famous. From under the hats came two long black plaits, reaching below the women's backs, with some having black stringy material hanging from them, to give more length, I supposed. With this they wore a large pleated, coloured skirt and either a lace shawl that hung down in a V at the back, making it look more like a tablecloth than anything, or an infant slung across their body in colourful striped material. Both the babies and the adults were rosy cheeked. I asked around about this and was told it's because there's less oxygen in the air at high altitudes, causing the body to produce more red cells to carry more oxygen to the brain, causing their cheeks to appear red.

I came out of my reverie with a jolt of the van and a young man telling me quietly that this was my stop. I handed over the few coins I had in my hand, waited for my change and hopped out of the van. I felt a little unsteady on my feet and queazy in my tummy. It was hard to know whether it was from the bumpy landing or the altitude. I wasn't feeling too bad, though, and set off to find a hostel. Walking through the streets, I found it hard to breathe. I would go to take a breath, only to have it cut short a quarter of the way through. It was incredible! I began to get a bit worried: I couldn't see any streets familiar to the guide book, and it was getting late. This was my first day in Bolivia, a country that people had made sound so scary, and I was pretty eager to find a place for the night. I walked up to a group of gentlemen standing by a smoothie stand.

"Perdon, do you know of a hostel close by?" I asked them in my terrible Spanish.

"Si señorita, just up the road." They motioned up a street to my right, between the two colourful smoothie stands with a woman standing at each one, wearing all white, rainbow-coloured fruit stains stretched over their middles.

"*Gracias,*" I replied.

"*De nada, gringita,*" one cheeky man replied. *Gringa* is the name given mainly to American women, and *gringo* for the men. There are many theories as to where this term originated, but the most logical theory dates back to a written document in Spain in 1796, where the word *gringo* meant a foreign person speaking in their native language or with a strong accent that made their speech impossible to understand.

I smiled politely and prepared myself to tackle the slight incline of the cobbled street to the hostel. Halfway to the hostel I had to rest and catch my breath. It was incredible. Every step took all of my effort, and I could only get sips of air into my lungs. I felt like I had aged one hundred years.

The hostel was nothing like I was expecting. It was dark, old and it looked as though I was the only guest. I handed over my passport and paid for one night, hoping to find somewhere a little more lived-in the following day. The señorita handed me back my passport with a warm smile and showed me to my room. It was equally dark until she turned on a flickering neon light to reveal two beds, a table and a bookshelf covered in dust.

"*Gracias,*" I thanked her as she left the room.

"*De que,*" she replied, which I thought meant, *for what.*

I swung my backpack from my shoulders and sat it on the bed. The layers of dust covering the bed sprang up and filled my nostrils. The hostel had a shower with hot water. I couldn't decide whether to have a shower before I went out to explore a little and have something to eat, or after. As usual, curiosity got the better of me, and I made my way out into the chilly evening air.

La Paz was something else. The city itself is almost four thousand metres above sea level, and surrounding the city are hills and mountains, the houses reaching up high above the city centre. As the sky grew darker the houses lit up like fireflies around the city. It was magical. The book I had read about Bolivia had some pretty horrific stories, so I was unsure of how late I should stay out and where I should be wary of. My hostel was really more like a guesthouse with not really any tourist help, so I didn't venture too far, although I did find some great local market stalls along the way.

I had withdrawn money at the airport and had expected it to last me at least a few days, if not a week, as I had heard how cheap Bolivia was. After an hour or so of shopping, I realized I was going to be in trouble: there were so many beautiful things, and everything was so cheap! And I was alone, which meant I could take all the time in the world looking at stuff that I (let alone an accompanying shopper) would never necessarily need. I took hours, wandering in and out of stalls, buying presents left, right and centre, and glorious warm garments made from alpaca fur. Just what I needed. I was taking it very easy up and down the hills of La Paz, being sure not to egg on any altitude sickness. From what I had heard, it is one of the worst things you can experience.

I wandered what seemed at the time dangerously around a few corners, being sure to memorise my way back. I came across a busy little stall selling potatoes and sausage. This was a typical dish from Bolivia called salchipapa, and it seemed like this was the place to get it. I ordered a plate and realized just how hungry I was. I took my salchipapa and made my way back home, eating the delicious creation along the way. It was pretty much just a cut up frankfurt, pan-fried with potato chips and mayo, but it was so tasty.

As I sat on my bed with my multiple bags of purchases, I got the pulling feeling in my stomach that I had left my passport at one of the stalls. Bags and gifts flew everywhere as I searched frantically through my things. The passport was nowhere to be seen. I grabbed the key to my room, hid my wallet in the pillowslip and ran as fast as I could for about two blocks, stopping only when I remembered how high above sea level I was and how important it was to take everything slowly. I stayed still for a few moments to see how my body would handle itself. I felt OK, but I could feel the start of a headache, which is not uncommon for me but can be a sign of altitude sickness.

I went slowly back to all the places I had visited. They were closing down for the night; I guessed it was too cold here to stay open much longer after dark. I arrived at the first place I had visited and the only place that I hadn't yet been to and it was closed. I tried to reassure myself that it would be there in the morning. If not, at least I was in the capital and could apply for a new passport easily enough. I walked slowly to an internet cafe to touch base with Mum and Yogi. The internet was cheap but the connection was terrible, so we just messaged each other through Facebook. Mum was making me laugh so hard but my lungs wouldn't allow for it; I felt as though I had emphysema.

I said my goodbyes to my loved ones and walked back home, ready for an early night so I could make an early start next morning to find my passport. As I moved all of the things from my bed onto the less comfortable one, I saw a small blue book poking out from under a pile of my shopping. It was my passport. I wasn't sure if I wanted to kick or kiss myself, but I definitely felt a huge wave of relief along with my headache as I snuggled in for the night. I couldn't help feeling extremely lonely, and I missed Yogi a hell of a lot.

Next day I woke up early, had a shower from a spout that came out of the bathroom wall like a hose, packed my bag, had a fresh-fruit smoothie from the rainbow fruit stalls for around eighty Australian cents and took a taxi to the next hostel, which was a completely different story altogether. There was a whiteboard with the names of all the guests and a list of all of the people who were waiting for a bed. I was too tired to try to search for something else and the place looked really nice, so I asked the gentleman looking after all the pushy backpackers to put my name down on the waiting list. He told me he would find out in around two hours. I sat down with my phone plugged into his computer, very excited to have some wifi action, when I noticed two guys and a girl asking questions I also wanted to ask about La Paz.

"But where can I go to party?"

"And here you have all of the museums."

"I don't want to go to museums, my grandma can visit the museums. I just want to know where I can party."

"And this is the witches' market."

"Oh, where is the witches' market?" I chimed in.

"Just here, you see?" the girl behind the counter said, as she penciled it out for me on a map. It seemed as though the Israeli guys in front of me only wanted to know where to party. The girl seemed really sweet and asked me what I was up to while I waited for a room.

"Nothing really," I replied.

"Would you like to come have some lunch with us?"

"Sure," I smiled back at my new friends. One of the guys was looking at me a little too intensely. I realized I would have to drop the boyfriend bomb pretty quickly.

"Where are you guys from?" I asked.

"Israel," all three of them replied.

"Oh, my boyfriend is Israeli."

"Really? Whereabouts in Israel is he from?"

"Well, his parents are from Roshpina, he grew up there until he was five."

"Ah, OK."

"Let's go," one of the guys said as he started walking towards the front door.

"Yes, I just have to store my backpack somewhere. I'll be right back."

I asked where I could leave my backpack, shoved it into the cupboard the receptionist had shown me and hurried back to my new friends; I didn't want to keep them waiting. While walking, we got chatting about where we had been and a bit about ourselves. Yahav, the sweet girl, and the two boys, Almog and Mayan, had just finished their service in the army. Two years for Yahav, because she was a girl, and three years for the boys. I couldn't imagine it. The supposed fun and free years of my new friends' lives were spent in the army, doing I have no idea what. They all seemed to have slightly different views on the topic. Yahav had hated the army and wished that she'd never had to go. Almog on the other hand said that he was happy that he went, that it taught him a lot. He'd worked on the field so I was guessing that he may have seen some heavy stuff. Mayan had worked in an office, so I think for him it wasn't quite as hard.

Before lunch we went on a mission to try to find a battery for the phone for Almog. We weren't having much luck, so we decided to go to another part of town, and there the strangest thing happened. People actually refused to serve us. I couldn't believe my eyes. These people who really needed to make money and have the opportunity to rip off tourists were refusing to serve us.

"What is going on?" I wondered out loud.

My new friends were talking rather hotly in Hebrew. "It's because we are Israeli," Yahav said.

"No, I don't think so," I replied, shocked that my new friends thought they were being discriminated against so openly. I was sure it was just because they were too shy to deal with foreigners. But after it happened a few more times and we could see that the store owners weren't shy but angry, I started to think maybe my new friends were right. It was crazy, though. La Paz had so many Israelis staying there.

"A week ago we were about to check into a hostel. We walked in the door, the guy behind the desk took one look at us, stuck both of his fingers up—it wasn't a peace sign—and said '*Viva la Palestine*'."

I looked at him in utter disbelief.

"It's true, I swear."

"No, I believe you, I just can't believe *that*." I was utterly disgusted. These three sweet young Israelis who, in my opinion hadn't had the easiest of lives, were being discriminated against because of the ongoing conflict between Israel and the Palestine.

We decided we didn't need a battery and that we were hungry. We made our way back to the main square. Here there were signs in Hebrew, and some of the store owners even spoke Hebrew! What a turnaround. It seemed as though the city was divided into two camps about Israeli travellers—the part that was cold towards them, and the part that was warm towards them and dealt with them daily. We were even lucky enough to stumble upon an Israeli restaurant, where we enjoyed a delicious lunch, after an hour's wait. (By the time it came, we were ready to eat our napkins.) Then we made our way back to the hostel.

The three Israelis had their names in the dorm room list, but my name was nowhere to be seen. The guy who was looking after the accommodation started to arrange what needed to be done for their stay, when he was interrupted.

"But what about her? She needs a bed too."

"But her name isn't here."

Shit, I knew I should have made sure he put my name down.

"But she is with us. Why can't you put her here?"

"So there are four of you? Here it says that you are three."

"Yes, now we are four."

I could see there was no way that I wasn't going to get a bed. Damn, those Israelis are hard to ignore! Somehow my name was scribbled into the room my new friends were staying in, and we all made our way there before the guy changed his mind.

"Thank you so much, guys!" I smiled.

"No problem, it's his fault."

Ahh, that Israeli accent, how much I had missed it!

We were all exhausted and spent the day chatting, and showering in the deliciously hot shower. That night there was a party at the hostel, and we all joined in. The next two days were a lot like this, along with ridiculous amounts of shopping in the markets and eating out at delicious and cheap restaurants. We did eventually make a trip to the witches' market, its streets lined with the strangest of things to purchase. The most disturbing would have to have been the dried baby llamas hanging from the store fronts. Yahav was a vegetarian and didn't even buy leather, so our visit to the witches' market was very brief. Grace arrived in La

Paz shortly after I had, and we met up a couple of times for shopping (even though she hates it) and a dance in my hostel.

My third day in La Paz was the day before Yurie's birthday. We were all to meet the following afternoon at the salt flats in the south of Bolivia outside a town called Uyuni. Grace and I were supposed to go together, but we accidentally booked different times. My bus was leaving at six o'clock that evening, and hers at ten, so we would also have to meet in Uyuni.

I packed all my gifts up to send home and headed out in the rain with my helpful friend Yahav to the post office. We knew we had found the right place when we were surrounded by long-haired, loud Israeli girls lugging enormous packages onto the scales, weighing in at an impressive twenty or more kilos, talking Spanish heavily laced with an Israeli accent. They were so cute!

Yahav read out one of the signs written in Hebrew on the post office door. It said: **It is possible for discounted postage for Israelis who are polite with us.** Ha! We were both giggling as we watched the young girls trying to express their courtesy to the old man and old lady dealing with their mounds of souvenirs. We were short for time and got my eight kilos of gifts posted as quickly as possible. Then we rushed back to the hostel and said our goodbyes. I took a taxi to the bus stop, made my way onto the bus and to my assigned seat, hoping that no one weird would sit next to me. Luckily for me, a young blond, nerdy but sweet-looking guy came walking up the aisle and rested his eyes on the seat number above my head.

"*Hola*," I grinned at him in relief.

"*Hola*," he smiled back.

We chatted for the next half an hour or so in Spanish until we were both tired and reverted back to English. He was twenty-two years old and from Colorado. He had been studying in Buenos Aires. I finished off

my empanada, took my famous motion sickness tablets that knock me
out (I was sure I was going to need them on this bus ride), bid my sweet
friend beside me goodnight and passed out. I woke up next morning
feeling like I had been dragged behind the bus rather than sleeping on
it. I rubbed the sleep out of my eyes and turned to my friend.

"*Buenos dias.*"

"*Buenos dias,*" he replied.

I looked out the window. We were completely surrounded by desert.

"Wow, it looks so beautiful."

My nerdy friend leaned over me, fixing his glasses back onto his face.
"*Si, muy lindo,*" he agreed.

At six o'clock in the morning, the air had a chilly bite to it. We made
our way past the six or so women offering tours to the salt flats. Other
than their suggestions for the best tour on offer, the town was in utter,
eerie silence. The style of dress here was different from that in La Paz.
The women still wore the plaits and the pleated skirts, but the bright
colours were replaced with pastels, and the bowler hats were replaced
with wide-brimmed, straw hats.

My friend from Colorado and I made our way to a coffee shop with
internet to try to figure out where we should stay and which tour group
to go with. He had to start his tour that day, whereas the girls and I
were to go on tour the next day. I also had to contact Grace to tell her
where I thought we would be staying for the night, in case I didn't find
her at the bus stop. We washed our faces, ordered breakfast and sat at
the overly-priced computers to organise the next few days in the desert.

After about half an hour, my friend and I said goodbye. I decided to
go the old-fashioned way of finding the cheapest place to stay—on foot.
I found a big run-down hostel that had two beds to a room, booked two
rooms for us four girls and then made my way to the bus stop to wait
for Grace. As the sun rose higher the earth and air warmed, bit by bit.

I licked my cracked lips and decided to go and buy a Chapstick; I had misplaced my amazing one, exactly at the time I would need it in this dry and desolate town. I had heard that the glare from the sun and the salt flats was blindingly bright, so I bought a pair of sunglasses while I was there.

15

Reunited

I sat at the bus stop and waited in the warm sunlight with an old homeless-looking dog. Grace was due to arrive in half an hour, but I was so tired I could hardly hold myself up. I leaned against the dusty wall behind me and closed my eyes, knowing I wouldn't be able to fall asleep. I sighed inwardly, grateful for the rest all the same.

Half an hour came and went. The sun started to get stronger, and the layers of clothes I was wearing became a little too stifling, so I moved into the shade. Another half an hour went by. Just as I was starting to worry, a bus pulled up in front of me, and through the window I saw the outline of my curly haired, curvaceous, smiling friend.

After a cuddly reunion, I led her to our hostel, where she checked in, after which we both decided to have a shower while the sun was out and there was still hot water. Afterwards we walked from our hostel to the main square to find a birthday cake for Yurie. There we came across what must have been the entire population of the tiny settlement of Uyuni watching a parade through the main street in celebration of The Day of The Sea. On March twenty-third, Bolivia annually celebrates its dour recognition of Sea Day, commemorating the loss of their coastal territory to Chile. Nobody seemed impressed to see us watching their festivities, so we made our way through the crowd as inconspicuously as we possibly could.

To our surprise we were in luck: almost all the stores were closed for Sea Day but the cake shops were open. We bought the biggest, pinkest cake filled with as much gross fake cream as we could find, along with a Dora the Explorer themed party pack, including hats, invitations, plates and cups. Our next mission was to find a place that sold alcohol. We hoped to find a bottle of champagne, and surprisingly we did. That afternoon the girls were to arrive, so we went about setting up Yurie's surprise party.

We met Yuki and Yurie by accident in the street, along with someone I didn't know then would turn out to be a new travel buddy and a special friend. This was Stephanie, the girl who had shared her biscuits with Yurie and me at the hostel, and who had informed me of Yuki's tardiness in catching her bus in Mendoza. We were filled with happiness, celebration and relief at being back together safely for Yurie's birthday. The girls hadn't had the smoothest trip on the way to us, with Yuki losing her wallet and with it her only credit card and access to money.

We walked with them to reception to check the girls in and book a bed for Steff for the night. Grace ran ahead of us to make a new invitation to our birthday party for Steff, while I led the girls slowly upstairs to our room, where we had arranged the plastic outdoor table with the champagne and cake and plates and cups lined up, along with some pink balloons. I handed out the invitations, Grace brought out Steff's invitation and my heart warmed at the smile that spread across Yurie's face at the small effort we had made to make sure she had a memorable birthday.

"Thank you so much, girls!" she cried.

We took photos of her cutting her cake. We ate the disgustingly sweet creation, and I would pay for it later. As the evening wore on we started to get hungry and decided to go to the restaurant where Grace and I had eaten a delicious and cheap lunch.

The restaurant looked scarily quiet, but going against my rule about eating in quiet restaurants, we stayed anyway. That night, even though I ate exactly what everyone else ate, only I spent the entire night in the bathroom with my reggae blaring, losing what seemed like litres of bodily fluids. The next morning I could hardly move. It was obvious that I wasn't going on a tour of any kind, other than from my bedroom to the not-so-nearby toilet.

The girls spent that day shopping, finding the best tours for us and checking in on me with bread and water, making sure I got something into my system. The aftertaste of that sweet birthday cake haunted me all day. Later that afternoon, I felt somewhat better and was able to go on the tour the following day. I also decided to join Yurie and Yuki on the short tour they had organised for early the next morning before the three-day tour to watch the sun rise over the salt flats. We would be back in Uyuni just in time to check out of our hostel and get ready for our tour into the desert. I was beginning to get excited at the prospect of something taking my mind off Yogi. While I was sick, all I could think of was being snuggled in his arms. Being so far away from him seemed like a cruel joke. I had seen incredible pictures of the salt flats and knew that it would take my mind off him, at least for some time.

We all had an early night and next morning, some time after three o'clock, I heard a knock at the door.

"Kristin? Are you almost ready?"

It was Yurie, and I was very much not ready, I was still asleep. I looked at the alarm on my phone and found that I had made the mistake of setting it for the afternoon. I threw on all the clothes I possessed, plus a jacket I had borrowed from Stef, and ran out of the room to meet the girls. We were running a little late and were worried that we would miss the tour. When we got to the front door, we ran into a problem that we hadn't planned on: the massive wooden door was padlocked.

"*Shit!*" I exclaimed, just as the old, frail-looking woman walked out from I don't know where, shushing us and asking where did we think we were going, and what were the Japanese girls doing with the blankets from their bedrooms.

"*Lo siento, señora,*" I apologised to the woman and explained to her that we were late for a tour and that we would be back by check-out, while the girls hurried back to their rooms to put back their blankets.

The old woman opened the door ever so slowly, chatting away to herself under her breath. We burst out of the door and ran up the road to where two jeeps were waiting for us. They handed us our gumboots—stylishly white—as we piled into the four-wheel drive. I had read to be careful when choosing tours for the salt flats. There had been many reported incidences of drivers being drunk and crashing into other tour jeeps in the desert. Even though I was feeling like death itself from the day before's vomiting and the early rise, I was hoping that death or injury wasn't waiting for me in the dark and starry distant desert.

I was the only Caucasian on the tour out of about fourteen people. There was one Korean girl, who could speak Japanese; the rest of the crew were Japanese. I had never seen so many Japanese tourists outside of Australia. The girls told me this salt flat was very famous in Japan and that many people would come all the way from Japan and only visit Uyuni on their short break, flying back to Japan two or so weeks after arriving in South America. The girls informed me that they had formed an entirely new group for the tour just so I could come. Previous to my wanting to come, there had been just enough for one group. Once I had said that I wanted to go, the girls put up a sign and advertised the tour,

aiming it towards the many Japanese tourists in Uyuni. I felt so blessed
to have two such caring friends.

We stopped on our way to the desert to change a tyre. I could almost
hear everyone in the car thinking the same thing: the time we spent
changing the tyre could have been spent in our warm beds, sleeping.
As soon as we were back on the road and driving out into the desert,
everyone started dozing off, anyway. The only sounds that interrupted
our much-needed slumbers came from that tiny friend of mine's nose.
Yuki and her famous snores. I have never understood how such a small
woman could make such a big noise.

The jeep started to slow as we arrived at the part of the salt flat
that was covered in water due to condensation from the night's cool air.
We drove on through the miniature lake for some time. It looked like
a dream. Words cannot come close to describing what I could see from
the jeep's window.

The jeeps came to a stop. Everyone took their time, bracing
themselves for the cold awaiting them once the doors were open to the
early morning. Our gumboots made a light, splashing noise as they hit
the shallow lake covering the salt flats. I blurred my eyes a little to erase
my pre-existing knowledge that there was a horizon, and could no longer
see where the star-filled floor beneath us met the star-filled sky above.

An orange, almost-full moon began to set. It looked like a sun
setting over a large lake, its reflection glowing brightly. Its full shape
glowed brighter orange the lower it sank and, as the sky got lighter
from the promise of the sun, the stars numbed out one by one. What
happened to our surroundings afterwards created a surreal feeling, as
though we were walking on the sky. We sat on provided plastic chairs in
the quiet of the salty desert and watched the sky and salt flat turn into a
haze of purples, pinks and blues. The more intense the colour became,
the quieter and larger-than-life the scenery became. No one stayed in

their seats, despite the cold and the exhaustion. I think it is safe to say that there were thousands of photos taken in that pre-dawn moment in time. As the sun rose, the sky's pastel colours eased to a less surreal backdrop, and we were back to reality.

I was among the first to give up on being the tough guy. I got back into the jeep, changed into my shoes, threw my sleeping bag over me and passed out, while the others took a million more photos. I was feeling surprisingly OK after the previous day and, after waking up on the trip back to Uyuni, I was able to force myself to eat a little bread and drink some of the water the girls had brought me.

We arrived at the hostel at nine o'clock. I had one hour to have a rest and pack my bags for the next tour. We all met at reception at a quarter past ten to check out, then we made our way to the tourist office where the girls had booked the tour. After meeting our tour guide, we set off into the desert for one day in the salt flats, where we could see nothing for miles but a floor of salt. We spent that night in a hotel made of salt after watching the sun set over the salt flats, which was arguably as beautiful as the sunrise. This time, though, we got to see it together, which made it all the more special.

The next two days in the desert we spent driving from one breathtakingly beautiful location to the next. I felt really unwell yet again for the rest of the trip, having lost a lot of fluids. At one of the places we visited for lunch, I urgently needed a bathroom. As there wasn't one to be seen, I had to run away from the group to a small outcrop of rocks and let it loose there, hoping no one would see—or smell—me, for that matter. Although I was feeling incredibly unwell, the girls helped me as much as they could, and I was still able to enjoy the tour.

We stopped at a red lagoon spotted with flamingos as this was their main nesting site, and later a gorgeous green lagoon. The colours of these lagoons were caused by the different minerals in the soil. We went to the Incahuasi Island, which was surrounded by salt flats and completely covered in cactuses similar to the ones in Mexican paintings. On the last day of the tour, at five o'clock in the morning we made our way to a volcanic site almost five thousand metres above sea level to watch the sun rise.

The site consisted of one geyser and a collection of bubbling, smoky pools of sulphur. Walking around the site, I had the sensation of being on another planet. The landscape around me, from what I could see through the hazy smoke given off by the pools, was rocky and barren. It seemed so uninhabitable and far from anything that our society knows or cares about. I felt like I had been able to experience something whose existence was unknown to anyone else.

We finished the tour and decided that, rather than going directly to La Paz, we would go first to a nearby town by the name of Potosi. It was supposed to be very cute and had been put on the map for its mining of silver. We started on our six-hour bus trip to Potosi. Around halfway, we stopped suddenly in the middle of the highway. The bus driver opened his doors and as many extra passengers as could squeeze into the bus piled on, even though our bus was already overbooked, with people sitting in the aisle.

Yurie and I were on the front seat. A young girl stood facing us with her back against the plastic window between us and the driver. To my right was a rather large elderly woman dressed in pastels, her two plaits swaying as she pushed her squishy buttocks rather firmly into my right cheek. Due to the sleepiness brought on by my motion sickness tablets, I was feeling a little grumpy at her inconsiderateness and tried to move as much as possible to send a message to the woman that her butt was not welcome. She must have gotten the message as she moved her backside slightly away from my face and struck up a conversation with me over her shoulder, informing me that the newcomers' bus had broken down and that a lot of them were going to have to take yet another bus once we got to Potosi, and that she was not looking forward to the trip ahead of her.

Up until this point, almost every Bolivian woman I had tried to have a conversation with had been quite short and rude. I had put it down to cultural differences and tried not to take it to heart, but the warmth I felt from the bum lady's smile moved me and was definitely so welcome. It made me feel much more at ease, and instantly guilty for my earlier impatience with her protruding buttocks.

After our little chat I turned and faced the front. A young girl around twelve years old was standing directly in front of Yurie and me. She looked as though she was about to throw up any minute. I knew exactly how she was feeling and why. She had motion sickness from facing the back as we drove. I was even starting to feel a bit unwell from turning to chat with my friend for a short moment. I offered her my seat but she looked more mortified by the fact that I was trying to speak to her in my terrible Spanish than the prospect of puking all over us. She didn't dare budge.

Yurie took out one of her motion sickness tablets and tried to give it to the girl. She didn't want a bar of that either until a few old ladies sitting on the other side of the aisle encouraged her to take it. She reached her small hand out and Yurie placed the pill inside. We realized that she didn't have any water so I gave her my bottle. She drank from it with her lips never touching the bottle. Then she tried to give it back to me, but I put my hand up to let her know I didn't need it and to keep it. She smiled and said an ever so quiet "*gracias*" and looked away as fast as she could.

Not long after this transaction, we stopped for a pee stop. None of us were happy to pay to go to a disgusting toilet so we walked over to some bushes and rocks on the other side of the road and peed altogether. Yuki's commentary on how nice it was to pee in the outdoors put Steff off.

"Yuki! Shut up! I can't concentrate!"

"Sorry, it's just that——"

"Yuki!"

"All right, all right."

We left Steff to get on with her pee; there would be nothing worse than getting back on that full and bumpy bus with a bladder bursting at the seams.

When we got back on the bus, I tried to sit on the floor so the little girl could take my seat. She sat down but must have felt guilty and ended up moving over to the edge of the seat to make enough space for me. I don't know how we did it, but the three of us sat and actually slept on that tiny front seat. I woke up about ten minutes or so before we arrived at Potosi to find the little girl asleep almost in my lap, holding on to me. When she woke, she straightened herself, looking a little shy but grateful for the nap she had taken on me. She was among the first to get off the bus. As she was moved forward by the impatient passengers behind her she looked back, sang out one last *gracias,* and with that she was gone.

We took our time collecting our things and getting off the bus. We were all a little cranky and extremely exhausted. Steff was still having problems acclimatising to the high altitude, and gave me a half-hearted smile as I let her get off in front of me, her teeth filled with cocoa leaves. We found a family-run hostel/travel agency with the help of the daughter of the hostel owner, who had been waiting for the likes of us at the bus station. After she had helped Yurie track down her brand new, unused, very expensive sleeping bag in the overhead compartment of the bus we had just gotten off, we felt inclined to at least have a look at her family's guesthouse.

We took a collectivo to the other side of town, climbed what seemed to be a mountain with our readjustment to the four-thousand-metre height of the city, after descending and reascending altitudes throughout the bus trip. Breathing was difficult. We needed to take a break every ten or so steps.

"Here we are." The smiling beautiful Bolivian motioned to us.

We took a look in through the doorway to see if what we were hoping not to see was there to welcome us.

Stairs. And plenty of them.

We glanced at each other. There was no other way but up. Slowly but surely, we made our way to reception where our pretty friend was waiting for us after she had practically pranced up the stairs. The mother also met us at the doorway and motioned to us to take a seat and to put down our packs. Before we had a chance to take a seat, though, the mother went into full swing with the array of tours that their company offered. I was exhausted in every way and was not at all up for the spiel this lady was about to unravel.

"Could we please just see the room? If any of us are interested in a tour, you can be sure we will come to you first with our enquiries," I said, although my proposition in Spanish was nowhere near as grammatically correct as that.

"Oh, sure. You must be so tired. Follow me."

And with that, we were on our way to the room.

We were shown a room with two single beds and what seemed to be a double bed. Yurie went to take a seat on this double bed while we made up our minds and fell straight to the floor. It was a semi-inflated air bed. We all erupted into a fit of giggles, while the mother waited for us patiently.

"What do you think, girls?" Steff asked.

We all looked at each other blankly.

"Can we just have ten minutes to decide what we want to do?" Steff asked the mother.

"Sure, just come down whenever you are ready to check in."

"OK, thank you so much."

Over a sandwich that we whipped up in the small musty room, Yurie, Yuki, Steff and I all decided that we wanted to keep moving and take a bus to La Paz. We cleaned up our crumbs, repacked some of the things that we had already begun to sprawl across the floor and headed off to tell our friends the bad news.

Grace was staying in Potosi but not at that guesthouse. She'd wanted to find a backpackers' with a bit more life in it and had come along with us.

"I'm so so sorry, but we are actually going to leave for La Paz tonight," Steff told the lady, handing her the few dollars we had all chipped in to thank the family for their help and hospitality.

"No, it's OK, you don't have to pay," the woman said, shaking her head, looking at the crumpled notes in Steff's hand.

We all insisted, though, and the sweet woman must have needed it, because she accepted. We walked Grace to the main square, said our goodbyes, not knowing when we would see each other again, and hailed a taxi to take us to the town's bus stop. When we got to the bus stop, the taxidriver tried to charge us double what he should, but I was in no mood to be scammed and placed the first agreed amount into his hand and walked away, as he shouted at us for more. We ignored his calls and hurried off out of earshot.

We had bought some maca, chia seeds and quinoa puffs earlier that day, so we ordered some milk and had all three together for dinner. This would be our staple breakfast for the weeks to come. That night, though, because I had eaten the mixture with warm milk, which did not agree with me, for the entire bus trip my stomach ached and pained like nothing else. We arrived in La Paz at sunrise. The city's beauty took my breath away yet again.

The next three days were similar to my last in La Paz, a lot of shopping and even more eating at delicious and cheap restaurants. I was looking thinner than I had ever looked in my life and took advantage by rewarding my poor body with as much yummy food as I could at the affordable Bolivian prices. We took recommendations from the guidebook on where to eat and found an all-you-can-eat vegetarian restaurant. It was delicious, healthy and only cost around five dollars per person. We also had plates filled with Mexican food for the same price, and Italian dishes with buffet salads for the same price. We even had a few three-course meals in local Bolivian restaurants that cost as little as one dollar seventy-five, including a drink.

Grace didn't end up meeting us in La Paz and instead stayed with a Bolivian family in Bolivia's capital Sucre, and took Spanish classes.

There was a growth of hair in my underpants that was starting to look pretty scary, so I stopped in at a salon on our last day in La Paz. The salon was always filled with Israeli girls getting hair wraps done in their long luscious locks. The signs on the walls of the salon were in both English and Hebrew and recommended the salon's services. Even the daughter of the salon owner had a Hebrew name. The mother walked me to a small dark room made of concrete out the back. This was divided from the store by a glass door which, thankfully, had posters of people sporting the last decade's hairstyles all over it.

I was instructed to take off my underwear and lie on what I had thought was a bench seat. I did as I was told, weary of the daughter who was in plain view of my girly parts.

"*No te preoccupes.*" She has seen it all before, the lady assured me.

"Oh, OK," I replied, still feeling very uncomfortable.

There was a small doorway on one side of the room. It was half-covered by sheets. I was desperate to go to the bathroom and thought that the doorway may have led to the toilet. I asked the beautician where I could find *el baño* before I got comfortable on the bench.

"Oh, I'm sorry, but it is too dirty."

"It's fine, I don't mind, really," I answered, but the lady only shook her head.

So I took my place on the bench, took off my underwear and let one leg fall to the side. I didn't know what sort of experience I was in for, pain-wise, with this fairly dodgy salon but I had rarely seen any places to get a Brazilian on my travels and I wasn't sure when I would get the opportunity again. Suddenly a voice came from the room that I had thought was the bathroom.

"Don't come in here," the woman answered in a panic. "Just stay right there until I say."

Hmm, interesting. Maybe that was why the woman hadn't wanted me to go to the bathroom.

The lady prepared the wax and started her mission on my girly parts. She was surprisingly quick and painless, although I was still counting down the seconds until the ordeal was over, keeping myself occupied by reading the notes of the previous victims. I couldn't be certain but I was almost sure from the way the notes were worded that they were written by Israeli girls. I read them over and over in my mind with an Israeli accent, missing Yogi and his mum Nava, wishing I could see them both.

My beautician's daughter was having a great time running backward and forward between the curtained-off room and the waxing room. She may have been used to seeing women's parts but she sure knew how to make a girl feel uncomfortable, peeking between my legs every time she came through the door. It also didn't help that every time she ran into the dark room where the voice came from, the person who was in there would whisper something to her. At one stage she even moved the curtain over so there was more opportunity for whoever was in there to see into the room, and my girl parts were facing right into the doorway.

When the ordeal was finally over, I quickly thanked the woman, paid her and made my way out of there as fast as I could without looking back, in case I came face to face with the potential peeping tom. I met up with the girls and decided to go one last time to the delicious Italian restaurant. It was hard to find such good Italian food in South America; we thought we had better make the most of it. We ate our pastas with great satisfaction and decided it was time to go back to the hostel, pick up a few last things from the markets on the way and check out of the hostel to take our overnight bus.

Just as we were gathering our things to leave the restaurant, Yuki made a noise of shock.

"My backpack—it's gone!"

"No fucking way," I replied.

We looked around the table, on the floor, behind the chairs and under the table in hopes of finding the backpack. It was nowhere to be seen. The first thing that came into my mind was that it had a lot of the only copies of many of our photos, as Yurie's camera had been stolen in Uyuni. It also had some of Yuki's medicine, along with, most devastating for her, her diary of our trip of almost two months so far.

We called the waitress over to our table and told her what had happened. She seemed to understand the situation straightaway and reminded us of the gentleman who had come in, sat at the table beside us and asked to look at the menu, only to leave shortly after. Of course we had no idea whether or not the restaurant was in on the whole ordeal, but all of us instinctively felt that it wasn't. Out on the street, it was pouring rain. We decided that the girls would take a taxi to the police station to report Yuki's backpack, while I would walk back to the hostel and grab our last bit of shopping. Then we would all meet at the hostel to take a taxi to the bus stop.

Half an hour before our bus was to leave, the girls got back to the hostel. They threw their things together while I organised a taxi to meet us out the front of the hostel. We found out that we were unable to go to Lake Titicaca, a beautiful lake that separates Bolivia and Peru on the way to Machu Picchu, due to protests and roadblocks. The lake was something we were all looking forward to seeing on our way to Cusco, and we were all very let down at missing out on the opportunity, considering how close we were. So instead we went directly from La Paz to Cuzco, the city where we would organise a tour to see Machu Picchu, the famous Inca ruins.

It was an extremely long bus journey but with my trusty motion sickness tablets I slept almost all the way to the border crossing.

16

Peru

It was around two o'clock in the morning, when we arrived at the border crossing from Bolivia. I woke from a twisting and turning sleep on our not-so-comfortable seats. Argentina had spoiled us a little with their *cama* and *semi cama* options. We piled off the bus, everyone looking a little worse for wear, and took our places in line to get our exit stamps. We were to go into the office we had been set down outside of, get our exit stamps, walk across the border and on a little to the Peruvian office to get our entry stamps. The bus would be waiting for us outside the Peruvian Immigration office.

Outside in the cool, dark night, right in the middle of these two countries, I was surprised to find many families huddled together, waiting for I'm not sure what. The children were playing, and the women were dressed in traditional Bolivian dress. I had been warned about the border crossings from Bolivia to Peru and hadn't expected to see these families sitting at the border. Were they living there? Waiting for someone? Wanting to cross?

I was feeling a little confused as to where to go for my stamps. A little boy no older than eight saw I was having trouble. He came up to me and pointed in the direction of a small building. His cheeks were pink, and he had a small scar just above one eyebrow. His clothes and face were covered in the dust that made up the pathway we were walking on.

"*Gracias, señor,*" I thanked him.

I started to walk in the direction of the building, and the small boy followed. I could see where this was going; this was this young boy's job. My heart dropped. As many times as I have seen children working under all sorts of conditions, it never got any easier to accept or comprehend. It was two-thirty in the morning and about ten degrees Celsius outside, and this little boy was showing stupid tourists like me how to get from one Immigration office to the next.

This was where my inner turmoil started over giving children money for their services. Of course it was different if I was ever in a family-run restaurant or corner store or something like that, where the children waited on the tables or served, while the parents cooked or managed the store. If I was to have been that stringent, I would have gone hungry quite a bit. But it started here with this boy on that freezing cold night in the middle of South America. I would no longer give money to children in these situations. Children of his age don't need money. Sure, their parents do—but *they* don't. And as long as travellers are supporting their parents' decision by taking their children out of school to work in the streets for them, they will do it.

In the past I have seen travellers hand over wads of cash to get rid of a child selling something. Sure, it is easy to grab a few coins from our pocket to shoo these children offering services away. But we are on holiday. We have time. We need to take some time out from our touring to buy this child something to eat—a warm jumper, a bottle of clean water. If the parents can't see their children as a way of income, they might just send them back to school. You never know.

Or maybe I am completely wrong and causing more suffering, although I feel much better knowing that I'm not supporting the uneducated life that this child will live by giving him money to pay his parents' bills. I feel that education is the only key to these children's success. Without it, the chances of their succeeding in life are very, very slim. Of course there may be children who are both working on the weekends and going to school, and this is a different story altogether, and I did come up against some cases like this in my later travels, which saw me buying certain items from children I was sure were going to school. But if I was ever in doubt, I just couldn't bring myself to do it. Maybe it just comes down to instinct and what feels right at the time, not what feels the easiest.

Outside the Immigration office I found a small stall that sold soft drinks and snacks. I bought a bottle of water and walked over to my little helper, who was already shyly holding out his hand. I shook it, thanking him muchly, gave him the water for his help and told him to try to go to school and that it was important. He nodded, gave me a big smile and thanked me back. Then he ran back to where he'd came from, most probably to try to get some money from the next weary traveller.

It was hard to swallow.

I walked into the office and made my way to the end of the queue for my entry stamp. I caught sight of the girls at the front of the line and called out to them. They turned around, looking relieved to see me and eager to get back onto the bus for some much-needed sleep. Eventually our bus came to meet us, and our group of around fifty people one by one found their seats and settled in for the last leg of our trip.

When we finally arrived in Cuzco, we were all in a very bad mood and in much need of more rest. But we had to wait three hours until we could do an early check-in. We went and sat on some beanbags in the courtyard, feeling too tired to talk. Suddenly I realized that I had left my card in an ATM machine in La Paz—a lot of the ATMs in South America ask if you would like another transaction after you receive your money, rather than giving the card before the money. I called my bank and cancelled the card. Luckily I had another card of the same type.

We checked in eventually, went upstairs for our included breakfast, which was delicious, and then all went for a shower, scissors-paper-rocking our turns. Even though we all felt like hell, we didn't have much time in Cuzco so we decided to go for a small walk through the city. It was postcard beautiful, with a huge main square surrounded by old buildings and a grassy park in the centre.

Walking through the streets, we were offered a massage for ten dollars an hour by a small, pretty Peruvian girl. We accepted, and after lunch she showed us to a small dodgy room separated by sheets. It reminded me slightly of the last beauty therapist I had visited. The massage itself was OK, although the music kept skipping. My masseuse must have been the one in charge of it. Every five minutes when the music skipped, she would disappear for what seemed a very long time (although it probably wasn't) trying to start the music again. I felt ripped off, but didn't say anything. Ten dollars for a one-hour massage is incredibly cheap.

Afterwards we walked to the nearby tourist office we had passed earlier and booked a three-day jungle tour to Machu Picchu. That night we had Chinese for dinner, and later that night I gave it all to the toilet bowl. Sick again. Next morning, when all of us girls were awake, a voice came from one of the beds.

"Who vomited last night?"

I raised my hand. Only Yurie could see me.

"No way!"

"Yep. Again."

"The Chinese?" Yuki asked.

"I have no idea. You guys ate exactly the same thing."

"Are you OK? Do you think you can go on tour today?"

"Yes, I'll be fine. It's not like last time, thank goodness."

I think we were all relieved by that. We went upstairs for breakfast and ate it as fast as we could. We were running late to meet our tour guide at the front of our hostel. It turned out there was no need: he was even later himself. Once he had collected us from the hostel, we followed him at a fast pace to where all the vans were parked, filled with tourists ready for this Jungle Tour. The Jungle Tour was either a two- or a three-night tour. It included bike riding, zip lining and hiking. The groups were split into two: the two-night group and three-night group. We were to see very soon that maybe the Jungle Tour was not the tour for us.

After we drove from one dodgy place to the next, with our guides collecting the bikes and piling them onto the roof of the van, we headed to the top of a nearby mountain. During the drive, one of the tour guides (who seemed a little highly strung and cranky), gave us the low down on what we were to do on this bike ride. He was barely audible over the sound of the van chugging up the mountain—passengers, bikes and all—and I hoped that what he'd said wasn't too important.

The view when the van came to a stop was utterly breathtaking. We were up fairly high and were surrounded by lush green forest with low misty clouds blanketing the trees. We piled out of the van and were each given a helmet, except for Yurie, as there weren't enough. We waited for another helmet to be dropped off to us by another van, even though the cranky tour guide was trying to hurry us off without her.

"We aren't leaving without her," we told him. Already we were beginning not to like the cranky tour guide. We were grateful that he was the guide for the other group and that ours seemed lovely.

The first worrying sign about this tour was that there were not enough helmets for everyone, and the so-called mountain biking was to be carried out on a steep, downhill main road, which was now being rained on. The second was that the cranky tour guide was now almost screaming at us girls for waiting for our friend to get her helmet. He told us that if we didn't make it to the checkpoint by one o'clock in the afternoon, the road would close for roadworks, and we would be left there until it reopened at five, with the rest of the group already at the hostel.

We told him again, more firmly this time, that there was no way we were leaving without Yurie, especially if there was a chance she would be left behind. Finally, the van with Yurie's helmet pulled up in front of us, threw the helmet to us, and we were on our way with the cranky tour guide of the other group and the driver of the van following closely behind, their lights on.

I started to get the feeling we were being hurried along, even now that we were on our way. I didn't have a clue what the time was, but the cold and the rain pelting down into my eyes were the perfect recipe for me to give up. We had been told at the tourist office that if at any time on this bike ride we wanted to take a lift with the van instead of riding, we could do so. I called out over the rain and the sound of our tyres splashing on the asphalt to the girls, telling them that I was over it, and pulled to the side of the road with Yurie following. Suddenly the van sped over to us, the door of the van swung open and the cranky tour guide jumped out before it had come to a stop.

"What are you doing? You won't make it in time! HURRY HURRY HURRY!!"

"But ... we thought ..."

"HURRY!" And with that he jumped back into the warm, dry van.

The other two girls had also stopped to put on their ponchos. Yurie and I followed suit, already completely soaked, as the rain slapped into our bodies and onto our heads. We pulled on the hoods of our ponchos, mounted our bikes and started back on the road. It was ridiculous; I couldn't see anything. The rain was going straight into my eyes, and I was blinking so much that they were practically closed. And we were on a main road, a lot of the way going down steep slopes.

At each turn there was a flooded causeway, and we had to slow down not to fall off, as the water came up to our pedals. All this and we had to go as fast as we could to make it to the checkpoint in time. We overtook the van, and I started pedalling as fast as I could. That was it, it was all for one now. I was freezing, soaked and had a bad feeling about zipping around on these hills in the wet. I wanted to get it over and done with as soon as possible. I didn't say a word to the girls, or even look around; I just pedalled as fast as I could. By this stage I think everyone was in the same mindset.

Suddenly the van following us overtook us. Strange. Thankfully, the rain had subsided a little. It felt as though we had been riding for quite some time. We rounded a corner and came face to face with two men. I thought this must be the roadworks they had been talking about. Around the next corner were traffic cones, trucks and a lot more workmen. I had a bad feeling. The road seemed to be blocked and everyone looked very busy. Was it one o'clock already?

"Sorry, you can't come through here," an overweight woman told us in Spanish.

"What? *Que?*" we all asked in a mix of English and Spanish.

"The road is closed, it closed at one o'clock. You will have to wait here until five o'clock this afternoon."

Yuki, Yurie and myself stood dumbfounded, but Steff was having none of it.

"No way. No, we are going through, we have to go with the rest of the group. They are all up ahead."

"No, sorry, you can't."

"Yes, we can and we will. Come on, girls." Steff's face was red. It looked as though she was containing a lot of anger.

The three of us followed Steff's lead. Yeah, take that! I thought bravely.

"*Policia! Policia!*"

We all kept riding on, slowly but steadily, picking up the pace as three men came over to us. As soon as they saw us they smiled and told us to go ahead and not to worry. At that moment two blonde girls rode past us, oblivious to what had just happened. I had no idea where they came from. Maybe they had had a break and we had missed them while we were pedalling with all our might, eyes closed and all.

Eventually we caught up with the other group and, even though we knew we weren't slowpokes and had had to wait for a helmet, none of the rest of the group were aware of this. So when we were told we were allowed to go by van rather than ride for the rest of the trip, considering that we already had the reputation of being the unfit lazy ones, we took the opportunity and rode with our nice tour guide, all of us ready to make complaints about the cranky one when we returned to Cuzco.

We arrived at our first stop in a small sleepy town by the name of Santa Maria, and checked in to what seemed to be a very small family home, then headed to a nearby restaurant for dinner. I was still feeling a little the worse for wear and, when we were offered an optional trip to visit some hot springs, I jumped at the chance. The other girls were excited to do so as well, and we all went back to our room to grab our swimmers. By the time we got to the hot springs, though, my stomach was doing backflips, disagreeing with the food I had just put into it. I was sure I wasn't going to vomit again because I had gone vegetarian yet again on this tour, but I think my tummy was just not up to its job just yet.

Feeling this way made it hard to enjoy the springs, although they were so beautiful. We were in the middle of the jungle at the edge of a mountain face. Lying in the warm sulphuric waters, gazing up, I was lost in what seemed to be a billion stars. Looking out to the horizon, I found that I couldn't see where the land finished and the sky began. There was nothing but blackness as far as the eye could see. From where we were, we couldn't even see the lights of the small village we were staying in. We soaked for around an hour at the springs and then headed back to our room. We had a big day ahead of us next day, so we all went straight to sleep.

At six o'clock the following morning we woke up to our alarms and headed for breakfast to the restaurant that we had had dinner at. We had a few choices and I chose pancakes, which, with my appetite back in full force, were very welcome and delicious. We had a short drive ahead of us to the site of the zip lining. We were told that if we didn't do the zip lining, which was an extra thirty dollars, we would have to walk eight hours to the next stop. So we all were in on the zip lining. Two young teenage boys were to be our guides and we had three zip lines ahead of us, all considerably long and across an incredibly dense and green valley. It was beautiful.

Yurie, Steff and I were all nervous, Yuki being the only one excited for the sport. She was first to go, then Yurie, then Steff and then me. Once I had taken off, I was fine, but when I got to the other side, I could see that Steff was not. She didn't know what had come over her but she was freaking out a lot. The next line was even longer and she said she wanted to go with one of the guides this time, which meant that she had to go first or last, and she chose last. So I went second last and, when I got to the other side, I set up the camera to film Steff gliding across the

Inca jungle. This time she looked to be enjoying it, she was lying out like Superman with her arms out. But as she got closer I saw that her face was red and she had tears pouring down her cheeks.

"Steff!"

She got to the platform a shaking mess. We had just discovered that Steff has a real fear of heights.

"I don't know what is wrong with me. It's crazy!" she exclaimed, wiping the corners of her eyes with the sleeve of her jumper.

"Are you OK? Can you do the next one?"

"Yeah, sure, I'll be fine. It was so much scarier lying down like that, I didn't know he was going to do that. I should be fine if I do it like the first time," Steff explained in her cute Swiss-German accent.

"OK, just let them know if you can't do it, Steff."

"OK, sure."

She got through the last line—just—and we found that we were back where we had started. We grabbed our things and climbed into the van waiting for us. Now we were to drive to a small village, have lunch in a restaurant at the village's train station, put our backpacks on the train and walk for two hours to Agnes Waters, the small town at the bottom of Machu Picchu. I was feeling really tired and paired up with a girl by the name of Tash, who was also taking the hike easy. We followed the train tracks through the jungle, talking about anything and everything. She was a delight to get to know, if only briefly.

Once we arrived and checked in, we all just lay on our beds, unmoving, even though we all needed and wanted a shower. Finally, we showered and met up with the group at the restaurant downstairs for dinner. It was an early night for us all, especially Yuki. She had decided that, rather than taking the bus up to Machu Picchu in the morning, she would trek up there, so she had to be up much earlier than we did.

The next morning we all got up, dressed ourselves in as many clothes as we could (though we would later find it was warm enough not to do so), and walked to the bus stop. It was five o'clock in the morning and still very dark, but thankfully nowhere near as freezing as we had been expecting. We stood in line for quite some time before we got to an empty bus. The sun was starting to rise and we realized that we would miss the sunrise from Machu Picchu, as the entrance to the site didn't open until seven o'clock that morning. We arrived before Yuki, which was strange, and waited for as long as we could before we'd risk missing our entrance to climb Huayana Picchu, something we had had to organise weeks in advance. Only limited numbers were allowed to climb the mountain which has a birds-eye view of the ancient city. We told a girl waiting for her friend who was walking with Yuki to let Yuki know that we had already gone in to save our places and would be just inside the entrance to Huayana Picchu.

We walked up a small slope, rounded a corner, walked through a few small ruins and then suddenly, right in front of my eyes was the almost glowing-green view of Machu Picchu. Not a word can come close to what my eyes had just fallen upon. I instantly welled up with tears as I drank in the sight of one of the wonders of the world. I had heard during my travels that Machu Picchu was nothing to be too excited about. I'm not sure which Machu Picchu they had visited. The one that stood in front of me that day was certainly something to be excited about.

"Kristin!" came the shrill voice of Yuki running up behind us.

"Yuki! Where were you? I'm sorry we had to leave, we were going to miss our spot."

"I know, I'm sorry. Robin was so sick, and we took so long walking up the hill. I'm sorry. How beautiful is this!"

"I know!" I exclaimed, wiping the tears from my eyes.

On our way to the entrance to Huayana Picchu, the four of us started to take the beginning of what would be hundreds of photos. We got to the entrance just as they were letting people in and hastily made our way up the hill. It was steep and narrow in many parts. We had to take many a breather. The reason we were in such a hurry was to make it down in time to take our included tour of Machu Picchu, which was due to start pretty soon. Along the way we found some wild strawberries and grabbed a few each. They were sweet and delicious and tasted nothing like those from our local supermarket back home.

We got to the first viewing point with no problems, except that Steff acted a little weird when we got too close to the edge. We didn't think much of it until we started climbing the very last part of the trail. Right at the top, when we couldn't get any higher and were completely surrounded by giant drops on all sides, right on cue Steff started freaking out completely. We started descending straightaway, going as smoothly as we could, comforting Steff all the way.

At one point I overheard the distinct accent of my fellow Australians not too far behind us. I had already overheard them at the first viewing point and couldn't help but smile on both occasions. Ahh, that accent. Incredible. It sounded so strange when I hadn't heard it for a while. When they got to us, I told them what was going on and that they could pass us if they liked. At this the older man and his daughter made their way over to Steff, he keeping his hand on her back and she talking calmly to her for the entire way through the steepest part of the descent until she was feeling a little more at ease. Eventually we let them overtake us and thanked them for their kindness.

We weren't going to make it to the next tour, so we started to take our time. Although we had a picnic packed for somewhere beautiful, we took a break to have something small and quick to eat; we were all starving. Afterwards we walked slowly through the ancient city without a clue as to what we were looking at. We found a place for a picnic, but were told to move on by a guard, who actually helped us to find a more secluded spot, where the other guards wouldn't notice us eating; no one was supposed to eat in Machu Picchu, for obvious reasons. We climbed the rocks to the place the guard had suggested and sat on the other side of them, as he'd instructed. The picnic was delicious—avocado, tomato and garlic bread rolls, mandarins and cake.

After our picnic we went for another walk through the city, taking hundreds more photos and finally taking the bus back to town. We got to the hostel in time to take our pre-booked train back to Cuzco, only to find out from our tour guide that the tourist office hadn't booked our tickets and it was too full to seat us. We had to stay one more night in Agnes Waters and take a train the following morning. We were all depressed over this as we had booked our accommodation in Cuzco for that night, and Yurie, Yuki and I had booked our bus to Lima for the following afternoon. This meant we only had tomorrow morning to really see Cuzco. Steff wasn't too worried as she was flying out from Cuzco later on in the week to her home-stay in Cartagena, Colombia.

We decided to go out to dinner and get drunk on the nation's cocktail, pisco sour, until late into the night. Our train left at five o'clock the next morning. Not one of us was thrilled about our alarm clocks blaring half an hour before that. We ran to the train station, and I'm not sure what the girls did for that ride, but I passed out for the entire trip; I only woke when the train came to our stop. I was ever so grateful that no one had sat next to me, and even more grateful to find a small packet of nuts in front of me, compliments of the train company. My stomach felt so empty I could have passed out. I almost cried when I dropped two of the nuts on the ground in our haste to find whoever it was who was picking us up from the train station and taking us back to our hostel in Cuzco.

"Krispin? Krispin?" came shouts from a small man with a moustache. He was holding up a sign that said *Krispin and Yurie*.

"That must be our guy," I said to the girls. We all burst out laughing.

"*Si! Soy Krispin!*" I called after the man, who was darting back and forth, shoving his sign in everybody's faces in a panic. Once he realized he had found us, he turned on his heels and started running in the opposite direction. He had another think coming if he thought that any of us were going to go any faster than a slow walk in our dreary, puffy-eyed, tired-leg state.

Sure enough, two minutes later he was running back to us. "Krispin! Krispin!"

"*Si, señor.* We are coming." I answered him, trying not to laugh. This poor man was obviously in a hurry, but there was simply no way we could go faster.

We got to the van just before our poor friend had a heart attack. We hadn't even closed the door when he began reversing out of the parking lot at full speed. We got to the city centre not long after that and took a taxi to the hostel. It was early morning and, because we had paid for the night before's accommodation, we were able to go upstairs to eat the included breakfast and use the wifi. We logged on to Facebook and found a message from Grace. She was in Cuzco! Not only that, she was staying in this hostel, although she was out organising her tour. We planned to meet up in the next hour, have a quick look around the city and have lunch before Yuki, Yurie and I had to take our bus to Lima.

It turned out to be a completely different trip from the one we had planned. Grace had done most of the trip alone, and in her place we had found Steff, although we were all excited to see Grace again. I spotted her curls before I spotted her, and she came bounding towards us through the hostel's gate.

"Darling! We have missed you," I breathed into her shampoo-scented hair.

"I've missed you guys, too!"

We spent the next few hours swapping stories until it was time for Yuki, Yurie and I to say goodbye to both Grace and Steff. How long for, we had no idea. It was hard, and none of the three of us wanted to get into the taxi. This time the taxidriver didn't try to rip us off, so he got a nice tip for his efforts. Our bus was very beautiful, and it was a *cama*. It was also supposed to have wifi, although that didn't work. The process for boarding was extremely thorough, and a video was taken of everyone as they boarded. We had our dinner and breakfast included, as on the Argentinian buses, and I passed the night away with one of my motion sickness pills and a glass of wine.

The trip was twenty-two hours long. We arrived in Lima at lunchtime. We had heard that the food there was amazing, and we were starving, so I picked the best-looking restaurant out of the *Lonely Planet* and, after buying our forwarding tickets to a town close to the border, I ordered us a taxi to the front door of the restaurant. Once there, we ordered three meals to share and could not control the moans coming from our mouths. It was so delicious—and pretty cheap as well. We didn't have much time before our next twenty-something-hour bus was due to leave and made it back just in time. Sometimes I really could not believe our luck.

Our meals were also included on this bus; it was the same company as the bus we had arrived on. We met a young man from Mexico, chatted with him for a bit, then I fell into my usual travelling sleep yet again. Next morning I woke up in my *cama* bus seat with a migraine. That was certainly not in my plans. I took one of the pills from Argentina and hoped for the best. The town we had arrived in looked incredibly dodgy.

We had planned to stay a day or two as it was beside the sea. We were all craving the salty air and sand between our toes.

Between my migraine, the effects of two twenty-something-hour bus rides in a row and the heat at sea level, which we were not accustomed to, we just weren't in the mood to stick around to see if we were safe here or not. Along with our new Mexican friend, we booked the next bus to the actual border crossing. This changed things dramatically as we hadn't made any plans for Ecuador whatsoever, thinking that we still had a day or two in which to plan. Our new Mexican friend told us of a city he was going to that seemed to be nice. Relieved at the thought of someone else organising things for us, we decided to follow him.

Turned out that this lovely city had only one thing to offer: the yummy lunch we had the following day in a restaurant close by our hostel. This delightful city went by the name of Guayaquil. It was hot, filled with smog and had nothing to do unless we wanted to take a boat out to the Galápagos Islands, which none of us had enough time or money to do. We discovered that our new friend was only going there to see if he could get any business there with his tour company. That was it. He soon realized that he indeed didn't.

We met a Canadian guy and his beautiful Colombian girlfriend, whom we shared the delicious lunch with. They knew Ecuador well, so we asked them where was the best place for us to go as soon as possible so we could get out of Guayaquil. They told us of a cute town that had hot springs, and with that we booked a ticket to the city of Banos. It was on the way to Colombia, where we were headed anyway. We took an overnight bus to Banos, so we didn't have to waste another minute in Guayaquil.

The trip was in two stages, even though it was only ten hours to our destination, meaning that in the middle of the night we were woken by the bus driver screaming out, "Banos! Banos!" We changed buses. Just as we were starting to fall asleep on this bus, we were again woken by the same call. We arrived in the early morning before the sun had risen and had no idea where we were going to sleep. We found a group of Israelis on the same bus, who were headed to a hostel they had heard was owned by an Israeli and would give them a good price. We were welcome to join them and took up the offer.

By this time we had been travelling for something like three days with one stopover in between and were feeling just a little under the weather. Our feet were moving of their own accord in the bright hopes of a comfortable bed. Luckily, there was enough room for everyone at the hostel, and we were allowed to check in straightaway. Yuki, Yurie and I had a room to ourselves, Yuki and I sharing a bed and Yurie with her own. We dived under the covers and stayed there until well into the morning.

For the next two days we absolutely spoiled ourselves. We went out to nice restaurants, went to a day spa and had a sauna, mud bath and our intestines flushed (an interesting experience), and in the night we visited the town's hot springs. By the third day we felt like new women. By chance, a guy Yuki had met in Argentina was staying in the same town. They met up on the second last day and, rather than taking the bus with Yurie and me to Cali in Columbia, Yuki stayed in Banos with her new friend, who just so happened to be Israeli.

So it was time for another goodbye at four o'clock the next morning at a deafeningly quiet bus stop. The three of us had not only travelled together for the past two months, but we had also lived together for the year before that. Yurie and I were our own little team now, and we were to experience what it was like for our very special bond to deepen even further into an everlasting friendship. After crossing the border of Ecuador and Columbia, we changed currencies yet again and took another bus directly to the airport of Cali, hoping to find a cheap flight to our new destination Cartagena, the same city that Steff had flown to only a week before.

We were going to see Steff again.

We found that it was almost impossible to get these tickets. In Latin America we needed an identification number for a lot of online booking, which of course, not being Latin American, we didn't have. We bought our tickets directly from the airline and at long last got a flight to Santa Marta, a town close to Cartagena. From this town we would first visit Tayrona National Park, which we had heard was beautiful, and then move on to Cartagena.

We arrived in Santa Marta after the sun had set. It was very warm and humid, and I could feel with all my senses that we were near the sea. I could barely contain my joy at this. The past week and a half of travel had taken its toll on us and some relaxing beach time was in order. At the arrivals gate there was a group of taxidrivers hassling everybody who walked past them to take their taxi into town. Of course it was incredibly overpriced, but according to them, it was the only way to get into town—until we rounded a corner where the rest of the Columbians were headed and found a public bus was waiting for a twentieth of the price.

I guess they have to try.

We took the bus into the centre of Santa Marta and found a nice hostel with a pool in the middle. This hostel and, we were assuming, this area in general had a very backpacking, touristic vibe, something we hadn't really seen for quite some time. We went out for a nice meal and came back for an early night, deciding to organise our stay here next morning, when we'd had some rest. Shortly after breakfast we met two other guys who were planning on going that day to Tayrona National

Park and we decided to team up with them. Their names were James and Robin.

James was from England, and Robin was from Luxembourg, although he had an extremely strong British accent from going to school in the UK with James. They were both very tall and very blond and attracted much attention from the drop-dead gorgeous Columbian women. I was reminded of how different it was to travel with a man. Not only was the attention from the locals lessened to a great degree, but the feeling of security was such an ease to my mind. I hadn't realized just how on guard I had been for pretty much the entire trip. I repaid the boys for this relief, whenever they needed a translator, with the Spanish that I had picked up along the way.

One thing I found incredibly disappointing was the unhelpfulness I found while in South America from the women. Some women would flat out not reply to my asking them for help with directions, even though at times I was alone, or it was dark and obviously dangerous for me. I would sometimes have to resort to asking men, the very ones I didn't want to know that I was alone and lost. The men that I travelled with, on the other hand, were helped not only by their fellow gender, having some kind of innate camaraderie between one another, but also and especially by the women. It didn't seem fair that women were so unsupportive of one another. We should have been the ones sticking together. I felt this way through much of Latin America and wondered if it had anything to with how sleazy the Latino men could be. Surely these women knew of their men's approaches towards women, especially foreign women. I guess they just felt threatened and the need to protect what is theirs. But still it was disappointing.

The bus ride to the park was quite an interesting one, with the boys' legs too long to fit behind the seat in front of them, and all of us flying into the ceiling with every bump in the road. We were the only foreigners on the bus, and I had the horrible feeling come over me of taking advantage of a developing country's beauty with my easy life. I wished in that moment, as I had many times before, that I wasn't so obviously a foreigner.

The national park was as beautiful as we had heard. There were camping places along the way, where we paid to stay the night in the tents or hammocks provided. It was a short hike between beaches and campsites along a somewhat deserted coastline, apart from the designated camping spots. We decided to give sleeping outdoors in a hammock a try, which was a very big mistake. For me, sleeping in a hammock was pretty much like giving up a night's sleep. Not only was it (surprisingly) freezing in the middle of the night, but also, rolling over was like rolling around in a giant spider's web. Never again, I decided, unless I'm desperate.

The next morning we went for another hike before heading back to Santa Marta. James and Robin were going to Cartagena as well that day, so we all took a transfer from our hostel to the city. The city itself was beautiful, with old colonial buildings and the old part of the city surrounded by a giant wall. I decided to stay on there for over a week and sign up for a week of Spanish classes. Yurie and I had only a few days left together before she was due to take her flight to Mexico. We spent those last days eating ice cream, partying with the guys and just walking the streets of the beautiful colonial-style city.

On our first day in Cartagena we went on a mission to try to find the same kind of delicious food as we'd had in Guayaquil, Ecuador. We walked the way to the city along the beachfront and came across a guy selling crabs. He talked us into sitting on one of the sun lounges on the beach, after assuring the owner of the lounges that we would later come back to give him business. The crabs looked delicious and we were both starving, but I was getting a bad feeling from the guy.

"How much for one?" I asked him after trying a sample, trying not to moan at its deliciousness.

"Five dollars for two halves, you can share one each."

I looked at Yurie; she seemed to be enjoying her sampled crab.

"OK, sure," we told him.

While eating our crabs, the seller sat as close to us as he could, trying to persuade us to buy more.

"No, we are OK, thank you, anyway," I told him, handing over the equivalent of five dollars.

"No, you need to pay me ten dollars! Look, you ate a whole crab each," the man exclaimed, pointing to shells on the sand near our feet.

So that was why he was sitting so close. He had somehow scraped the meat out of a crab into the halved shells of an entire crab. I knew he had already ripped us off in the first place, although I was happy to pay for such delicious crab, but I wasn't in the mood for tricks.

"No, you tricked us, this is all we are paying," I said firmly, upset at his behaviour.

I took Yurie by the arm and left without a backward glance. We never found the delicious type of food we were searching for and ended up eating KFC. I always tried not to eat from McDonalds or KFC while travelling, but desperate times call for desperate measures, and it was cheap.

On the eve of Yurie's flight, we were both incredibly sad. We had gotten so close and were not yet ready to say goodbye. We went out for a final meal that was not at all nice, but we didn't care. We were just grateful for our last evening together and for the friendship we had formed. At three o'clock next morning, I walked her to her taxi with tears in my eyes. We gave each other one last hug, and that was it. Her yellow taxi disappeared into the distance and she was gone. I went back to my room to find the sweetest note that anyone had ever written to me on my bed. Even though the room was full of people, I could not contain my sobs.

I stayed on for one extra week to complete the Spanish course I had enrolled in. The day after I completed it I took my flight from Cartagena, Colombia to Panama City, Panama.

17

Central America

The flight from Columbia to Panama was the scariest flight of my life. Just after the stewardess had served our drinks, the pilot announced that everyone had to stow away their tray tables and for the staff to take their seats. Seconds after the announcement, the plane jerked left, right, up and down so hard that the tea of the man two seats across from me flew out of his cup and all over me. That same song came flooding into my mind, the one sung by Alanis Morrisette, and I had to use all my willpower not to panic. Usually, when encountering turbulence, I gauge how intense it is by the other passengers' reactions; I'm never sure whether I'm panicking for no reason. Looking around me, I could see that my fellow passengers were just as spooked as I was. Not long after the turbulence, however we landed, a little shaken but all in one piece.

I was feeling incredibly nervous that I wouldn't make it to Nicaragua in time for the start of my internship. I had three days to get there by bus. This meant driving north from Panama City through Panama and then through Costa Rica up to my destination city Managua, Nicaragua's capital. I made my way hastily to the airport's information desk and got as much information as I could about transport. I was to take a bus from the airport to the main bus station. From there I could take an international bus.

I walked outside and was greeted by a taxidriver. I told him that I needed to take a bus into the city's centre. He told me that the bus station was quite a walk but he would have a taxi take me there for free. He called over another taxidriver and instructed him to take me to the bus stop free of charge, which the man was happy to do. I thanked the taxidriver as he dropped me off, not really understanding what had just happened; I was sure there would be some trick. But the taxidriver at the airport had really just wanted to help me out. I smiled inside and out.

There was a foreign couple at the bus stop. I asked them in Spanish where they were going. They acted strangely for a moment but eventually came over and spoke with me in English, although they were from Spain—which I thought was odd. It seemed as though they didn't want anyone else to understand our conversation. They told me that I needed a special card to use the transport here and that the guy they were standing with was accepting money from them and letting them use his card.

So I couldn't just pay the bus driver. Shit. I asked the man beside me if he minded doing the same with me and he accepted. Phew. So lucky. When we got onto the bus, I went to give the guy who had spotted me my fare money and realized that I either had fifty cents or a twenty-dollar note.

"*Un dollar,*" my friend informed me.

I gave the man the fifty cents that I had, grateful that we were at least dealing in dollars and asked him if he had any change. He didn't. I went from person to person on the bus. It turned out that the entire bus didn't have any change for twenty dollars.

Figures. South America *never* had change.

I really could not afford a short bus ride for twenty dollars. Things were looking pretty bleak. The man didn't look like he was going to let me off the fifty cents, and I didn't expect him to, anyway. Eventually a young man got up from his seat and walked over to the driver and paid the remaining fifty cents for me. I was so lucky, I couldn't thank this boy enough. I wrote him a note telling him that if he ever came to Australia he would have a place to stay, with my email address scribbled down as a means of contact.

In hindsight that is most probably the most arrogant thing I have ever done, and I cringe at the thought of it now. I had no idea who this guy was. The fact that he could spare fifty cents by no means meant that he could afford a plane ticket to Australia. Oh well, can't take it back now.

I moved to the front of the bus and asked a lady if she could let me know when we were close to the main bus station. She told me that she was getting off at the same stop and not to worry. When I told her I was worried about my buses to Nicaragua, she seemed to take it as her mission to get me that bus. When we arrived at the ticketing office for international buses, there was no one to be seen. There was a queue of people complaining that they had been waiting for two hours without a peep from anyone who worked there. My new friend was in a hurry and couldn't wait with me. I told her not to worry and thanked her for her help. People from Panama were proving to be incredibly hospitable.

Finally, a woman showed up to her shift on this rather warm afternoon to a fairly unhappy, sweaty crowd. Eventually it was my turn and I found that I couldn't get a bus until the next day. I was devastated. I was sure that I wouldn't make it to Managua in time; I'd wanted to get there at least one day before. I took a taxi to the nearest hostel, which was completely booked out, and then took another taxi from there to a kind of guesthouse. I talked with mum for a while. She got incredibly worried when my battery ran out in the middle of our conversation while I was getting hassled by a drunken elderly gentleman from Brazil. My phone finally charged and I called her back as soon as I could to let her know that I was OK. It must be so hard to be the mum of a traveller, especially a daughter.

I got an early sleep, ate my included breakfast the next day, which was huge and delicious, and took a taxi to the bus station in preparation for my two-legged, forty-hour bus trip. I decided to keep my bag on me as the seats looked uncomfortable. That way I could put my bag at the foot of my seat and rest my legs on it. This turned out to be a good choice: we were stopped three times during the trip to have all our bags searched and our names checked off a list. I had never had a bus trip like it. I was the only foreigner on the bus travelling alone, and the only girl. Two other male foreigners travelling together later commended me on my bravery for travelling alone here.

At the first roll call, our bags were laid out in front of us. A dog ran from one to the next, searching for drugs and I'm not sure what or if anything else. I was delighted by the authenticity of the experience when listening to the names being called out.

"Rodriguez."

"*Si.*"

"Sanchez."

"*Si.*"

"Lopez."

"*Si.*"

"Garcia."

"*Si.*"

It went on like this. Names notorious for this region of the world.

We stopped for a few hours in Costa Rica at a bus station in the middle of the night. I was exhausted but couldn't sleep. I had made friends with a girl from Panama and an old man from Honduras. We chatted until the time to check in for our bus. When I got to the check-in desk, I was told that my bus had left hours earlier. Oh no, I could have been out of here ages ago! I'd just assumed that I was on the same bus as my friends from the last bus. Luckily, though, I was given a seat on their bus at no extra cost. It was a sight for our sore, tired eyes when that bus rolled in, and we all collapsed into our assigned seats.

I made it to Managua city that morning. I said goodbye to my new friends (who also seemed to have respect for me travelling alone) and set out to try to find the closest hostel. I had read in the guidebook that one was within walking distance. I headed off in its direction. I found it, only to realise that it was too far from the city centre. I decided to pay two dollars a night more and stay in a hostel in town. It had a pool, and I felt much safer there. I had heard a lot of things about this city, none of them good.

I had arrived a day before I was to start my internship. What on earth was I worried about?

My first two days in the city's capital was a bit of a culture shock in comparison to the other warmer Latin countries I had been to so far. In Nicaragua almost everyone wore jeans and T-shirts, despite the extreme heat and humidity. Eyes were constantly on me, possibly more than ever before. The city of Managua was really only a stopover for tourists; hardly anyone ever spent more than one night there, as I was to find in my eight-bed dorm room.

I needed to buy some more modest clothing, so the morning after I had arrived in Managua, I looked up where I could find a market. The entire trip there was an incredible experience, not only because the streets in Managua aren't named, but also because they are navigated by cardinal directions and reference points. Where Columbian buses had strange stuffed animals hanging from their roofs or sitting on their dashboards, Nicaragua's buses had stickers ranging from Power Rangers to Star Wars characters on their windscreens, along with colourful tape wrapped around their steering wheels. Everyone seemed to have their money ready before they were even on the bus.

The type of bus I got onto was referred to by the foreigners as a chicken bus, although I never figured out why. These buses had bench seats and looked like the school buses in old American movies. I gave my money to the driver, and he gave almost all of it back to me; I had no idea how much the fare cost. It turned out to be a whole twenty-five cents. I took my place standing directly by the driver and asked him over the reggaeton blaring from the speakers if he could let me know when we arrived at the markets. He smiled at me and told me he would.

Holding onto the rails above me, I watched as an old woman got onto the bus. She paid the driver and gave him some mangoes, obviously a regular customer. He motioned to the front of the bus. She placed them on the dashboard and smiled at me as she made her way past. I looked to where the bus driver had put the coins that she had handed over. In the middle of his steering wheel was a magnet as big as the one in the space cowboy's chest. The driver stuck the coins there in an arrangement of what I could make out was twenty-five cents. This was to make giving out change easier for the fifty-cent pieces handed to him, I supposed.

In that moment, as the bus threw me around to the hip-thrusting music and I tried my hardest not to bump into anyone near me, I felt that I was exactly where I was supposed to be. Never before had I had that feeling. Like the coins coming and going from the magnet on the bus driver's steering wheel, I felt I had been drawn to all those different places all over the world to bring me exactly where I was: to realise a dream I had had all of my life. I was finally going to help people in need and start the ball rolling for whatever other human betterment that was to come. This was all just a dream only days ago. It's amazing that once you are pro-active about something, it will happen. Start speaking about it, researching it, planning for it, even though it seems that it will never happen, it really can and will.

I got to the market unscathed but a little overwhelmed by everything. There were a fair few homeless beggars at the market, one of whom tried to come up and eat yet another mango that I had purchased first stop off the bus. Fourth mango for the day—I would have given it to him but I was too in shock to register what was going on. Nicaragua would be the country where I ate the most fruit I have ever eaten in all my life. That morning I had bought three mangoes peeled and sliced for two dollars.

I had travelled alone from Panama to Nicaragua fairly directly. The only other time I had travelled alone was in Spain, Greece and on the tour in Europe. I was feeling very on edge and paranoid about everything. Each day that I survived without anything going wrong I felt very thankful. I kept hearing terrible stories about this city, which didn't help at all. I had heard of a girl who had been picked up by a taxi and dropped in the middle of nowhere, where two men were waiting. They beat her up, stripped her of her clothes and took them, leaving her in the middle of the street, naked.

Outside the country's capital, though, was supposed to be much safer and calmer. But I was here for a reason. It was definitely my destiny to be here and I had a good feeling that nothing would go wrong because of this.

The market was big, dusty and not exciting at all. It had mainly household goods and nothing that a tourist would want or need, other than the experience of going there. I searched high and low for clothes, but they were all far too expensive. I asked a boy if he knew of any second-hand clothes stores, and he gave me directions to where I could find some. I found my way to the second-hand store and was met by a toothless woman at the entrance.

"*Hola,*" I smiled at her.

"*Hola,*" she replied.

I set about finding some modest clothes. I found some black overalls two sizes too big for me, a long floral skirt, a white singlet and a pink, short-sleeved shirt. That ought to do it. I paid for my purchases and made my way back to the hostel long before dark. I was too scared to go out after sunset and rarely found myself doing so. I still had one more day before I would start at the Earth Education Project, so I took the opportunity to venture around a neighbourhood that was one of the most dangerous in Managua. Of course I didn't know that before I followed my new friend there.

My new friend was the lady I'd been buying mangoes from. She also sold cigarettes, phone credit, sweets, some kind of small, cherry-sized fruit with a large round seed inside that tasted like port, which you eat accompanied by a large amount of salt. She also ran a mean barbeque, her main revenue being from her delectable *churrascos*, a grilled meat that was so tasty I was always left wanting more.

Her small stall was made of a few pieces of wood for a table, which displayed a rainbow spread of colourful sweets and other types of tempting but not so tempting snacks. I can't remember her name, but she was always so happy as she sat across from me at the mango stall, ignoring my attempts at Spanish, telling me animated stories in Spanish, spitting words at me, though I had only very vague ideas of their meanings. They must have been funny; she was usually giggling as she told her stories.

I told my new friend that I was starving, and that I was looking for somewhere cheap and yummy to eat. That was it, she was on a mission. Like most Latin people, the thought that someone she was in the company of was hungry was just unthinkable. She told her daughter and granddaughter, who also worked at the family stall that she had to take me some place to eat. She showed them where the money was hidden, and a few other things I couldn't quite catch. Then she grabbed my hand to cross the noisy, horn-blowing, ever-so-busy street. When we arrived at the store that used to sell the typical dish that she so wanted me to try, a little girl told us that they didn't sell it anymore but that across the road they did, although now it was too late and we would have to come back *mañana*.

Mañana, *mañana*, *mañana*. Tomorrow. I was soon to learn that *mañana* was the Nicaraguans' favourite word. Along with many other warm and tropical countries, the people of Nicaragua moved just a tad slower than those of cooler lands, arrived to appointments *solo un poco tarde*—just a little late, and put things off for *mañana*, which rarely, if ever, came.

On hearing the store was closed, my new friend grabbed my hand and pulled me back towards her stall. I felt a little awkward holding hands with my forty-eight-year-old new friend. Being white, with long blondish-brown hair and an obvious Anglo face, I got enough attention in South America as it was. I didn't need the added attention for being a twenty-six-year-old woman who couldn't cross the road without holding a local's hand.

My new friend quickly informed the family back at the stall that she was taking me home to give me some lunch because "*Ella tiene hambre*"— she is hungry. Leaving the bills of lesser value, she grabbed the few five-hundred cordoba bills out of a pile and stuffed them down her bra. Then she grabbed my hand, and off we went again. She explained to me that her house was really close to her business, and it was.

We walked off the main road, and I was surprised to see the road turn from tarred to dirt. The houses looked very much like slums. Another two blocks up and we found her house, where she, her two daughters, one of their husbands and their two children lived. Once through the locked gate to the front of the house, I was immediately greeted by a five-year-old boy with a massive hug, and a small wave from the grumpy looking two-year-old. I waited out the front of the house, sitting on a red plastic chair, the seat of which held a puddle of water that seeped into my overall bottoms, while my friend served up the lunch her daughter had already prepared. She came outside with our plates and announced proudly, "*Lingua con salsa.*" My stomach flipped. Tongue with sauce. Shit. There was nothing I could do but smile and say, "Mmmm, bueno, let's eat!"

I dodged the tongue for my first few mouthfuls, keeping my attention on the kids fighting over a small handmade toy, a great distraction from what was going on inside me. Luckily I found an opportunity to drown my tongue in tomato sauce when my friend ducked inside for a moment. I don't usually eat tomato sauce, but today it was the best tasting condiment on the planet. I made it seem that I was so hungry and enjoying the meal so much that I downed that baby as fast as my flippy-floppy stomach could handle.

After our lunch my friend brought me inside the house. Finding the words to describe her house is difficult. I had been to some poor people's houses and shacks before, but this was just so unexpected. The front room which seemed to be the living room was just big enough to fit me and the two kids inside. It was occupied by a sagging couch, lights that were unplugged and a long mirror. This was the only real indoor area of the house. We walked through to the next room. I had trouble working out whether or not it was a backyard, a laundry, bedrooms or a kitchen. It turned out to be a combination of all these things. There were hardly any defined walls; most of the rooms were divided by sheets and were open to the elements.

The sink was also the washing machine—there is a technique to washing the dishes so as not to get food in the laundry water or laundry water in the food water. Who would have thought it would be so hard. I took over from my new friend and started slowly and carefully washing our dishes. The family got a lot of enjoyment out of watching me do the washing up—at least I could contribute back in some way for my tongue lunch.

After I washed up, my friend brought me out to her dirt-floored bedroom, one side of which was completely open to the backyard and, as she told me, got extremely wet in the wet season, which was now on its way. She kindly showed me where the toilet was if I needed it, which luckily I didn't, then told me to sit on her bed. She pulled out a comb, laughed a little too eerily, and then started to comb my hair, which had its fair share of knots. Every time she came to a knot, she tugged down so hard that it brought tears to my eyes until she found its release, bringing the comb successfully through to the ends of my hair, all the while chuckling in that same eerie tone.

I didn't know that this neighbourhood was dangerous before entering it, but this was still Managua, and I always had in my mind that something could go very wrong at any time. So I have to say, at this point I was starting to question my friend's orientation. Luckily I received a call from a friend I was going to meet and had an excuse to leave. I said an *adios* and *gracias* to everyone, and my friend walked me to the point where my other friend was waiting for me; she later let me know about the neighbourhood I had just lunched in.

I couldn't help but smile. Actually I think this made me smile even more. When I thought of how poor and unfortunate these people were, yet they had invited me into their home, fed me and even brushed my hair. This was an example of the human spirit that is lacking in many of our lives.

The day I was to meet the women at the The Earth Education Project workshop I was so nervous. I didn't really have a great idea of what to expect, and my Spanish was most certainly not up to scratch. I took the bus to the stop closest to the centre and walked the remaining half a block. The sun seemed extra warm that day, and I was sweating uncontrollably. I didn't seem to have body odour though, in spite of this Central American heat; it must have been something in the food. I basically ate beans, rice and fruit. That was it. Although it was a bit boring in the beginning, I soon found myself craving it and certainly missing it. Not to say there weren't many other dishes to try. It was just that these were the healthiest cheap options I could find.

I walked up to the centre's white gate. Although it was padlocked, the main doors to the building were open and I could see the women working on their arts and crafts.

"*Hola,*" I called out.

"*Hola,* Kristin!" A beautiful curvaceous woman smiled as she walked towards the gate to let me in.

"*Mucho gusto, Ana.*"

Ah, this was Ana, the on-site manager. I would be working with her on my assigned tasks, along with another woman Silvia the admin clerk, although she wasn't in that day.

"Chicas, this is Kristin. She will be here with us starting next week."

"*Hola.*" I searched the faces of the girls.

"*Hola,*" some of them replied.

Wow, was I nervous. The women seemed very shy and, if I hadn't known any better, very uninterested. These women sitting here before me working on their arts and crafts had come from a life that I and many others cannot even begin to imagine. For their entire lives they had lived, worked, eaten among, scavenged over, cooked on and raised families among the country's largest rubbish dump. A place so dangerous that very few people would dare to go. A place that would have smelled of rotten food and burning plastic, with scavenging animals living as neighbours, and no education or access to any of the leisure activities we believe to be our rights to enjoy.

These women had not had the opportunity to go to school, to drink clean water, to know of social skills or etiquette. They could not read or even write their own names. Many of them had endured years of domestic violence; this was the type of world these women came from. The rubbish dump was called La Chureca, which is slang for city dump.

There had been a number of NGOs working in the area, trying to get the people out of the poverty in which they lived. Six years earlier, La Chureca had a visit from Maria Teresa Fernandez de la Vega, the vice-president of Spain, while she was on an official visit to Nicaragua. She was disgusted with the way the people lived at La Chureca and planned to develop a thirty million dollar project to clean up the city's rubbish dump. This did not get under way until some time later, meaning that the women I worked with were still living in the dump until three months before I arrived, when the dump was sealed and homes were built for the people.

As incredible as this development was for La Chureca, it meant that the women's livelihood disappeared under the dump's seals. They could no longer make money by selling the products and by salvaging what they could. That was where The Earth Education Project came in, and where an amazing Swiss woman by the name of Andrea stepped onto the scene four years ago. She opened a workshop and hired a team of women in the most need. The women received staples for their work, depending on what they had made, along with reading and writing skills and computer workshops. Not only were the women making a living, but they were learning skills for life.

The handicrafts made by these women were incredible. They recycled paper to make greeting cards, gift bags, jewellery, bowls, plates and coasters, which were stylish and impressive. Most of the men from La Chureca worked at the recycling plant, and until not long ago the workshop was at the rubbish dump site itself. Now the workshop had moved to a building near the women's new homes. That was where I was right then, face to face with these beautiful and strong, white-smiled souls.

The girls not only learned how to make jewellery. They also learned social skills and working skills, how to keep a job by being reliable and understanding the nature of the workforce. Almost all of the women who came to the centre eventually left for paid work. It was an incredible transformation.

I sat with the women, watching what they did, feeling very self-conscious about my ever-so-fortunate life and my continuous mistakes in their language. I stayed for only an hour on my first visit. I would have liked to stay longer, but I wasn't sure what I should do; I had been told to come in for only an hour and then to come in for a full day the following Monday. I bade them all good bye, receiving not too much attention in return, and left feeling lighter and more determined about my stay here.

My assigned tasks for EEP were fairly simple. I was to video the making of the new products, cut and edit the recording to make a short clip explaining the process and what EEP was all about. Then I was to travel to a nearby city to interview the founder of The Pure Earth Project, who worked with reafforestation and turtle conservation alongside EEP. I was to film the planting of a tree, and also help with presentations of EEP to the hotel and school that donated their paper to them.

My time in Nicaragua were emotional, rewarding, tiring and satisfying all at once. I started to fall in love with the country and inevitably the people. From my first experience to my last, the bus rides would be my favourite and most frustrating part of my day. Sometimes the buses were so crowded that if I wasn't near the door for my stop I wouldn't be able to get off. But even then, among the sweaty bodies in the stifling heat it was bearable with those blaring, hip-moving tunes. It was just impossible not to feel good. During my stay in Nicaragua I felt like I was so deeply immersed in the culture that I actually had to *search* to find something that wasn't typically Latino. In the beginning it was of course scary, but by the end of my stay here, it was my second home.

The one thing that did get annoying were the stares I got from all corners; I just stood out like a sore thumb. I couldn't do anything without feeling as though I was being watched. One thing I really missed while living in Managua was picking my nose. I could never just have a little indiscreet pick because, no matter what, there were always eyes on me.

Over the next weeks I slowly got closer to the women at the workshop, receiving less giggles and more words. Maudalia in particular picked on me for my terrible Spanish, if only to make me feel more comfortable.

"Do you only wear skirts in Australia?" she asked me cheekily one day. It was true. That was pretty much all I had worn to work. It was so hot I couldn't bear the thought of wearing jeans like the rest of the city.

"Hmmm, no, I did have a backpack with more clothes, but it was stolen in Argentina."

"Really?" I had all of the girls' attention by then. I flushed crimson and told them that it was OK, and that I was just happy nothing else had happened. Seriously, with what these women had been through, my petty theft experience was almost embarrassing.

Apparently Maudalia thought differently. Next day, while I was in the office working on the videos, Maudalia knocked on the door.

"Kristin?"

"Yeah?" I turned, relieved to have a break from the computer screen.

"I have some clothes for you. It's not much but at least you will have something to change into."

Maudalia was about five-foot-three. I felt as though I had to bend in half to engulf her in the biggest hug I had ever given to anyone.

"Maudalia, you didn't have to."

"I know, but I wanted to."

It was really, really hard not to cry. I had visited the new houses that had been built for the families at La Chureca just a few days earlier. Because it was so dangerous, even though it was her day off and even though it was one million degrees outside, Maudalia had come to show me around. I had met her two children and remembered the adorable daughter wouldn't let go of my hand. These people literally had nothing. They lived from day to day, and still Maudalia gave me clothes almost literally from her back, as I'm sure up until EEP these women were wearing clothes they found in the rubbish dump.

"*Gracias, Maudalia, muchissimas gracias.* You are too sweet."

My internship soon came to an end. On my last day I organised cake and juice for everyone. I had wanted to buy everyone a massage, but the founder of The Pure Earth Project advised me that the cake and juice was more suitable as it would be unfair to give the women just a taste of luxury. I could definitely see where she was coming from.

Just as I was finishing up, I was called out to the workshop room. The girls had pushed all of the tables together and there were plates filled with a Nicaraguan dish called *vigaron*—a dish of pork rind, cabbage and uca. This along with *nagatamal* were my two favourite typical dishes from Nicaragua. Silvia had prepared it for all of us. I had grown quite close to Silvia. Most of the trips I made away from the centre were with her. Her nickname for me was *chela*, meaning blonde. I was going to miss her and was saddened at the thought of not knowing when I would see her again. I had also grown close to Ana, and we would constantly joke about Nicaraguan women pointing with their lips! It was incredible. When Nicaraguan women were busy with something in their hands, or sometimes not busy at all, when pointing to something, they would pout their lips in the direction of where they were trying to point! It was amazing!

I stood in front of the group of wonderful women and said a few words of thanks to them for being so kind and accepting, after Ana had done the same for me. To my surprise the girls got up one by one with a gift they had each been working on throughout the last week for me. This was just too much. The tears welled in my eyes. I had not had enough time with these women and I was determined to do more for them and make sure this foundation would get as much support as it deserved. The people of Nicaragua, especially those women, opened my heart wide and I feel forever grateful to have experienced the selflessness and lightness of these beautiful people.

I had been given samples of the girls' products by Silvia and Ana so I could try to find a non-profit organisation in Australia to sell them in and expand the foundation even further, so that more women could have the opportunity for this empowering working environment. I took my bag of gifts, my bags of sample products and my open heart and said a last goodbye to my sweet friends. This was not the last they would see of me, I was sure of it.

18

Coming Home

I had two weeks in Mexico and four days in San Francisco before my final flight home to my love. Although I fell in love with both Mexico and San Francisco, my heart and mind were already in Australia.

I had learned what I came to learn. I had spent time in a foundation that had been started from scratch, and I was determined to do so myself. I saw that it was possible and that in not too much time I would be on the right track to starting something big to help people as well. This was all I wanted—my man and the opportunity to make a difference.

I made incredible friends along the way, who only further showed me that I was on the right path. I met an amazing Argentinian boy by the name of Nico in Mexico, who would later help me create a website for searching places around the world where it is possible to do charity work or give a helping hand in some way. I also met and stayed with a musician by the name of Robin in San Francisco, whose band Naked Soul, does charity work around the clock, and who let me stay free of charge in his house for my entire stay, even though we had never met. I had met his friend on my trip to the Pure Earth Project interview, and he had asked Robin if I could stay with him.

My last day at Robin's house I was completely filled with nerves: I was almost home! I could not get the butterflies to die down. All I could think about was that heart-shaped face and those creamy brown eyes. Yogi. Yogi, the boy who had captured my soul. We had breakfast with Robin's friends and father, and Robin's housemate Jameson sweetly offered to take me to the airport. I had a flight from San Fran to LA and then a flight from LA to Australia.

We ended up getting to the airport five minutes after I could check in. There was no way for me to make it on that flight. I was *beyond* distraught. I had booked my ticket so I would land the day before Yogi's birthday, along with a hotel for the night I arrived and his birthday night. If I missed my connecting flight, I would get there a day late. I was given a standby ticket and made my way directly to the gate. I walked straight up to the lady at the counter, trying to remain as calm as possible.

"Hello, ma'am," a friendly Asian American greeted me. My guess was that she was Philipino. That's when you know you are getting old, when people start calling you *ma'am*.

"Hi, how are you?" I asked, smiling to hide my panic. I kept up my manners, even though I felt like I was going to pass out.

"I'm very well, thank you. What can I do you for you today?"

"Well, I have lost my flight to LA and I am on standby for the next flight. If I don't make that flight, it means that I won't make my connecting flight from LA to Australia. And it's my boyfriend's birthday and I haven't seen him for four and a half months and——" Tears began welling.

"Australia, well, you *are* a very long way from home. I'm not making any promises but I will do everything I can to get you on the next flight."

I believed her. Usually in these situations you get the feeling that you're being told exactly what you want to hear, but this woman seemed too sincere for that.

"Thank you so, so much."

"You're welcome, ma'am."

I walked over to the seat closest to the desk, sat and stared at the woman for what seemed like an eternity, my stomach churning the entire time. My breathing was extremely shallow, I felt as though I would faint. I had to make that flight. The long journey ahead of me was only bearable knowing that it was just a matter of hours until I saw the man I loved. The thought of those hours turning into one more day was unimaginable. And I would miss half and possibly all of his birthday.

The lady beside my friend at the counter started reading out the names of the standby people who had been accepted onto the flight. I sat staring with all of my strength at those women. One by one, names were called for all the lucky travellers, except mine. I couldn't bear it. There was no way. I walked up to the counter and waited as an Australian couple explained that they were on the next flight, but they were scared of a delay and wanted to get on this flight to avoid missing their connection in LA as well. That hardly seemed fair to me, but then again, I had missed my flight, so who was I to judge. The lady the Australian couple was talking to was the one I had spoken with earlier. She seemed sympathetic to their case and eventually gave in. As she was writing their names down she reached under her desk and took a boarding pass, and looked at me.

"I'm sorry. I have been so busy. You were first on the list. I had already printed this out for you and saved it here."

"Oh my god! Thank you, thank you, thank you!!" I almost reached over the desk and hugged her, but thought better of it. I took my boarding pass and could barely wipe off the grin that was reaching from ear to ear. I ran over to one of the stores that sold chocolate and bought the biggest box that I could afford. I ran back to the counter and handed it to the woman.

"No, you didn't have to do that," she said, stunned.

"Neither did you! Thank you so much!"

And with that I proceeded to the boarding line, all the while trying to get one last eye contact with the lady who had just made me feel like the luckiest girl in the world. But she was too busy dealing with other desperate passengers. I found my seat and put my things in the overhead compartment, all the while with the same stupid grin on my face. I wanted to scream out to everyone that I was the luckiest girl in the world.

Shortly afterwards, we landed in LA and, as my bag was checked through, I went straight through to security and on to the gate, where I waited only an hour before boarding my final flight of the trip, the flight that would bring me to him. How strange it was going to be to smell him again, to look under those soft lashes into his golden chocolate eyes, to feel his soft, smooth skin on top of me. A thousand butterflies were again released in the pit of my stomach at the thought. He was the one. I knew it. He was the person I had dreamed of my entire life.

After our in-flight meal, I was surprised to find that I was feeling sleepy with all the excitement of getting the flight and being only hours away from my love. I grabbed my pillow, took out the sleeping bag inside it and stuffed some clothes in it. There were only two of us in the four-seat row, so I took advantage of my yoga exercises, curled up into a comfy ball and fell into a fitful sleep. I woke up maybe forty times that night, each time glancing at the screen above me with the picture of the map of the world and a yellow dotted line tracing where we had come from. Each time the dotted line grew longer and the gap between us and Australia became smaller.

We were to arrive at eleven in the morning. I had to force myself to eat breakfast; I was feeling far too excited for food. I was sure Yogi wouldn't have eaten. He already had trouble eating breakfast as it was, without driving to Brisbane to pick up the lover he hadn't seen for four and a half months.

The plane landing on my home soil couldn't have been more welcome to me. I was home, safe and sound, and minutes away from the arms of my love. Immigration and security was a constant flow, hardly a queue at all and, before I knew it, I was on the escalator down to the baggage-claim area. I reached the bottom of the escalator and felt him before I saw him. It turned out the baggage claim area was also the arrivals gate. There, leaning against a wall was the tall, handsome familiar soul that I had denied myself for far too long.

"Yogi!" I screamed. Well, I think I did. It may have just been in my mind. I ran and jumped into his arms, wrapping my legs around his body, his broad shoulders holding me close.

"Kristin," he breathed into my ear.

I was home.

Being back home with no flight plans, overseas adventures or savings to be saved in sight was a little daunting after five and a half years. I had been chasing cultures, languages, horizons and summers for quite some time. Never in this time did I think I would be settling in Australia to stay. But having a real love, I couldn't care less where I was. No amount of wonder and adventure could drag me away from this boy again. And my true destiny of helping people worse off than me didn't need me to live permanently away from home.

I could do it all from here.

I have continued with my studies in international relations in preparation of making a big difference, and have been lucky enough to find an opportunity to work with the refugees close to the town that I still call home Byron Bay while studying. I hope that this will one day open doors for me to start my own foundation. Although if not I will be more than content to continue to help those coming to Australia through the difficult transition of migrating to a foreign land. I feel that my experiences travelling have taught me the utmost love and compassion for those coming here after what could have been many years of all kinds of violence. Each day that brings wondrous miracles only pushes me further and convinces me that it is the right path. I don't know what my future holds and I have much more to experience in the field. I have sponsored a little boy Robiul from Bangladesh, in honour of the five year old me that had tried to send cheezles in an envelope to Bangladesh after seeing the children starving on TV.

The growth I have experienced over the last five and a half years and voyages across forty countries is something that I could never have imagined. One thing it has shown me is that if there is something you want badly enough, you can have it. All you need to do is start the motion; everything will flow after. In one way or another, it will come. Although there will be many times when you think everything is going wrong, if you are on your true path, you will see in retrospect that it was going completely right. Time and time again, you will be shown that, until you believe it. Then, no matter what problem you are faced with, you can know it will turn around again, that this, too, will pass.

END

my website for the purpose of this book is
www.hearttravel.org